RHODA KADALIE is a columnist for *Business Day*, *Die Burger* and *Beeld*. Trained as an anthropologist, she worked from 1976 – 1995 as an academic at the University of the Western Cape, where she founded the Gender Equity Unit. She presented papers at numerous international conferences, in countries ranging from the USA, the Netherlands, Germany and Sweden to Japan, China and Brazil. In 1995 President Nelson Mandela appointed her Human Rights Commissioner. She investigated and reported on rights violations in prisons, places of safety and on farms. In 1998 she served as head of the District Land Claims Unit for the Commission on Restitution of Land Rights. Since 1999, Kadalie has been the executive director of the Impumelelo Innovations Award Trust which rewards initiatives that improve service delivery and eradicate poverty in South Africa. She has received Honorary Doctorates from the University of Uppsala, Sweden, and her alma mater, the University of the Western Cape. She is also the recipient of the Human Rights Award, Toronto, Canada and the *Rapport* and *City Press* Prestige Award for Inspirational Women. Kadalie serves on a number of boards, including those of the South African Institute of Race Relations, the Institute of Ethics in South Africa and the Ash Institute for Democratic Governance and Innovation at Harvard University in the USA.

RHODA KADALIE

IN YOUR FACE

Passionate Conversations about
People and Politics

Tafelberg

Tafelberg
An imprint of NB Publishers
40 Heerengracht, Cape Town, 8000
www.tafelberg.com
© 2009 Rhoda Kadalie

All rights reserved
No part of this book may be reproduced or transmitted in any form or by any electronic or mechanical means, including photocopying and recording, or by any other information storage or retrieval system, without written permission from the publisher

Set in Adobe Jenson Pro
Cover design by Anton Sassenberg
Cover photo by Michael le Grange
Book design by Nazli Jacobs
Index by Mary Lennox

Printed and bound by CTP Book Printers, Cape Town, South Africa
First edition, first printing 2009

ISBN: 978-0-624-04730-8

I dedicate this book to
my daughter, Julia,
my parents, Joan and Fenner,
and my beloved Helen Suzman.

Table of Contents

Acknowledgements, 1

Forewords:
- Helen Suzman, 3
- Njabulo Ndebele, 5

Introduction, 7

Thoughts on South Africans (Heroes and humorists)
- SA still has a knack for engaging or enraging slogans, 13
- Hero to zero for media darling Patricia de Lille, 15
- Tutu's clerical peers fail to speak in his defence, 17
- Ramaphosa's rich talents equip him for top office, 19
- Sisulus embodied noble principles, 21
- What you sow, you shall reap, 23

Transformation (Troubled Transformation)
- A coconut knocks on the door of the Native Club, 26
- ANC's transformation is nothing but hogwash, 28
- And SA's new black elite said: 'let them eat pap', 30
- Just a nuance away from smash-and-grab looting, 32
- Local solutions to halt SA's sure slide into chaos, 34
- We cannot dismiss reasons whites give for leaving, 36
- ANC creates new diaspora with race-based laws, 39
- State must act now to plug brain drain, 41
- Poor excuse for failure develops a life of its own, 42
- The point is delivery, not the race of the deliverer, 45
- 'Victim' psychology finds expression in attacks, 47
- Silence around murder of Somalis speaks volumes, 48
- Media and politicians abuse race card for own gains, 50
- The racism debate obscures other issues, 53
- Is the Native Club another Broederbond or will it

plug intellectual vacuum?, 56 ■ Video uproar betrays culture of double standards, 59 ■ Notion of African campuses too glib, 61 ■ Opera clicks with African students, 64 ■ Transformation minefield far from easy to negotiate, 65 ■ Is empathy really a better gauge of aspiring doctors than high marks?, 68 ■ 'Contrary' rulings explain ANC assault on judges, 70 ■ Brave judge won't slide on the Hlippery Hlophe, 72 ■ Sorry, this is just another divisive fad, 74 ■ Patriotism soured by dashed expectations, 76

Women (Abandoned Sisters)
■ Sisters in power give ordinary SA women little joy, 79 ■ SA's women leaders leave their sisters in the lurch, 81 ■ What we black women ought to tell this president, 84 ■ Abuse of women a blot on 'new SA', 86 ■ Let's get real about improving the lives of women, 88 ■ Double standards muddy the waters of Zuma trial, 90 ■ Tshabalala-Msimang gives women a bad name, 92 ■ Mother Theresas bring comfort to the needy, 94 ■ Back to the barricades, sisters, 96 ■ Women's rights the victim of sordid saga, 99

Ruling Alliance (Party Poopers)
■ We must shed notion that only ANC can save SA, 102 ■ Intolerant ANC ignores biggest threat to its power, 104 ■ No vote of confidence for Mbeki's 'Party of Death', 106 ■ A clouded national psyche revealed after acquittal, 108 ■ More to ANC's grassroots revolt than Zuma case, 111 ■ Criticise the president and cross his sycophants, 113 ■ Political parties with a personality disorder, 115 ■ Use your vote to fight a one-party state, 118 ■ Supine MPs blow chance for people's Parliament, 122 ■ ANC compounds porcine heritage of ally NNP, 125 ■ SAs big-mouth communists offer no real solutions, 127 ■ Power at any cost has backfired on ANC, 129

Western Cape (Stormy Cape)
■ On the Cape Flats, Madam sings its own De la Rey, 133 ■ Bring back the old Cape gang, regardless of cost, 135 ■ Moves to undermine Cape coalition bode ill for SA, 137 ■ Stalinist cabal

parodies ANC's promise in Cape, 140 ■ No gentle use of power from this mayor, 142 ■ Public servants can lead us by example, 144 ■ Politicians score points as tik lays waste to coloured youth, 146 ■ The rise and rule of the Cape Flats war machine, 148 ■ Atlantis a telling example of state not hearing poor, 151

Good Governance (Stumbling State)

■ A crime that many of SA's ministers keep their jobs, 154 ■ Blind lead the blind through a moral wasteland, 156 ■ Mbeki's silence rotten as Land Bank dirt piles up, 158 ■ Mbeki resting on laurels that few can discern, 160 ■ Democratic charade misses the point of dialogue, 162 ■ Evil depth of SA's crimes calls for drastic measures, 164 ■ President must get to grips with crime, 167 ■ Hard-won freedom must not remain a paper tiger, 169 ■ Trusting Mbeki on Selebi takes a leap of faith beyond most of us, 171 ■ Unrest, gags and insults call back unhappy past, 173 ■ Death of John Muller, a hero who shamed the ANC, 175 ■ Babies perish even as ministers lead charmed life, 177 ■ HIV sufferers still left out in the cold, 180 ■ When presidents go paranoid, NGO's beware, 181 ■ Ministers rate 'I' for in competence on my card, 184 ■ Inquiries aplenty, but none into ANC abuses, 186 ■ Government for the people rings hollow, 188 ■ Society pays the price for neglecting prison reform, 190 ■ They may kiss babies, but beware, 192

Media (Media Meekness)

■ Dumbed-down SABC still its ANC master's voice, 195 ■ Now the media thinks it can silence 'whingers', 197 ■ Journalists also close ranks, 200 ■ 'Consensus politics' just a way to silence dissenters?, 201 ■ Smug white journalists strangers to democracy, 203 ■ 'Ja baas' media shirks uncomfortable questions, 206 ■ Embedded scribes grovel to new elite, 208 ■ Afrikaans press carries torch of brave journalism, 210 ■ Déjà vu on SA Bootlicking Corporation TV, 212 ■ So sue, but Zikalala's partiality is beyond doubt, 214 ■ Hackneyed digs at Zille expose our gutless media, 216 ■ ANC desperately covering up Hout Bay sleaze, 218

Foreign Affairs (Foreign Fumbles)
- Tainted foreign policy at the root of SA's woes, 221 ■ Oscars for Mugabe and SA's 'internal Zimbabwe', 223 ■ Support for Mugabe brings SA no benefit, 225 ■ From liberation heroes to rotten paranoid thugs, 227 ■ Down a familiar path into the heart of darkness, 229 ■ Funny how well Cape Flats manners work in the US, 231 ■ Nepad's peer review system needs to be given real teeth, 233 ■ Glossing over truth on Aristide does SA no favours, 235 ■ An unfortunate historical amnesia, 237

Love her or loathe her: Readers' sentiments
- Kadalie kudos, 240 ■ No new ideas, 240 ■ Gutless media, 241 ■ Pap and wors, 242 ■ Kadalie pushes her own agenda, 242 ■ Mbeki still in denial on AIDS, 243 ■ Race still a factor, 245 ■ ANC bashing, 245 ■ Credit where due, 246 ■ Over the top, 247 ■ Columnist bias, 248

Cracking the whip: Rhoda's letters to newspapers
Why single out Shaik family? 249 ■ Blatant racism, 249 ■ Media destroyers, 250 ■ Time to stand up, 251 ■ Bunch of clowns, 252

Glossary, 253

Index, 255

Acknowledgements

THIS BOOK happened because many people believed in it when I was deeply sceptical: my readers across the country who kept asking me to publish my columns; members of Parliament who regularly sent comments either endorsing or cursing depending on the party to which they belonged; my parents beaming proudly whenever they saw their daughter in print but who feared for her safety; my brothers, some who were supportive, and others who felt their careers were jeopardised by association; my daughter, Julia, ever trusting of her mother's righteous indignation when others rebuked her; her boyfriend, Joel, one of my most loyal readers long before I knew him.

Milton Shain, Millie Pimstone, Marianne Thamm, Suzanne Vos, Anne Routier, Jeff Lever, Njabulo Ndebele, Tony Leon, my colleagues, and my beloved Helen Suzman encouraged me to keep on writing when I felt uninspired, tired, and bored with ANC politics, or wanted to opt out for fear of sounding repetitive. It was often the column I was most displeased with that got the most comments. Soon these friends became a necessary sounding board, highly valued when they were least aware of it.

My greatest mentor, the late Anthony Holiday, for whom writing was the product of blood, sweat and tears, shaped my thoughts through much teasing and laughter when I was most inarticulate. He made me appreciate the value of every word, every sentence, and every paragraph. Intolerant of sloppy thinkers, he agonised for days over one sentence and I marvelled over the results captured in some of the finest columns this country has ever seen.

The person who actually got me writing was Diana Russell, who spent a sabbatical in my house in the late 1980s, writing one of her many books. Whenever I returned from a UDF or UWCO meeting outraged at the Stalinism of the left, she would say, 'Rhoda, write it down.' 'But I cannot write,' I would complain, whereupon she would urge me to write it down as I speak. Thus began my struggle with writing. She, thankfully, undid the damage all the years of apartheid education inflicted upon my porous brain. She will probably be surprised to read this, and be even more surprised that her advice has been translated into a book!

The greatest disincentive to putting this book together was to wade through the hundreds of columns I had written since 1987. It was my colleague, Candice Jansen, who took the bull by the horns and eagerly volunteered to sort them, classify them, and sort the fan from hate mail. I shall never forget how she spluttered and gasped while reading through stuff she was too young to understand when they were first published. She made me realise that, for people like her who were too young to remember the cataclysmic political events that shaped our past and future, my columns were an ongoing chronology of events about people and issues. She was so excited about this book that her enthusiasm became infectious. Walking endlessly, always smiling, from our offices to those of NB Publishers in the raging southeaster, to convey messages to the publisher, she, more than anyone, deserves my heartfelt gratitude and thanks.

One friend in particular convinced me to publish my columns – referring to them as the 'wet-market of ideas' – so I finally gave in and am forever grateful to him for his persistence.

Finally, I wish to commend publisher Erika Oosthuysen and her team, always respectful and responsive to my dumb questions, for putting this volume together.

RHODA KADALIE

Foreword

RHODA KADALIE and I first met some fifteen years ago when we were both appointed as members of the Human Rights Commission. It did not take long for us to realise we had shared values and shared prejudices. We immediately recognised each other as fellow spirits where human rights priorities are concerned, and have remained firm friends ever since.

A glance at the index of this remarkable book reveals Rhoda's wide interests and strong convictions, which range far and wide from her training as an anthropologist at the University of the Western Cape. I have been an avid reader of her forthright articles which have appeared in the press since 2003. Rhoda does not pull her punches, whether she is dealing with a powerful politician or a corrupt civil servant. South African readers have enjoyed her hard-hitting articles for the past five years and this book provides a great opportunity for other readers to catch up, so to speak, on Rhoda's indictment of politicians and government's failure to deliver on its promises of 'a better life for all'.

In Your Face – Passionate Conversations about People and Politics will make an excellent gift for anyone who is interested in South Africa's transformation from apartheid to democracy, the country's turbulent present, or its unpredictable future.

HELEN SUZMAN
October 2008

Foreword

RHODA KADALIE'S writing never evokes a neutral reaction. It is either liked or disliked. Between this fraught continuum, the gamut of reactions to her opinion columns over the years is reflected in some pieces in this new publication whose very title evokes Rhoda Kadalie's expository bearing: here are the basics of truth-telling. Reading her is guaranteed never to be a dull moment.

South Africa since 1994 has never seen a dull moment. Change has driven the excitement at the heart of our public life. Policy changes in the entire range of national life were a key feature of the Mandela presidency. Implementing those policies can be said to have been the key objective of the Mbeki presidency. Indeed, change has been a consistent feature of our national life in the last fifteen years.

The lively witness of Rhoda Kadalie's pen has been in synchrony with South Africa's unrelenting change. How has our engagement with that change, a central feature of our dramatic history, been shaping our national character. Public figures, private or public organisations and institutions, have an enormous capacity to shape and influence public opinion and behaviour. That is why in a democracy it is mandatory that they deserve our closest scrutiny.

Rhoda Kadalie is one of South Africa's public agents on behalf of that mandate. The import of her focus on any public figures who happen to be in her sights is about their credibility, their judgement, and the choices they make against the standards they have declared themselves to be measured against. They can either affirm or condemn themselves in their expressed thoughts and actions. Thought and action in public figures are self-defining. By the time Rhoda Kadalie writes about them, they have already assessed themselves, even though at times they may want us to believe what is contrary to the real visual or conceptual import of what they have done. This disparity is what raises Rhoda Kadalie's ire.

The same goes for the behaviour of organisations and institutions: their credibility, judgement, and choices, and the often lack of consistency between self assessment and the actual reality of the outcome of some of their actions.

I once thought that her unrelenting forthrightness could eventually be dismissed as her 'usual thing'. That has not happened. What rescues her writing from the predictability of sameness is precisely the varied reactions it evokes. They guarantee the freshness of impact. It is a total package of forthrightness, passion, strong belief, strong-mindedness, and unflinching witness.

And so, *In Your Face – Passionate Conversations about People and Politics* is guaranteed to please, annoy, embarrass, amuse, unnerve, anger, frustrate, empower, cajole, and even revolt. Profoundly, Rhoda Kadalie invites you to yourself, to your own thoughts and feelings, and their implications for your own interactions with the world around you. For this reason, she will always make you look over your shoulder. She performs a vital service to ensure a lively and self-aware democracy.

NJABULO S NDEBELE
October 2008

Introduction

THIS BOOK of columns is a tribute to the power of last-minute writing. Inspiration seldom responds creatively to deadlines but the scramble for a column the night before deadline is saved so often by the unscrupulous politician who, in the nick of time, determines one's script. Ranging from the inspirational to the analytical, most of my columns are sheer gut responses to a government that has failed to live up to the promises so easily made during election time. And, after fifteen years of democracy, we are once again at the crossroads, frantically seeking solutions to the challenges that face us.

If anything, these columns portray a deep sense of the African National Congress' (ANC) betrayal of those who overwhelmingly voted it into office in 1994. Today the poor and the marginalised feel particularly aggrieved and as a feminist activist I align myself fully with their cause. Having grown up in District Six and Mowbray (my family being the victim of forced removals) I became involved in the struggle so that my daughter and future generations would live free from the shackle of repressive domination. My feminism was cultivated at the University of the Western Cape (UWC), a university that openly aligned itself with the mass democratic movement. Campaigning actively for the inclusion of women as full and autonomous citizens in public life and the discourse of democracy, I set up an institution to advance the position of women, the Gender Equity Unit in 1993. It designed policies and programmes intended to transform the institutional culture of UWC. At the time, liberation chauvinism reigned supreme. The going mantra was 'liberation first, women's liberation, second'. Often dismissed as a 'bourgeois, liberal feminist' for daring to suggest that the abolition of apartheid did not mean black male domination, the challenge was to stay the course in a country where our male comrades frequently claimed that 'women's liberation was divisive of the national liberation struggle'.

Feminist voices continued relentlessly into the constitutional negotiations and played a pivotal role in the final design of the Bill of Rights, billed today as one of the most progressive in the world for women. Trained in Women's Studies and Development and having studied the position of women in post-colonial societies and their continuing oppression after liberation, I was determined to continue my voice post-liberation. During Nelson Mandela's reign and my stint at the Human Rights Commission there was much opportunity for women to engage in a new political discourse and seek ways to translate our progressive constitution into enabling legislation. This sense of opportunity and freedom was short-lived. Under the subsequent Mbeki reign, the ANC steadily grew intolerant of criticism and divergent views. The president would single out individuals who dared to criticise him and it started with a vicious attack in 2004 on ANC activist Charlene Smith, expert journalist on women's health and HIV/AIDS. I was astounded at the silence of the sisters, many of whom refused to support Charlene not because they disagreed with her cause, but because she is white. I consequently wrote many columns taking up women's issues and the failure of women Parliamentarians to prioritise feminist interests above party political interests.

Under President Mbeki's erratic rule, a time of political unease, many comrades who fought for democracy and freedom shut up in face of those who rewarded the acquiescent with position and patronage. Those of us who refused to be silent became the enemy. The stage was set for politicians who blamed all their misdemeanours on the media and public commentators, but never themselves. Some pundits were even blacklisted by the South African Broadcasting Corporation (SABC). I then veered into writing about everything and anything that smacked of political opportunism, government ineptitude, and corruption. All over the place people succumbed to political pressure for silence, urged to be forever grateful to the ANC for ushering in our liberation, no matter how corrupt and self-serving public officials were. With others, I, too, became targeted by former political allies, for simply appropriating the right to criticise government.

Journalist, Evelyn Holtshauzen so presciently commented, early on in our democracy, that: '... our adolescent democracy, (sadly) is still under threat by those who fear to speak. But while previously it was fear of the state, today it is fear of not being politically correct that keeps us silent. This is a far more sinister threat to democracy.' (*Cape Times* June 5 2001)

The effects of this self-censorship could be felt throughout the body politic of South Africa and played itself out in both the macro- and micro-political spheres in strange ways, captured in the anecdotes below.

- For ten years I served as a member of the Board of the Community Law Centre at UWC, an organisation that was very politically active under Dullah Omar's leadership during the heady days of apartheid. At one of our board meetings as I walked into the room, I was accorded what had become a customary greeting: 'Here comes the loose cannon!' It was a reaction to the provocative columns I had been writing to the newspapers the week before, calling on Manto Tshabalala-Msimang, minister of health, to resign. As much as many in that room detested her, not one dared to say so. These epithets – 'unguided missile', 'traitor', 'reckless' – the list was endless – were hurled at me by former colleagues and comrades who found my columns embarrassing, but who were never prepared to debate them in public.
- Even editors succumbed to political pressure. In 2002 I phoned John Battersby, then editor of *The Sunday Independent*, informing him that I should like to have an open letter published in his paper, calling on the minister of health to resign for her mismanagement of the HIV/AIDS pandemic. He promised to put it on the front page. Contrary to his promise the letter did not appear that Sunday, but was replaced by a small article informing the readers that I had called on the minister to resign. Readers called to ask where the open letter was. On contacting Battersby, he confided that he had sent my letter to the President's office for comment and that they 'blew a fuse about it' so he decided not to publish it. When I conveyed my annoyance he published it the following Sunday at the bottom of the page as an ordinary letter with some editing.
- Nicoli Nattrass, Professor of Economics at UCT, was asked by her funders to present her research – a fiscal analysis of the costs of denying anti-retrovirals to people with HIV/AIDS – to a group of government officials who were attending a workshop dealing with various aspects of fiscal policy. When Nicoli presented her research, which was construed by the ANC participants as anti-government and unpatriotic, she was shouted down to such an

extent that her session was brought to an abrupt halt by the organisers. Silenced by the mob, inferring that as a white person her research had no legitimacy, she left in disgust.
- Two years ago, when Ebrahim Rasool referred to coloured people who voted for the Democratic Alliance as coconuts, I wrote a column condemning his racism. Cape Talk subsequently invited me to spend an hour at the radio station to respond to questions from listeners. Cape Talk's journalist called me a few days later, reporting that they were taken out to dinner by some ANC politicians who asked them not to invite me ever to the station again. They invited me the next day to debate with a politician just to show that they would not be beholden to political pressure! Such behaviour evokes Benedict Spinoza's warning in the 17th century that: 'once we make crimes of opinions, we are moving towards tyranny'.

Sadly, the free flow of ideas had become bedevilled by a range of pressures that have come to haunt our fragile democracy. The tyranny of political correctness, the tyranny of the majority, the fear of being called racist or disloyal. Embedded journalism and vested interests became standard discursive devices used to stifle independent critical thought. They contributed to the deluge of self-censorship one detected in the media, in public life, and around dinner tables.

Patronage, access to jobs, or a promotion and access to power so easily determined what one said and did not say. The silence of ministers and civil leaders around the HIV/AIDS debacle was a case in point. No-one in the cabinet dared question the president on his stance on the virus and many were prepared to suspend their intellects in defence of the president. The more people submitted to this tyranny the more it became a way of life. These 'mechanisms' impeded freedom of expression and association and to some extent had the same effect repressive legal obstacles had on activists denied free speech under the old regime. Slowly but surely George Orwell's warning became a reality: 'If freedom of speech is taken away then dumb and silent we may be led, like sheep to the slaughter.'

And so like sheep, we feared being called 'racist', 'right-wing', 'a sellout', 'disloyal', 'a traitor' and 'unpatriotic'. These epithets were so powerful that many were prepared to sacrifice the truth. Even academics feared to ply their trade in public, lest they be construed as reactionary. 'One gets branded so easily' was the stock answer from former colleagues who were the most vocal during the struggle. It was so bad that one of the authors of the Medical Research Council (MRC) AIDS Report confided at a private briefing that the AIDS situation was so terrifying that he would not contest the statistical findings of government commissioned research, even if flawed, since the AIDS crisis demanded such urgent attention of government that quibbling would just further delay treatment to dying patients.

Whereas my feminist voice had been nurtured and cultivated during the struggle and by the struggle, I was suddenly expected to shut up after 1999. One is often silenced in the name of guarding the national interest (increasingly a euphemism for consensus and conformity). But who determines what is in the national interest? Is it not in the national interest to admit that HIV causes AIDS? Because a president chooses not to do so, does it therefore cease to be a national priority? By the same token, does the president's prioritisation of race make it an issue of national interest? Does that mean that racism is a priority to the nation when people rank unemployment and poverty as more important?

JF Kennedy's words ring true more than ever: 'Conformity is the jailer of freedom and the enemy of growth.' Politicians know that whoever controls the media controls the mind. Inspired by Stalin that, 'ideas are more powerful than guns. We would not let our enemies have guns, why should we let them have ideas,' government has made the public broadcaster its prime target. The ANC conference at Polokwane was a watershed event in the ANC's political history and hopefully the control of the SABC will be reviewed. Mbeki's demise came sooner than expected, and similarly the ANC split caught the pundits off guard.

This selection of columns mostly records events during Mbeki's reign and the effects his erratic rule has had on state institutions, the media, and the public in general. For example, through board and senior appointments he controlled the SABC. His attempts at political and economic transformation often backfired because they were so firmly embedded within a nationalist framework cloaked in language of the African Renaissance and Black Economic Empowerment. Billed as the gender-sensitive president, in reality, Mbeki failed women in his policies on crime, women's health, sexual violence, and HIV/AIDS. He also failed the poor. High rates of unemployment, unmitigated poverty, and the chronic failure to deliver basic services to the poor, were underscored by the thousands of protests against service delivery recorded around the country.

The political trajectory of that era is captured under specific headings that cover the wide range of issues addressed. 'Heroes and humorists' deals with prominent South African personalities: some inspiring, some who transcend challenges with humour, and others who had greatness thrust upon them. 'Troubled Transformation' includes a collection of columns exposing the belly of the beast of under-development despite the rhetoric of transformation and social justice. 'Abandoned Sisters' focuses on how powerful women betrayed their sisters once they tasted power. 'Party Poopers' focuses on how the ANC failed to deliver on the various mandates of the Freedom Charter to the poor. Moving from the general to the particular, 'Flat Cape' looks at local politics in the Western Cape, and the next chapter isolates specific incidents of how the corrupt state ruined major institutions and reduced whistle-blowers to helpless victims of state power. Centralised control required the manipulation of the public broadcaster and the chapter on the media, 'Media Meekness', regales readers with vignettes of how the SABC became a sorry casualty of both the paranoia of absolute control and the suppression of opposing voices. The final chapter, 'Foreign Fumbles', gives examples of how the obsession with centralised control steadily spread its wings in wooing like-minded rogues and pariah states to bolster Mbeki's attempts at continental control through Nepad and the African Renaissance.

In Your Face – Passionate Conversations about People and Politics ends with readers' responses to my columns and includes both fan and hate mail and confirms Orwell's dictum: 'In times of universal deceit telling the truth (is) a revolutionary act'. The question now is: what will happen under President Motlanthe's interim presidency and after the election in 2009? Will a swing to the left mean a curb on freedom of speech and expression so typical of leftist governments and dictatorships, or will we enjoy the greater freedom that goes hand in hand with being anti-Mbeki, anti-autocratic and pro-democracy? I wait with great expectations for something better. Jacob Zuma dares not disappoint because my pen is ever ready to strike back.

RHODA KADALIE

Thoughts on South Africans
(Heroes and humorists)

☞ **SA still has a knack for engaging or enraging slogans**
Business Day April 29 2004

I WAS AGONISING over what to write for today's column while watching Freedom Day celebrations on television, when a poster leapt out from among the masses: The ANC will rule until Jesus Come.

Amused, I wondered how long the fruits of Liberation before Education will be with us. On this slogan, the movement was divided. Some argued liberation first, others insisted education is liberation. Some followed their hearts, the results of which are clear!

We are now free, and the need for the African National Congress (ANC) to educate the masses is more urgent than ever. No doubt, with education, our language too will be liberated. Politicians should never underestimate the indelible prints their slogans leave on the masses.

So, grammatical or not, our slogans either enrage or engage.

Even through the pain of struggle, South Africans never lost their penchant for witty and humorous slogans, no matter how bad the grammar.

I am reminded of the launch of the United Democratic Front (UDF) in 1983. The meeting was delayed by serious overcrowding. Some people were even hanging from rafters. After many appeals from security guards for people to descend from the rafters, a typical Cape Flats voice shouted impatiently: '*Manne, manne, klim nou van die* beams *af, ons wil beginne* history *maak.*'

And so we made history, marching and protesting against the laws that determined where we lived, where we worked, whom we married, where we swam, where we ate and even where we worshipped.

From the masses emerged Dr Allan Boesak, leader of the UDF, hero-worshipped for his bravery, oratory, and charisma, until he fell. Accused of having an affair while hosting Ted Kennedy, the UDF called on him to rebut the allegations, convinced the security police were framing him. A mass meeting was called to a hall in Mitchells Plain where Boesak would repudiate the allegations.

Needless to say, the hall was chock-a-block, filled with comrades and voyeurs alike. Unable to find a seat, I remained outside with the proletariat. As was customary, Boesak, draped in a red cloak, made his dramatic entry, at which point the crowd broke into a spontaneous chant: 'Boesak, Boesak, Boesak'. The vagrant next to me, all fired up, joined the chorus: '*Dit is van laat jou Broeksak, Broeksak, Broeksak!*' My day was made because for once I did not doubt the allegations.

In the 1980s when the reproductive and gay rights debate was raging in the liberation movement, a graffito appeared on the walls of Observatory, a leftie Cape Town suburb: 'Lesbians unite in armed snuggle!' next to 'Comrade unite in armed struggle'.

Even in our saddest moments, humour kept us going. As when Albie Sachs lost his arm in a bomb blast in Maputo, the grief that engulfed us was lifted by a macabre but funny slogan on the walls of Cape Town: 'Albie Sachs, the ANC's one-armed bandit'. It was made so much more palatable by Albie's amused acceptance of it.

When the ANC called on the masses to make SA ungovernable, the graffiti on the walls of Orange Street reminded us every day that 'A naartjie in our sosatie' (anarchy in our society), while inconvenient, might be one of a number of strategies to bring freedom.

Soon after, when Robert Mugabe condemned homosexuals as lower than beasts, the gay lobby came out in full force, protesting against his visit to the World Trade Centre in Johannesburg.

One slogan proclaimed: 'Mugabe go home, Zimbabwe needs a queen'; another pointedly read, 'To MuGaybe or not to MuGaybe'. Funnier than that is rare.

Fortunately, the gift for sloganeering has not left us post-1994, as was evident at the recent doctors' march to Parliament. 'I am Manto-negative', signalled how many doctors felt about the health minister's inability to govern the health sector and her equivocation on providing antiretrovirals to the masses.

I shall never forget just before 1994, a huge mass rally was held at the University of Western Cape. The entire mass of students sang a most moving rendition of Nkosi Sikelele. From the back of the main hall, a voice croaked: '*Manne, julle kan darem sing, al het julle nie eers stemreg nie*', and the audience broke into laughter.

We now have *stemreg* – the right to vote – and the world is at our feet. Hopefully the crowd's cheering for Mugabe as he ascended the stairs of the Union Buildings to join the celebrations is not symbolic of what it means to have an overwhelming *stemreg*. A regrettable blot on the festivities in Pretoria.

☞ Hero to zero for media darling Patricia de Lille
Business Day 23 March 2006

PATRICIA DE LILLE, the feisty politician, is in the doghouse.

The darling of the media before March 1 2006, she is now the pariah of politics, having earned the titles Patricia de Liar in the *Citizen* and *Mampara* in the *Sunday Times*.

That is because she lied blatantly, saying she would not back the African National Congress (ANC) or its mayoral candidate for Cape Town, Nomaindia Mfeketo, and then doing so at the 11th hour. She continues to deny this, contrary to all media evidence.

De Lille's fatal flaw is that she believed the image the media created of her. Desperate to have a black opposition leader, the media promoted her, throughout the election, as the honourable black opposition leader this country needs and overlooked her enormous political ineptitude.

The significance of this nail-biting contest for mayor in the City of Cape Town is that it exposed the leader of the Independent Democrats (ID) for what she is – egotistical, immoderate and politically irresponsible.

As the former chief whip of the Pan Africanist Congress (PAC), De Lille's trademark was sound bites. Excellent at hurling political bombshells, her street-fighting ability masked the unsophisticated politician she really was. Her lack of political restraint from the time she served as a loyal member of the PAC to her current status as leader of the ID has exposed the irascible political conduct that led to her decline.

For years the PAC protected De Lille. It was entirely predictable that the day she started her own party, she would be unmasked. Those who feel betrayed today, and who voted for her in good faith, failed to see that her actions during the negotiations with opposition parties were consistent with her long political trajectory.

Already during Codesa, De Lille showed her true colours with words that have come to haunt her: 'No, we (the PAC) are not in favour of power sharing and if we get some kind of majority in the constituent assembly, we will say to hell with whatever they agreed in the negotiations.'

In her relation to the Democratic Alliance (DA), she was and still is completely untrustworthy. She often used them for protection against the ANC, and would abuse them when things were not in her favour. In the *Financial Mail*, she implied – like Ebrahim Rasool – that, by voting for the DA, coloured people in the Western Cape had lost their racial identity and had voted for 'the oppressor'.

'The bottom line here is not an ideology but race. I can't explain why, to use the liberation phrase, "the oppressed should vote for the oppressor". Inside myself I've said it, "I know I am an African", but many of our coloured people still need to come to terms with this.'

De Lille is incapable of seizing the moment. Relishing her role as 'kingmaker' during the mayoral contest, she pranced around like a queen smelling power for the first time. She tried to outfox the smaller parties by overplaying her hand and lost in a battle where one of her own betrayed her.

Overestimating her own political prowess, she became a liability to her ally, the ANC, to whom she promised much. But why would De Lille sacrifice so much if there was not a quid pro quo – especially given rumours she was offered a deputy minister's post? Why the sudden love affair with a party she has sought to embarrass at every opportunity? Is she not like all 'crosstitutes' who are in politics for personal gain? 'An honest politician is one, who, when bought, will stay bought,' to quote US politician Simon Cameron.

If De Lille wishes to survive she should jettison the cult of personality around which the ID has built itself and do some hard political work to earn her credentials. The arms-deal bombshell was marred by her failure to follow through properly. She did not study the joint committee's report on the arms deal, nor did she participate with Raenette Taljaard and Gavin Woods in the subsequent standing committee on public accounts meetings to expose the major gaps in the report.

One cannot ignore Parliament and spend a great deal of time on the golf course and expect one's political credibility to stay intact. After all, it is Parliament that pays her salary. In an interview in 2002, De Lille stated openly: 'I am only going to spend 10% of my time in Parliament, which means I'll be a de facto absent member. I've decided I've got better things to do.'

What may seem like courage and principle – a phrase she used ad nauseam throughout the discussions – is stubbornness and a failure to compromise when it is the right thing to do. Using this refrain in the negotiations, as though it was a mark of integrity, provoked a rebellion among her gatvol supporters, one of whom remarked: '*Kyk hoe lyk haar principles nou!*'

☛ Tutu's clerical peers fail to speak in his defence
Business Day March 31 2005

DURING THE EARLY 1990s, a woman student was raped in a residence of the University of the Western Cape by someone from outside the university. Students were enraged and vowed revenge. In heated vigilante action, they yanked a suspect off the streets, dragged him into the hostels and beat the daylights out of him. No one could control them and Archbishop Desmond Tutu was called in to deal with the mob. Realising that no priestly admonition would help, he waded into this storm of attackers and literally took the victim's head under his arm, trying to ward off his assailants, who were intent on killing him. Tutu himself was boxed left, right and centre, but persevered until he wrenched the man from the mob.

This fearless priest has saved many from being necklaced and lynched by angry mobs. His courage knew no limits as he took on the National Party government, pointing out how its Christian national ideology was at odds with Christianity. Filled with righteous anger, he would alert the world to what was going on in SA, relentless in his opposition to apartheid at mass rallies, church meetings and student marches.

Today, with the government he fought for in power, the Arch is not changing his tune. He is a priest and prophet, and his job is to deal with unpalatable truths, no matter at whom they are directed. It pains Tutu to castigate his own. He suffered when Winnie Madikizela-Mandela could not say sorry. He suffers when he sees the ruling elite enriching itself at the expense of the poor. He suffers when people die of AIDS with little being done about it.

Tutu continues to do what God wants him to do: to be a prophet regardless of the consequences, continuing in the footsteps of those who have gone before, of those who were persecuted by their own for their allegiance to God and the truth.

Like Daniel, who was thrown into the lion's den for his prescience and his commitment to God, so too is Tutu being thrown into the den of African National Congress (ANC) loyalists intent on bringing him down a peg or two. This Nobel laureate is being vilified for warning us gently that we are straying from the very ideals that brought us our liberation.

And what does he get? Comrades who use every tactic in the ANC book to discredit him. 'He was never a member of the ANC; he has scant regard for the truth; he does not know what he is talking about; he is ignorant and uninformed' they say. The most preposterous of all accusations comes from Butana Komphela, chairman of the portfolio committee on sport, claiming Tutu's views of transformation in sport amount to high treason. And that from a *laaitie* who probably was not even born when Tutu started his opposition to white domination! It all sounds very much like PW Botha, who not so long ago called Tutu 'a demagogue in bishop's robes'.

Bishops should not belong to political parties. For Tutu, loyalty to God and to issues of justice precede loyalty to the party. When one reads Tutu's collection of sermons and his experiences in politics as a priest, one realises that he, unlike many of the struggle priests, remained true to his calling. Throughout his career, he chose God above Mammon.

In his preface to the book *Aliens in the Household of God*, Tutu reveals a man very few of us know – an unusual response from an elder breaking new ground in his compassionate, Christ-like response to the issue of homosexuality. Why is the Anglican church kicking up so much polemical dust about a matter Tutu has total clarity on? Tutu is a mensch and any attempt to vilify him will boomerang.

I have seen many marches where Tutu locked arms with other religious leaders – such as Bishop Mvume Dandala, the Rev Lionel Louw, the Rev Colin Jones, the Rev Allan Boesak, the Rev Chris Ahrends, the Rev Frank Chikane, Rabbi Cyril Harris, Imam Gasant Solomons, Father Smangaliso Mkhatshwa and the Rev Courtney Sampson – against the repressive apartheid state.

I have yet to see one of these clerics come out in defence of him. The courage that prevailed before 1994 has dissipated, with the clergy seeking greener pastures in the secular world, reluctant to criticise lest they jeopardise their chances of benefiting from the state's largesse. Herein lies the demise of the prophetic voice, kept alive mainly by Tutu.

☛ Ramaphosa's rich talents equip him for top office
Business Day July 27 2006

I AM glad that Cyril Ramaphosa's name has been added to the list of African National Congress (ANC) presidential hopefuls for 2007. His candidature would be a pleasant neutraliser to the alternatives, who are too ghastly to contemplate. Many might unfairly disqualify him on the grounds that he is too rich for the job and that he might use his economic power to enrich himself even further, or use it to leverage resources for his empowerment pals or the ANC, in the same way that Silvio Berlusconi, tycoon and prime minister of Italy, became notorious.

Berlusconi was a prime example of how a convergence of business and political interests is bad in politicians. Big business, at the best of times, behaves like a whore. It attaches its body to any government as long as it can use it to further its own ends.

The evidence since 1994 has been disconcerting. The very same businesses that sucked up to the apartheid government are now cosying up to the ANC and have been quite ruthless in using the ruling party in a system of patronage that is rather embarrassing to behold.

For every corrupt politician, there is a corrupter, and complicit businesses often recede quietly into oblivion when corruption is exposed, with the government portrayed as the only villain in the transaction.

Big business in Zimbabwe generally supported Robert Mugabe to the hilt until they could no longer sustain the relationship and left quietly when his largesse dried up.

Ramaphosa's political credentials are well known and I need not list them here. But what needs to be emphasised is that while his rapid rise to wealth keeps being mentioned, people forget his proven track record as head of the Constitutional Assembly. His management of the constitutional process during a tight schedule from June 1994 to May 1996 is worth the highest order SA can bestow on anybody.

Putting together a constitution in a politically fractured country was a new and risky undertaking for SA. Politics was volatile and even though the 1994 election was relatively peaceful, tensions remained. The right wing had just emerged from a brutal destabilisation process; similarly, the resistance movement had to cease all revolutionary activity.

Politicians were still fighting about the property clause; the issue of abortion and customary rights threatened to derail gender solidarity; the debate around proportional versus the constituency-based electoral systems was heated; federalism versus centralised control provoked divergent responses; yet Ramaphosa held the process together with his amiable, gentle, yet decisive demeanour.

His relationship with Roelf Meyer was legendary. He managed the wide chasm between the ANC, the National Party, the Democratic Party, the Freedom Front, the Pan Africanist Congress and others with aplomb.

He could defuse the growing tension between divergent views with even a lame joke and have everyone in stitches. He pulled in the expertise and resources of the best constitutional experts into the six theme committees and I shall never forget the flurry of activity, debates, conferences and workshops between the politicians and the nongovernmental organisations trying to get to grips with what a truly representative South African constitution would be, with a Bill of Rights that would be unique to SA.

What this entire exercise demonstrated was the willingness of political actors across wide divisions to work together and reach a compromise. People whom many of us wrote off as dinosaurs were now in the fold and talking to each other. Four months before the May 8 1996 deadline, 68 issues were unresolved and there was great concern that the deadline would not be reached. Even by April 22 1996 there was no consensus on the death penalty, the appointment of judges and the attorney-general, language, local government, proportional representation and the floor-crossing issue.

By April 1996, there had been 298 amendments but the entire process went swimmingly under Ramaphosa's capable leadership, so that by May 8 1996 the text was completed. March 1997 was the culmination of a difficult process, ending with more than seven million copies of the constitution distributed in eleven languages all over the country.

For these reasons, Ramaphosa is ideally suited to bring that experience to bear on bringing the ANC together again, with its political contenders, into an inclusive society united in its goal to drag SA out of poverty.

Ramaphosa has economic power. What he wants now, it seems, is political power, not for its own sake, but to use it to take SA in a different direction – eliminating economic inequality, creating a culture of tolerance, and building a healthy civil society that will work together to support and sustain a different kind of democracy to the one we have now.

He would not hesitate to bring committed activists and experts back into the fold to utilise their skills in ways that would benefit SA. The task is not easy, given that he is perceived to be a ruthless Randlord, but I hope that by now he is so tired of making money that he will truly focus on the poor, the unemployed, the landless and the huge army of HIV-infected people.

Lest I forget, Ramaphosa had a fair amount of political groupies who swooned over him, obeying his every beck and call. Everyone wanted his attention and while he loved the grovelling, work got done around him. If he stands for president, we might just be in for one of the most exciting dispensations this country has seen. I am sure the country will rally around him despite some minor misgivings.

Sisulus embodied noble principles

Business Day August 5 2003

'HE TOWERS above all of us with his humility and intrinsic dignity.' – Nelson Mandela. Walter Sisulu's passing, sadly, is the beginning of the end of an era in the African National Congress (ANC).

Described as a postmodern feminist by his daughter-in-law, Elinor Sisulu, one can comfortably call him the grande dame (I don't know the male version) of ANC politics. Amina Cachalia called him a selfless, nonmaterialistic comrade, a sentiment echoed by Ahmed Kathrada.

George Bizos praised him for his sacrificial service, a model to young people, who would do well to imitate him.

Former president Nelson Mandela movingly talks about how their lives were intertwined for the past 62 years. 'We shared the joy of living, and the pain. Together we shared ideas, forged common commitments. We walked side by side through danger and tribulation, nursing each other's bruises, holding each other up when our steps faltered. Together we savoured the taste of freedom. His absence has carved a void. A part of me is gone.'

What an epitaph.

Mandela's pain at losing a bosom pal is poignant and one senses his apprehension that Sisulu's death signals the slow demise of a camaraderie typical of comradeship in those days.

Reading Sisulu's history, one cannot help but notice that he was born, ironically, the year that the ANC was formed. He had a difficult young life, moving from job to job to survive. His quest for dignity as a black man automatically attracted him in 1940 to the ANC – the home then of the marginalised and oppressed.

Those were difficult times, the decade before and after the Nationalist Party took over. Sisulu's militancy and uncompromising nature were understandable given the tyranny with which resistance was met.

His life was a product of turbulent times, yet he remained a devout family man, husband and comrade throughout his life of hardship. The '50s and early '60s were marked by police intimidation, harassment and imprisonment, culminating in the treason trial in 1963.

In looking at this eventful life, one cannot help but link Sisulu with his wife Albertina, a stalwart partner who encouraged him to continue his political commitments through the ANC Women's League and the Federation of SA Women when he was banned.

A great political couple, they complemented each other. They managed to keep marriage and family together despite the disruptions and threats to their lives. Their intense political involvement enriched their family in ways that we will never be able to measure. While Sisulu was in jail, Albertina's small nursing salary provided for seven children, her own five and two of her sister-in-law's. As a member of the Federation of SA Women, she was jailed while still breast-feeding her ten-month-old baby, banned for five years and placed under house arrest for ten years.

In 1981, Albertina was arrested for speaking at the funeral of Rose Mbele, one of her patients. At the trial she was even blamed for the ANC flag that draped Mbele's coffin. The judge's statement at her sentencing signalled how the law at the time saw her and Walter as one: 'You allowed yourself to be used by the ANC by allowing yourself to be introduced to the public as Mrs Walter Sisulu, the people's secretary.' She was sentenced to four years in prison for being Mrs Sisulu.

The Sisulu history is an example of an effective and heartwarming political symbiosis, of a couple who embodied the noble principles of the Freedom Charter and what the ANC represented. In a cynical world where marriages and relationships don't last, the Sisulu partnership, under extremely difficult and trying circumstances, is writ large on the political canvas of history.

We say *hamba kahle* to an ANC cadre who gave the movement the grace, dignity and humility I hope will be kept alive with renewed vigour in the party. In the words of Bizos: 'SA has lost a great man. He has left us with a legacy of what it means to be a great citizen.'

☛ What you sow, you shall reap

Mail & Guardian April 2 to 8 1999

I WISH TO RESPOND to Farid Esack's condemnation of Judge John Foxcroft's ruling against Allan Boesak ('Used and discarded like a condom', *Mail & Guardian* March 26 to April 1 1999). As a religious teacher and gender commissioner whose primary concern should be with establishing the rule of law and morality in a country where crime is the order of the day, he sets worrying precedents.

Esack knows he is treading on dangerous ground, hence he seeks conscious justification for illogical arguments. His basic argument is, given Boesak's stature and the horrors of apartheid, Boesak's crime pales into significance, hence he should not have been sentenced. And what right has this judge of yesteryear to judge our inimitable cleric?

Boesak has been condemned by many as yet another senior ANC official found guilty of theft and fraud. More seriously, a point missed by many, the man is a highly trained theologian and dominee, who strayed from his calling through his lust for power, money and women, in that order.

Ironically, his conviction coincides with that of the president of the Baptist Church in the United States who was found guilty of fraud of enormous proportions. The difference, however, is that the Baptist president publicly apologised to his wife, children, church and nation for his misdemeanours. There was not one iota of remorse and repentance in the fibre of Boesak's being.

The tragedy about Boesak is that his attraction to Mammon made him forget that his talents lay elsewhere. And a gifted theologian he was. As a chaplain of the University of the Western Cape in the 1980s, he never lacked an audience. I, too, was astounded at his polished enunciation of one of the complex utterances of Jesus: 'I come to bring a sword not peace.' The man, therefore, is to be pitied for, like a Shakespearean tragedy, his fall has been occasioned by his lust for power, regardless of all his other talents.

It was clear to many in the struggle that his intoxication with his meteoric rise to power would be the seed of his destruction. If he 'felt called to be an instrument in the hands of God', why did he succumb to the temptations of the world? To be called and to feel used are different things, and reflect Esack's muddled thinking. Boesak cannot be a victim while also wanting to be an instrument.

While his oratory skills and courage were not doubted, Boesak engineered his own leadership and his own detention in ways that kept many dinner conversations going. There was a way in which apartheid forced greatness on all us, and Boesak's ego was ready bait for this. Why this sudden emphasis on his exceptional leadership when many of his friends gossiped endlessly about his newfound opulence, his self-conscious vanities and his affairs?

As a humble cleric, with a sudden rise to fame and easy access to funds, he sowed the seeds of his downfall by submitting to pleasures of the flesh. And for this he is solely to blame. Beyers Naudé, Desmond Tutu, Cosmos Desmond, Paul Verryn and many other struggle priests did not let the side down.

Boesak was indeed called, but refused to listen, unlike Tutu, who regardless of whatever situation he found himself in, stuck to his calling. While Tutu can be criticised for often failing to distinguish between his role as a secular head of a state institution, the Truth and Reconciliation Commission, and as a priest, he should be respected and lauded for never reneging on his calling. Boesak strayed and refuses to take responsibility for his actions. What's more, he gets support from key people in society whose rise to power have equally blinded them to what is right and what is wrong.

Boesak deserved the sentence meted out to him because he stole from the poor to enrich himself. Analogies with the sentence meted out to Angelina Zwane's killer are opportunistic at best. When Freddie Steenkamp was jailed for six years for a similar offence, there was not a peep of support from politicians and sympathisers. No, because *he* was the skelm, not Boesak, and *he* was responsible for Boesak's downfall.

But now that Judge Foxcroft has proven otherwise, the analogy is expediently used in the media to urge the transformation of the judiciary. So the judge becomes the villain, and is implied to be racist, an instrument of the untransformed judiciary.

The judiciary is there precisely to guard against public pressure and mob justice. All who are found guilty of crime should be treated fairly, a basic tenet of the constitution. Justice is no respecter of title, and one's struggle credentials should in no way exonerate one from the application of the law.

To suggest Boesak is the 'fall guy' is to deny his own agency in his downfall. To link his sentence with Cassinga, Lusaka, Gaborone, Sharpeville, etcetera, and amnesty for murderers and political criminals, is to miss the point and blame the judiciary for the political compromise made at the World Trade Centre.

It is precisely because of the amnesty provision that it is incumbent upon us, especially on human rights activists, to uphold the rule of law and to seek its enforcement equitably.

Esack fails dismally in trying to make a case for Boesak by invoking inappropriate analogies. In this exercise he deliberately suspends his logic for reasons that are understandable, but totally unacceptable.

Boesak is not the first great man who has fallen. The great king David also did, but he said, 'Woe is me for I have sinned.'

Boesak seems to have forgotten Christ's warning that what you sow you shall reap. Hopefully he will ruminate upon these words during his quiet times in prison. Or perhaps, by some stroke of political manoeuvring, incarceration might escape him too. This, I fear, is the intention of Esack's article.

Transformation (Troubled Transformation)

☛ A coconut knocks on the door of the Native Club
Business Day June 1 2006

HI. I'M Rhoda Kadalie and I should like to apply for membership of the Native Club.

Your credentials, please?

I am short, black and female.

You qualify on short and female, but not on black. Are you black as in ANC black? Or as in UDF black?

UDF black.

Sorry, the latter does not apply.

Why not?

There is too much rainbow in that black. To qualify for this club you need to be black black.

How do you determine that? Do you use the pencil test, the nose test, or the head test?

No, those tests were used under apartheid.

Which tests do you use now?

The Native Club admits only those who can write, spell, and think.

Oh, I thought race was central.

No, you need only write what we tell you to write, then you'll be admitted. You see, that is what is meant by black.

Oh, now I understand – you mean black consciousness. But Steve Biko's motto was 'I write what I like', even though he was the leader of the Black Consciousness movement.

Yes, but he was black and unconscious – that is why he was never in the ANC!

The Natives are restless again, and this after ten years of democracy. I keep wondering what will calm them down, but I have no way of knowing, since I, as the resident coconut intellectual, will never be admitted to this august body of thinkers. They remind me of Sabra (the South African Bureau of Racial Affairs), the apartheid government's think-tank of non-Natives, who thought about the Natives all the time, to the point of wanting to control them.

They taught at the University of the Western Cape and were sent there to rein in the restless Natives. But the Natives were cheeky and picketed and marched and burnt down the buildings. Ungrateful lowlifes!

No matter what the Natives did, Sabra persevered in their pursuit to understand them. The cheekier the Native, the more tantalising they were to these pale intellectuals, whose inspiration came from their founding fathers – Strydom, Diederichs and Verwoerd. They said funny things about the Natives all the time, even though they found them a nuisance. So obsessed were they with them that they even created a whole ideology about how to keep them in their place.

Some of the things they said about their *bêtes noirs* – *noirs* in more ways than one – were extremely entertaining. Ben Maclennan reminds us what they said about the *noirs* – one could easily have mistaken them for jolly hotnots.

'I know the Native, I speak the Native tongue, I am familiar with his customs ... I know his habits. Knowing the Native as I do, I can assure the committee that the Native wants apartheid.' (Capt GHF Strydom, National Party Aliwal, House of Assembly, 1948.)

'We do not believe the Native is really a communist at heart. He is not able to form a conception of the ideology and of the dialectical materialism of their doctrine.' (Dr N Diederichs, National Party Randfontein, House of Assembly, September 9 1948.)

'Does the honourable member believe for one single moment that in the Native mind there is no such thing as a national consciousness? Of course every Native has the consciousness that he is a Native.' (Minister of Native Affairs, Dr HF Verwoerd, House of Assembly, May 28 1951.)

'Mr Lovett, a former general manager of the Native labour organisations of the Transvaal and Free State Chamber of Mines, said the real barrier to political, economic and social equality between Natives and Europeans in SA was not primarily based on distinctions of colour. It was formed by a natural gulf between, on the one hand, large groups of Native races that were only emerging from the darkness of barbarism and, on the other hand, the civilised groups, which were chiefly represented by the European population groups. He divided the Natives into five groups – the primitive Native, the responsible dressed Native, the irresponsible dressed Native, the semi-educated Native and the educated Native.' (*Optima*, journal of the Anglo American Corporation, quoted in the *Cape Times* March 10 1955.) (From *Apartheid, the Lighter Side*.)

There you have it – five different kinds of Natives. I can perfectly understand why the Native Club wants to retain its pet name. 'NC' is the perfect logo for those Natives who want to continue with the closed community of ideas that many of us gave up a long time ago.

☛ ANC's transformation is nothing but hogwash
Business Day November 10 2005

HAVING BEEN in the US for two weeks, I come back completely out of touch with what has been happening in SA.

Clueless about what to write in my next column, I peruse past newspapers and feel sickened to see the continuing Zuma-Mbeki melodrama, the slightly more intriguing spy saga, the Imvume and UN food scandals taking on international proportions, and Scopa (Standing Committee on Public Accounts) yet again snatched from the official opposition.

Corruption in municipalities abounds and protests around delivery continue amid reports of gross underspending. In the Western Cape, the SAPS takes sides between Rasool and Skwatsha, and shoots at and assaults peaceful protesters. Like Pieter-Dirk Uys, I remain grateful to the politicians for writing my script.

Let me remind you of a few incidents that struck me as related and which point to an increasingly heavy-handed police service that defies the very essence of Batho Pele. Police fire rubber bullets and tear gas at the poorest of the poor as they protest about typhoid deaths and raw sewage flowing across their streets and through their homes – while fat-cat African National Congress (ANC) councillors cream it off the top. What is frightening is not so much what we have come to, but where we are headed.

Our police, military and secret services, no more or less arrogant than their apartheid-era counterparts, are increasingly brutalising the vulnerable in our society – seemingly with impunity and with full approval from the top.

For example: 'Safety and Security Minister Charles Nqakula has settled a R1.3-million damages action by a restaurant owner, his assistant and two customers after police and paramilitary officials assaulted them in full view of members of the public in 2002.' This from the *Cape Times* September 9 2005.

The case against the minister was brought by the owner of the Mandola Restaurant in Observatory, Johan Dyssel, his assistant and two customers. They allege, without demur from Nqakula, that members of the police and paramilitary personnel arrived at the restaurant, without a warrant of arrest, broke down the door, assaulted four people by hitting them with fists, rifle butts and truncheons, swore at them and kicked them as they lay on the floor, damaged the restaurant and detained Dyssel and his assistant for two days. During their illegal incarceration the restaurant was looted – possibly by the very people who had deprived them of their rights. While paying out the R1.13 million – not his money but yours and mine – Nqakula bizarrely, but in true apartheid tradition, alleged the arrests were lawful and, in the true apartheid-era ethos, there has been no indication of any action taken against the thugs responsible.

The military seems just as keen in this regard. In August, 72-year-old Simon's Town pensioner Felix Baddely was awarded R60 000 – your money and mine – after Adm George Mpafi had him arrested by military police and confined to a police cell for a night without food or blankets. Baddely's 'crime' was to knock on the door of his neighbour, the admiral, at 9.30 am, and ask him if he could stop his dogs from keeping the neighbourhood awake through repeated nights by their barking. Mpafi was rewarded with a promotion to Pretoria where he now struts his stuff as head of external affairs for the defence department.

On January 13 2005, the decades-old South African Museum of Military History was raided by a combined force of SAPS and military police. The curators, Susanne Blendulf and Richard Henry, were accused of having, among the more than 40 000 exhibits on display, 'suspicious, stolen, military vehicles'. Though they were unarmed and offered no resistance, our crack squad of commandos felt it necessary to lead them away in handcuffs. The museum director, John Keene, was at home recovering from an eye operation. He too was arrested, incarcerated and refused medical treatment even though it was explained to the goons on duty that this could result in his losing an eye.

They were only released after the public prosecutor refused to prosecute them.

Keene was rushed to hospital for an emergency eye operation and a subsequent operation was also required. Defence Minister Mosiuoa Lekota praised the quick and efficient actions of the police.

The perceptions of an increasingly concerned international community were summed up by Helmoet-Römer Heitman, local representative for Jane's Defence Weekly. He described the arrest and incarceration of the three curators as 'medieval'.

Transformation – the ANC's buzzword – is nothing but hogwash.

☞ And SA's new black elite said: 'Let them eat pap'
Business Day August 19 2004

IN OUR HEADY rush to majority rule in the early 1990s, the trade unions made us honest, playing a major role by their inexorable dismantling of apartheid in the workplace.

Now they are keeping us honest as manifest in trade union federation Cosatu's recent articulation of the obvious fact that legalistic black economic empowerment is, in effect, simply black elite enrichment.

They, like others who care about the future of this country, see that President Thabo Mbkei's two-nations concept is fast taking on a different guise. No longer is it just the rich whites and poor blacks.

Now it is the chosen sons of the African National Congress (ANC) at the trough versus the millions on welfare and in the social grants queue.

The anomalies are glaring and as obvious to all. In less than a decade Patrice Motsepe has acquired more wealth through empowerment than Pick 'n Pay's Raymond Ackerman has acquired in half a century through hard work.

Putco's shareholders rebelled against the iniquity of Saki Macozoma's company Safika acquiring 28% of their company's equity at a discount of 96% not least because there was absolutely no benefit for Putco's 4 000, mostly black, employees.

Their temerity enraged Smuts Ngonyama. Similarly enraged was the president when Sasol's Pieter Cox had the nerve to suggest empowerment had a downside. I would have thought the billions of rand in overseas investment being lost when details of government's mining charter became known proved the point.

Yet while most here see empowerment as serving, but not sating, the avarice of the party-anointed, what do international investors say? At a recent Cape Town Press Club function, Robert Guest, Africa editor of *The Economist*, said that empowerment was seen abroad as nothing more than a traditional slice for Africa's elite and part of the cost of doing business on the continent.

In his book *The Shackled Continent* he notes that in SA a favoured place at the perimeter of the trough is not gender-specific, and the wives of those so aptly described as 'the new Jacobins' are not precluded from getting their snouts into the gravy.

What is then striking about the ANC's nouveaux riches is that they are not using their unearned, risk-free, patronage-derived largesse to benefit SA's wellbeing.

I am not even sure the newly rich set up scholarships, academic trusts, endowments for faculties of medicine or libraries, provide grants for environmental or historic heritage conservation, or back the deserving and needy.

The message to the poor from the black economic empowerment 'capitalists without capital' who pay nothing upfront for their massively discounted shares – the new Marie Antoinettes and their spouses – is thus clear: 'Let them eat pap!'

We need a united opposition that will fast replace black economic empowerment with poor economic empowerment, and stop the rising Russian-type oligarchic mafia owning it all.

Last year empowerment deals exceeded R42 billion, and will top that this year. With reference to those she admiringly called 'the gentlemen of empowerment', mining minister Phumzile Mlambo-Ngcuka has said they should not be shy to say they are 'filthy rich'.

However, filth comes at a price. The Kenyan government discovered this recently when its approaches for aid and investment were memorably equated by a British diplomat with 'vomiting on our shoes'.

I challenge Mbeki and Ngonyama to give us a single example of how shackdwellers adjoining the section of the N2 travelled by overseas investors between Cape Town's airport and its central business district have benefited from broad-based empowerment. Perhaps they can also explain to us how it differs in principle from the ubiquitous cronyism in Africa.

In the light of those sentiments, I note Public Enterprises Minister Alec Erwin hopes to achieve foreign direct investment (FDI) of 2% of our gross domestic product (GDP) in the coming years. This compares with our present FDI of 0.5% of our GDP.

With about eight million people unemployed and a disturbing number of jobs having been lost during our 'ten years of democracy', it is a target we must reach.

However, given the odium being created here and abroad by the ANC's 'black elite empowerment' policies, one's reluctant response must perforce be: dream on Alec and please stay clear of the shoes of potential investors!

Just a nuance away from smash-and-grab looting
Business Day September 2 2004

THIS RELUCTANT sequel to my column on black economic empowerment a fortnight ago was inspired by the latest shenanigans of the former head of the Industrial Development Corporation, Khaya Ngqula.

He hit the headlines in the *Sunday Times* not only for his appointment as the CEO of the ailing South African Airways, but also for his recent divorce, a soapie from hell, it seems.

Off with a young Miss Universe SA to his apartment in the south of France, he has had to pay his former wife R5 million in the divorce settlement. She apparently asked for R25 million.

The man, no doubt, has money. With several homes in the best areas and a family trust allegedly holding R21 million in investments, the wife obviously knows his assets.

The question I want answered is how do some board members and senior executives involved with the corporation – a state institution, constituted by an act of Parliament and financed by the state – amass this amount of wealth within such a short time and presumably pay taxes?

The corporation's role as a national development-finance institution is to stimulate economic growth, industrial development and economic empowerment at national and regional levels. But all I see is economic growth and the empowerment of the usual suspects to whom expensive divorce settlements are but minor irritations. The corporation has been mired in previous corruption allegations, which have surfaced again.

If half the energy and creativity put into the frenzied compiling of empowerment charters could be used in curbing crime, AIDS and unemployment, SA would be a happier, safer place for all. Every endeavour – bar prostitution, it seems – is getting its empowerment charter, and even the latter, I am sure, will soon be targeted!

Zaireans who experienced the Mobutu Sese Seko era in Congo have a name for beneficiaries of such charters: 'grosses legumes' (big vegetables). Anyone who has read Michela Wrong's eloquent analysis of that era, *In the Footsteps of Mr Kurtz*, will be aware not only of the term's origins but of the disturbing analogies between the big vegetables in equatorial Africa and the situation in southern Africa.

For those who haven't, the following extract: 'In 1973 Mobutu decreed that foreign-owned farms, plantations, commercial enterprises – mostly in the hands of Portuguese, Greek, Italian and Pakistani traders – should be turned over to "sons of the country". That was followed by radicalisation, in which the largely Belgian-controlled industrial sector was confiscated.

'The result was an obscene scramble for freebies by the burgeoning Zairean elite. Thousands of businesses, totalling around $1billion in value, were divided between top officials in the most comprehensive nationalisation seen in Africa.

'The social class known as the "grosses legumes" – a term used by ordinary Zaireans with a mixture of resentment and awe – was born.

'The proceeds were spent on luxury items with imports of Mercedes-Benz hitting an African record one year after Zaireanisation. Ordinary Zaireans, supposed beneficiaries of the process, watched in shock as businesses closed, prices rose, jobs were doled out by new bosses on purely nepotistic lines, and shelves emptied.

'After a few weeks the big vegetables could be heard asking when the Portuguese and Greek businessmen who had left the country would be coming back to stock the warehouses.

'But in the west, outraged parent companies had halted supplies, and frozen credit to their former subsidiaries.

'Until Zaireanisation, the economy had grown by an average of 7% a year. Look at the graph of just about any indicator and there, in 1974, is the sharp peak, followed by a long, slow unstoppable swoop that continues to this day.

'For the population, Zaireanisation's impact was to extend beyond the immediate commercial crisis. The belief that something could be had for nothing, the looter's smash-and-grab mentality, had been endorsed at the very highest level of society.

'Before Zaireanisation, corruption, while a problem, had seemed to observers on a par with that witnessed in many other emerging African states.

'But, in the generalised climate of impunity created by this botched economic experiment, sleaze – whether practised by the lowly breadseller or the Mercedes-driving big vegetable – was about to become the most striking characteristic of Zairean society.'

While the African National Congress would bridle at the suggestion that the 'looter's smash-and-grab mentality' motivates today's empowerment deals, others would say the difference between it and Mobutu's programme lies only in nuance – Zaireanisation was the threat-induced handover of wealth the recipients had done nothing to create, and empowerment is the legally induced handover.

☛ Local solutions to halt SA's sure slide into chaos
Business Day April 24 2008

THE FRONT-PAGE story in *The Weekender* last weekend on the exodus of South African doctors was alarming. According to *Productivity SA* and the *2007 IMD World Competitiveness Yearbook*, SA is among the 55 countries with the highest brain drains and worst skills shortages.

On nearly every major international index, SA is either lagging or sinking deeper into the quagmire. This is hardly surprising. It is the logical conclusion of a deeply failed education system unable to compete in maths, science and technology with other African countries, despite its more advanced status. It is the result of a failed affirmative action policy that alienates skilled labour from our shores, and an aggressive black economic empowerment policy that promotes black wealth by stealth, regardless of merit. And more seriously, it is about professionals choosing life over death, in a country where murder, robbery, rape and hijacking have become national sports.

There is nothing more hurtful than seeing South African-educated doctors, nurses, pharmacists, physiotherapists and engineers leave for first world countries such as Canada, Britain, Australia and New Zealand. It is too simplistic to say those who emigrate are unpatriotic. Who wants to leave family, friends and the country of one's birth, especially when it is one of the most beautiful in the world? Our hospitals are in steady decline, the clinics are no better and the burgeoning burden of disease makes working in healthcare a living nightmare. And even though the health minister has made primary healthcare a priority, local clinics are the places where the dignity of many, especially the poor, is regularly affronted and their health rights infringed.

Equally, municipalities all over SA are collapsing due to the exodus of engineers and technicians, worsening the precarious sanitation conditions in informal settlements and the rural areas and causing the development of infrastructure to lag behind. The '2007-2008 National Capacity Assessment Report', released by the Municipal Demarcation Board, revealed that '74% of district municipalities performed less than 50% of their functions. In the same period 53% of all local municipalities performed less than 50% of their functions.' This same report reveals that most municipal managers lacked the experience to perform optimally, a situation worsened by the fact that a large number of senior positions are vacant.

On the Human Development Index, we have actually moved downwards due to our shocking infant mortality, maternal mortality and life expectancy rates. With eight-million people infected with tuberculosis and more than five million with HIV/AIDS, President Thabo Mbeki and his cabinet have been tolerated for far too long. Under his leadership, every public institution has been destroyed – the public protector, the Land Bank, the Independent Complaints Directorate, the SABC, Telkom and Eskom.

This rapid slide into chaos can only be halted by Mbeki's competitor, Jacob Zuma, and his cohorts. Zuma's victory at Polokwane has to be a victory for the salvation of this country, if it means the beginning of a new dispensation of public service, citizen participation, good governance, political competition, service delivery and a selfless leadership that puts the people first.

The problems that plague our country can be addressed. Two weeks ago, the Impumelelo Innovations Award Trust hosted a two-day workshop on skills training, education and employment, where our award-winning projects presented their examples of best practice to an audience of 90 delegates. Over two days we witnessed solutions to the maths, science and engineering problems in the country; to the exodus of doctors and nurses; to the literacy and numeracy problem in the rural areas; to basic adult education; and the use of arts and crafts in job creation. This workshop demonstrated that there are African solutions for African problems. We need look no further than the Impumelelo database.

☛ We cannot dismiss reasons whites give for leaving
Business Day October 5 2006

THE TOPIC of the John Perlman radio talk show on Monday, 'Victims or Villains', was the ultimate provocation to a white woman who called in to complain of another show, also hosted by SAfm, which she believes fuels anti-white sentiment.

Host Nikiwe Bikitsha went ballistic at the accusation, claiming it was the show's right to encourage debate, but then rudely cut off the caller, who complained that the title itself was loaded.

Nikiwe, who is generally calm and polite to her callers, lost it with this woman. It was obviously a sore point. Were the one-million whites, who were leaving, according to *Rapport*, victims or villains? The report published by the South African Institute of Race Relations, based on an analysis of the 'Statistics SA Household Surveys from 1995 to 2005', said that the main reasons given for emigrating were crime and affirmative action.

Many callers phoned in accusing those who leave of hankering after their apartheid past and being unable to come to terms with a country where they were no longer the privileged. Some accused the emigrants of outright racism, of not being committed to transformation and the development of the country. Those who balked at these accusations called in to tell of their children, friends and relatives who have left against their will, as their options were increasingly becoming limited. The rampant crime and the racist application of affirmative action were cited as reasons for leaving.

The number of whites who have left since 1995 is astounding. According to the 2005 census, approximately 841 000 white South Africans have left, leaving the current white population at 4.3 million. The cohort that leaves is apparently between twenty and 40 years old, with children. The frequent complaint – that they are being punished for apartheid, which many felt they were not responsible for – should be taken seriously. Indirectly punishing white people for the past is a betrayal of our negotiated settlement. We cannot afford to let our economically productive citizens leave, nor can we afford a shrinking tax base, given that our economically active black population is dying like flies of AIDS.

It is easy to make negative political capital out of this phenomenon, when in fact we should be extremely worried that an important, highly skilled sector of our population is leaving – not to speak of the coloured and Indian professionals who are also disappearing at a rapid rate. This loss is particularly serious in the public sector, where whole layers of medical, technical and engineering skills have gone. It takes about eight to ten years to grow and nurture experienced engineers, doctors or technicians, and to lose them because of affirmative action is to throw the baby out with the bath water.

While affirmative action is seen to be an important political imperative, there seems to be denial about the havoc it is wreaking on the economy and the public sector. Skilled labour is scarce, not because there is a paucity of qualified people, but because we drive skilled people out for stupid reasons. SA is one of the least successful countries in Africa when it comes to producing black students who are literate in maths, science and technology. The poor matric results attest to this as well as the fact that few teachers in black schools are properly qualified to teach maths and science. Add to this the moratorium placed on employing white male academics in some universities, and we are really in trouble.

Given the challenges facing our country, we ignore the 'purge' at our peril. The consequences for the economy and the public sector are dire and when a whole sector of a population feels unwanted, from a constitutional point of view, their rights to a livelihood and economic activity are under threat.

I am convinced that most whites who leave do not want to go and that they feel driven out by crime and affirmative action. We forget that it is government's duty to create the kind of society in which people want to stay and contribute. And there are many who do stay at great cost to themselves. A sound case can be made for affirmative action when properly applied, but when vacancies in the public sector amount to thousands, government has to find ways to seriously stem the tide of current emigration levels.

Dance for All, for example, is a ballet company set up in the townships to train black youth in classical ballet and a variety of other dance forms. Two of SA's premier retired ballet dancers, Philip Boyd and Phyllis Spira, set up studios in the black townships, the Cape Flats and in the rural areas specifically to train black dancers and so provide job opportunities for those who formerly have been excluded from the profession. Spira, as well as some of the other members, were brutally attacked at one of the studios in the townships, but survived.

This is but one story of committed white people who go out of their comfort zone to teach black people in the performing arts, a profession formerly preserved for whites.

In appealing to our loyalty, the African National Congress too often confuses loyalty to the country with loyalty to the government, and when people criticise government's failure to protect them from rampant crime, they are labelled unpatriotic, racist and against transformation. But no amount of political rhetoric of ubuntu, of African Renaissance, of transformation, of empowerment, will hold educated and talented people behind when opportunities abound overseas. The availability of jobs, access to public transport and the freedom to enjoy the public sphere are increasingly becoming attractive to people who want better prospects.

Unlike many of us who do not have the option to leave, or who choose the beauty of SA above our safety, others choose life and freedom and I certainly do not blame them for it. My daughter is well on her way to becoming a villain.

ANC creates new diaspora with race-based laws
Business Day September 30 2004

DO EVERYTHING you can to retain the skills and expertise of professionals. This was the sage advice proffered recently to the African National Congress (ANC) by Mozambican President Joaquim Chissano.

I was reminded of this by a typically pithy and cogent letter to this paper recently by former *Sunday Times* editor Ken Owen. He averred that while SA's current situation in no way justified Afro-pessimism, the bottleneck being created by a shortage of skill and expertise was one of the greatest challenges this country faced.

That bottleneck affects every sector of our society, but specifically the poor. Millions of rand sit unused in government's coffers, Eastern Cape is a basket case, dozens of municipalities are dysfunctional, once world-leading institutions such as the Red Cross Children's Hospital and the Onderstepoort Veterinary Research Institute are in decline and pensioners die in endless queues.

This took me back to a function I attended few months ago at the University of Cape Town. The guest speaker was Pallo Jordan, accepting a posthumous award on behalf of his late father, Dr Archibald Campbell Jordan.

In 1957 AC Jordan became the first black African to receive a PhD at UCT.

After being refused a passport in 1961, which would have enabled him to utilise a Carnegie travel grant to tour universities in the US, he went into exile. He later became a professor in the department of African languages at the University of Wisconsin-Madison, where he died in 1968.

He was one of the first of a new black diaspora created by apartheid legislation such as the Job Reservation Act, and for the next half-century SA would be immeasurably impoverished as the brightest and best of our black talent moved abroad, depriving the country of their talents, energies and patriotism.

Ironically, everything indicates the ANC is creating a new diaspora with similarly race-based labour laws. More than a million of SA's expatriates live in Britain alone. Close on that number has left since 1994 for countries from Canada in the north to New Zealand in the south.

The ANC justifies this legislation on the basis of a need to implement 'representivity', a word that does not even exist in the dictionary. This is not without precedent. On coming to power, the Nazis promptly tabled and passed laws that limited the entry of Jewish students to universities to 1.5% of new applicants because this reflected their proportionality within Germany's population at that time.

Hendrik Verwoerd advocated the same principle because the Afrikaner, impoverished first by the Boer War and then the Great Depression, was unable to compete with the better educated English speakers in the professions.

He advocated a quota system in which both groups would be represented 'according to its percentage of the white population'.

There is not a white, coloured or Indian in this country who, if not personally a victim of affirmative action, does not know someone who is.

Ask Govin Reddy how he felt about being overlooked in 1998 in favour of his subordinate, the ineffectual and subsequently replaced Hawu Mbatha, for the post of SABC CEO. In my case I am haunted by the memory of a former colleague, a white lecturer at the University of the Western Cape, whose PhD now qualifies him to work as a security guard.

The purpose of such race-based legislation, whether implemented by Adolf Hitler, Verwoerd, Idi Amin, or Robert Mugabe, is to remove competition. What it does not do is ameliorate conditions for the poorest of the poor as those now dying an agonisingly slow death of starvation in Zimbabwe – without causing Mojunku Gumbi any loss of sleep – will testify.

And so history repeats itself.

Just as the ANC intelligentsia, the likes of AC Jordan, left the country in their thousands in the sixties, seventies and eighties, so whites, coloureds and Indians now leave the country in their tens of thousands, hoping to make a new start in countries where their skin colour and ethnic affiliation will not disbar them from progress and prosperity.

In time, they, like AC Jordan and Boer War freedom fighters banished to Ceylon, will die, lonely in exile, their gravestones poignant, enduring testimony to the South African government's racial exclusivity. If I were Thabo Mbeki, I would use the skills of whites in particular as their contribution to reparation in SA. As it stands, no one benefits.

And the poor will continue to suffer. *Aluta continua.*

☛ State must act now to plug brain drain
Business Day September 11 2003

RETURNING from a recent trip overseas, I sat next to a young coloured man who was on his way to Cape Town from London. Looking very much like one of us I asked him whether he was coming home to SA from a holiday. He said that he was on his way to visit his family in Grabouw.

I probed further curiously and asked him what he did for a living. 'I teach maths to British kids,' he said very proudly in his unmistakeably plattelandse accent.

And where did you study? 'At the Pentechnikon in Bellville and then on to Cape Tech and now I am doing postgraduate studies part-time at UCT.'

'But why are you not teaching in Grabouw where people like you are needed?'

'Because the education department treated me like a child, disrespectful of my career ambitions, blocking my access to promotions not because they were mean but simply because they were *slapgat*.

'All I wanted to do was to teach and give back some of the skills I acquired through hard work to my community but I was tired of being shoved around. When I saw an advertisement for a maths teacher in the UK I applied, doubtful that I might even be considered. I have been there now for almost two years and I've already had one promotion and have gained a lot of experience at the two British schools I have taught already.'

He also said, with some sense of achievement, that it was great being part of the global community of educators and that in his short space of time in the UK, he had travelled to Paris and Amsterdam. 'If I had submitted to (department) tyranny I would have rotted in Grabouw and only dreamt of Paris and Amsterdam as vague possibilities.'

Surely this is not the kind of teacher SA, let alone the platteland, can afford to lose? That he was Afrikaans speaking with a smattering of English did not deter the British from employing him. They recognised his abilities as a good maths teacher, first and foremost, and knew that after a year he would make a great maths teacher.

I have no doubt this young man will be followed by his peers and relatives to the UK where the fruits of knowledge, international travel, information technology and future career prospects seem extremely tantalising. And so, when I read in the *Cape Times* (August 18 2003), that almost 31 000 nursing posts are vacant, not to speak of the doctors and, allegedly, 8 000 teachers leaving in droves, then surely government ought to take stock of the situation.

The department needs to take steps, not punitive, to lure these people back and keep them here where they can make enormous contributions. What incentives are in place to keep our professionals here?

Incentives are not the only thing. Government needs to develop a deep respect for what doctors, nurses and teachers do – they often work at the coalface of extreme levels of poverty and underdevelopment. More importantly, conditions conducive to those who long only for a satisfying career are perhaps the best incentives to entice them to stay.

As long as salaries are not market-related, let alone having to vie with dollars and pounds, the brain drain will continue unabated until drastic measures are taken. Gauteng has 7 976 nursing vacancies, KwaZulu-Natal is short of 6 098 nurses, the Free State of 4 234 and Western Cape of 2 533.

Blaming the British, Canadians and Australians for 'raiding' our talent is futile. The lack of resources and inhumane conditions should be addressed with some urgency.

Coercive tactics such as compulsory medical service and imposing certificate of need provisions on doctors wanting to set up a hospital, clinics or surgeries are counterproductive.

Unless we seize the day, it will soon be too late to attract brains to the drain!

☛ Poor excuse for failure develops a life of its own
Business Day August 24 2006

A SMALL REPORT in the *Sunday Times* (August 20 2006) caught my eye. It looked insignificant but captured an issue at the heart of government's inability to deliver services to the poor.

'Youth body says it lacks capacity' is the story about the National Youth Commission complaining to MPs that it does not have the tools or 'capacity to achieve our mandate... Our research directorate is a joke compared with other government units.'

What an admission.

Almost blaming Parliament for their inability to do their work, these *laaities*, who earn more than professors (more than R500 000 a year), were appointed to high office by the ANC simply to co-opt them into the ruling elite lest they stray into Zuma's path.

Whatever the political reasons, many are far too young and inexperienced to do the job, and use the excuse of 'lack of capacity' as though it is unrelated to their abilities.

The same goes for the South African Local Government Authority (Salga), the National Development Agency and the Umsobomvu Fund. Millions of rands have been wasted on these organisations – their role being to build capacity – when the very people running them lack the skills and competencies to carry out functions they are meant to perform.

Business Day recently exposed former Salga CEO Thabo Mokwena's gross mismanagement of the body. And the auditor-general commented on exorbitant wastage under his command. Parliament's oversight body, Scopa, finds it difficult to keep track of misappropriations at this and similar bodies because, complains chairman Themba Godi, of perennial turnover of senior government officials, who despite bungling move on to the next job before they get found out.

And so this phrase 'lack of capacity' has developed a life of its own, a euphemism for the appointment of unskilled, unqualified, and incompetent people under the guise of affirmative action. By their own admission, these highly salaried, BMW-driving youth lack the qualifications to do their jobs. It has become commonplace for government to employ underqualified people, often political appointees, to top jobs, but then employ consultants, researchers and academics to do their work for them. Countless houses could have been provided with the money these institutions have wasted. Instead of taking up space in newspapers to counter John Pilger, government's Trevor Manuel and Joel Netshitenzhe should address this rampant wastage.

The government is its own worst advertisement for affirmative action. Project Consolidate is an admission that affirmative action has failed.

Debate on scrapping provinces is another acknowledgement that the incumbents (political appointees mostly), and equity-at-any-cost have affected delivery adversely. The more that local and provincial government fail to deliver, the more government thinks it should centralise. This politically inspired view denies that decentralisation, citizen participation and democratic decision-making at local level enhance rather than detract from effective service delivery.

The City of Cape Town, under mayor Nomaindia Mfeketo and city manager Wallace Mgoqi, was incompetent and wasteful because the most heinous affirmative action and procurement policies (compounded by secret forms of governance that excluded the public and opposition parties) destroyed capacity in that municipality.

The country cannot continue on this path, and has to find a better way to implement affirmative action. Government has to acknowledge that political appointments are not the same thing as affirmative action.

Second, affirmative action is not about redress, because we cannot make up for the travesties of apartheid but we can adopt measures to make equal opportunity a reality for those discriminated against.

Affirmative action should not exclude white people but should create a balance between what is needed and who is the best person to do the job. So if I were the president, I would employ rather than alienate skilled whites precisely so they can make up for the past – those with the best skills and privileged education should contribute to rebuilding SA by using the skills that advantaged them.

Third, affirmative action means appointing on the basis of merit, skills and qualifications of those formerly excluded. It does not ever mean getting rid of incumbents, no matter what their race, gender, or ethnicity.

For affirmative action to succeed, it has to go hand in hand with relevant selection and recruitment procedures; proper induction of new employees; continuing training and development of staff; transformation of the organisational culture; establishing special training programmes; and periodically setting goals and timetables for achieving diversity.

'Lack of capacity' is the result of policies based solely on race, gender or disability, and is responsible for municipalities collapsing and the decline of efficient services to the poor.

Affirmative action is a human-rights violation when unskilled people are foisted upon the poor, who need effective service delivery most.

☛ The point is delivery, not the race of the deliverer
Business Day March 17 2005

IN COMMON political parlance, 'transformation' has come to mean: is the organisation black enough? One is never sure that 'black enough' includes coloured and Indian. As for whites, they are redundant and may as well leave. But that is beside the point.

As far as government is concerned, the 'representivity' of an organisation is of the least concern, while they pretend otherwise. But in actual fact, transformation refers to more than racial demographics. It means the complete renewal of an organisation or a society, in form and substance. The *Cambridge International Dictionary* defines it as the complete change of appearance or character of something or someone so that they are improved.

When we talk about the transformation of the judiciary, it should be more than just a racial head count. A recent editorial in this newspaper noted the urgent changes needed to revolutionise the courts and the justice college, and to improve the management of the legal system. Citizens expect a legal process that is rigorous, fair and precedent-setting, in line with the constitution. It matters least what colour the judge is.

The same applies to the public service. Transformation means *Batho Pele* in action, a responsive government that provides services promptly, efficiently and respectfully to the public. It means a police force that is incorrupt and good at preventing crime; it refers to a health service that serves the sick efficiently.

While demographic profiles of organisations have changed, not much has changed in terms of real transformation since 1994, if recent *Special Assignment* programmes are anything to go by. They have featured programmes exposing corrupt, lazy, unresponsive, unaccountable officials in home affairs, the housing and welfare sectors, health and the police, and these were mainly blacks.

That is not to say that white people are not corrupt. The point I am making is that black does not necessarily mean transformed. The increase in black appointments has not improved the situation; if anything it has worsened it because black arrivals often lack skills and qualifications. Token appointments mean little and are of no consequence if they do not transform the organisation in question.

When a person of Cape Judge President John Hlophe's stature writes a report calling certain colleagues racist, citing unconvincing incidents to justify his allegations, then 'transformation' is exposed for what it is – the last resort of the incompetent. Is the race card used to cover up his feelings of inadequacy or has he genuinely been offended by his white colleagues? If so, he should come up with better examples and institute proceedings against offenders. After all, he is a judge.

Finding a racist in the public sector today is like looking for a needle in a haystack. White public officials are so politically correct they will not even use the word 'black' for fear of being labelled thus. So, when Hlophe calls Jeremy Gauntlett a racist, it is the ultimate insult to the advocate, who is so politically correct that bending over 'blackwards' comes as naturally to him as drinking water from a tap.

When professors Malegapuru Makgoba and Sipho Seepe were exposed recently for allegedly committing plagiarism, Makgoba's immediate response (according to *Die Burger* March 10 2005) was that these sorts of allegations led to polarisation, inferring that white academics were instigating a campaign against black academics to destroy them. But nobody told them to plagiarise.

When powerful, highly trained black men blame racism for their failures, they are no different to Robert Mugabe, who after twenty years of misrule still blames colonialism for his dictatorship and political failures.

To deny racism exists is like denying the sky is blue. Sadly, accusations of racism are made mostly about personal issues. They are rarely prompted by the poor services blacks receive at the hands of the public sector.

The racists are those people who steal public money to enrich themselves. The racists are those who steal linen and medicines from hospitals. The racists are those who refuse to relinquish power when their time is up.

The time has come for us to take responsibility for our own destiny – or are we forever going to inhabit the citadel of 'victimhood' and give substance to the saying that democracy gives everyone the right to be his or her own oppressor?

Unless we black people embrace democratic power and govern confidently, we will remain victims and confirm the worst suspicions of the rest of the world – that when we have power we do not know what to do with it.

☛ 'Victim' psychology finds expression in attacks
Business Day May 22 2008

EVERYBODY IS SHOCKED at the attacks on foreigners in Gauteng. In September 2006, I wrote a column condemning not only the murders of 31 Somalis in the Western Cape within two weeks but the police for failing to bring the murderers to book. I also warned that we would ignore these atrocities at our peril. At the time, senior police officers claimed that these were ordinary criminal attacks and had nothing to do with xenophobia.

Alexandra is now a cauldron of hate against those who seek refuge here and who cross our borders illegally, because those who do not have will blame those who are perceived to be a burden on the already scarce resources of the state. They see rising unemployment, the housing crisis and dire poverty as direct threats to their survival and retaliate against those closest to them, but who are considered 'other'.

This is compounded by the ineptitude of Home Affairs Minister Nosiviwe Mapisa-Nqakula, which has added fuel to the fire. She is completely out of her depth, displaying the worst incompetence imaginable. Unable to foresee the consequences of her inaction and that of her department, she plodded on until all hell broke loose, blaming the anger, among other things, on the 'exploitative wages' paid to these people by 'exploitative employers'.

All kinds of reasons have been proffered for the xenophobia, but no one dares to explore the deeper psychological stuff that is going on here. And it has to do with our inability to deal with the race question constructively. Not so long ago, I said President Thabo Mbeki's inability to deal with Robert Mugabe was because he has not dealt with his 'inner Zimbabwe'. An obsession with race has been the defining feature of his rule, and his design of an African Renaissance was a poor attempt at dealing with the legacy of racial discrimination. It became his excuse for the mismanagement of SA; for blaming reports of corruption on the white media; for castigating those concerned about HIV/AIDS as being obsessed with black male sexuality; and for shutting up complaints about crime as an elitist preoccupation.

And so when that video from the University of the Free State emerged, the government, the media, writers and certain institutions went to town, condemning the entire university as racist, barbaric and anti-black, instead of doing a thorough investigation into how the video was made, why black women participated, and why it was released at the time it was.

This one-sided portrayal of victimisation perpetuates and feeds into the 'woundedness' of black people and breeds an entitlement often lacking in refugees and immigrants. It breeds an ethos in victims that they can never be wrong and, given the circumstances, are 'owed' a livelihood. And when refugees and foreigners leave their countries for whatever reasons and come here and make it, it challenges the victim status quo. The lesson these outsiders teach us – not to depend on the government and not to expect handouts – goes against the inclination of those hard done by to find a solution to deprivation.

This in no way justifies the government's lack of responsibility towards the poor, the alienated and the deprived, but it does mean that if this entire society is to be healed from years of racial discrimination, the government, political parties and civic organisations should take the lead in minimising the kind of conflict that arises in situations of dire poverty, uncontrolled immigration and competition for scarce resources, such as jobs and housing.

The constitution gives the lead on how to deal with this, and obliges the government to act. Democracies fail when their *raison d'être* is to be reactive. A visionary government would have averted the kind of disaster we are witnessing. With our political history, we have the absolute wherewithal to prevent our communities from descending into such lawless crimes of hatred. We should stop exporting our truth commissions and start here. If anyone deserves a Nobel peace prize, it is Bishop Paul Verryn.

☛ Silence around murder of Somalis speaks volumes
Business Day September 7 2006

WHEN, NOT SO LONG AGO, the *Sunday Times* carried headlines that Africans were more racist than any other group in SA, the backlash was astounding.

It is commonly assumed that the oppressed cannot be racist and discrimination is the preserve of white people and the powerful. But genocide and ethnic cleansing in Africa have put the lie to these assumptions. Virulent attacks on immigrants and refugees testify to the fact that those of us who have been discriminated against know how to give those whom we consider the 'other' – and an economic threat – the same if not worse treatment.

It brings to mind Mahmoud Mamdani's book on Rwanda, *When Victims Become Killers*, which warns that when simple prejudices become transmogrified into hate crimes and later ethnic conflict, the consequences are difficult to reverse. Closer to home, the shocking news of serial murders of Somalis is worrying. Within a matter of weeks the media has reported 31 murders of Somalis in Cape Town. These hate-crimes against immigrants and refugees merely trying to make a living are the ultimate expression of xenophobia – against people who have learnt to transform their desperate situations into entrepreneurial activity.

More astounding is the failure of the police to get to the bottom of who is perpetrating these murders, especially given the promises made by Safety and Security Minister Charles Nqakula and Western Cape MEC Leonard Ramatlakane that the police would be proactive in fighting crime. If ever there seemed to be an easy case to handle it is this, yet the lack of political will speaks volumes of the police's own xenophobia and failure to treat these killings seriously. These murders follow a pattern and they seem to be happening in confined areas (Du Noon and Masiphumelele), yet police have failed to arrest anyone.

One would think that two murders within a week would propel the South African Police Service into action, but after 31 deaths, Nqakula and Ramatlakane are still clueless as to who the killers are, only acknowledging that it must be xenophobia. The official lethargy is astounding and just another demonstration of the state's own prejudices. The police urgently need to round up suspects, investigate the circumstances and offer rewards for information. Can we imagine the outcry if 31 Germans or French were killed in such close proximity? There would be a national outcry and the police would find the perpetrators in no time.

The silence of the Human Rights Commission is even more disappointing, given that they held hearings into xenophobia in 2004, the report of which was published in June this year. As is so typical of the commission, the recommendations in this report are so wide-ranging, vague and cumbersome that they are difficult to implement. Identifying the causes of xenophobia is easy and this report does so eloquently. Finding solutions and a clear programme of action is the challenge and requires the commission to be proactive in fulfilling what they are meant to do – protect and promote the human rights of all, without fear or favour.

This report admits up front that the SAPS and home affairs department are perceived to be the most xenophobic against asylum seekers, refugees and immigrants, and are often guilty of violating the rights of black immigrants to be in this country. Yet the commission has failed to monitor and report on ongoing cases of xenophobia. When one most expects action from the commissioners, they are silent, nowhere to be found. Forever busy with political campaigns of very little relevance, the commission loses wonderful opportunities to institute test cases, and hold government institutions accountable to the most vulnerable people.

The opening paragraph of the report states: 'A country's human rights record is judged by how far it respects and protects the human rights of the most vulnerable,' yet the commission has been complicit in keeping our human rights record dismal. Perceived to be a threat to poor South Africans, the Somalis have become the butt of their frustrations – often with deadly consequences.

The commission's high-sounding recommendations to combat xenophobia – such as setting up a refugee council, initiating public awareness campaigns, working with the Southern African Development Community's human rights agencies, ratifying the international convention on the protection of refugees and migrant workers, inter alia – will achieve nothing unless the commission takes up test cases, monitors abuses and killings, holds Parliament and government accountable, subpoenas the police for their failure to act, and calls on the relevant ministers to account. Anything less is a gross dereliction of duty.

☛ Media and politicians abuse race card for own gains
Cape Argus September 15 2003

IN HIS NEW BOOK, *Beyond the Miracle - Inside the New South Africa* (Jonathan Ball), Allister Sparks touches briefly on the way the race card is all too often falsely and maliciously used against whites and how vulnerable they are to it.

It is, he says 'a factor that is revealing itself more and more as the inhibitions of oppression fade, and which poses its own threat to the realisation of the rainbow dream.

'It reveals itself in power plays in the scramble for advancement. Black South Africans have a lien on the collective guilt of their white fellow-countrymen, which equips them with a devastating weapon with which to demolish any white competitor for a job, or white critic of government policy.

'All they have to do is label the competitor, or the critic, a racist... The target of this charge has no way of countering it. There is no defence. And the more successful it proves to be, the more frequently it is used.'

What South Africans should realise is that this tactic is increasingly exploited by whites to suit their ends. An article in the *Cape Argus* on August 29 2003 is a case in point.

'Thugby Ethos Will Keep Us Divided' by 'political analyst' Richard Calland reeked of hate speech, blatantly misusing all the emotive clichés to ratchet up animosity against white Afrikaners.

Shortly after condemning him, the ANC and some newspapers scrambled to apologise for their attacks on 24-year-old Blue Bulls lock forward, Geo Cronjé.

Newspapers like *Rapport* and the *Sunday Times* established that there were no previous examples of racism in Cronjé's rugby CV. And in keeping with their ethical codes, they interviewed people of all races in Cronjé's home town and elsewhere who said he had never behaved with anything other than scrupulous courtesy to his fellow South Africans.

How starkly this contrasts with the approach taken by Calland, journalist and senior employee of the Institute for Democracy, who said: 'It is not that it is hard to imagine that such people still exist. But that they should be so crass, so downright ignorant, as to express their racist souls in such a banal and blatant way, is incredible...

'How resolute is Straeuli in his own convictions about diversity and racism?... And does he ever pause to consider why so many black people continue to actively despise the Boks?...And as for you Mr Cronjé, not only are you not fit to be a citizen of this country. Go home to your laager. And good riddance.'

I am not alone in being angered by the way Calland arrogantly assumes the role of spokesman for enlightened Afrikaners. Writing that the Cronjé incident made Cape Talk presenter Nigel Pierce appear justified in his own 'crass comment' about 'thick hairy Dutchmen', he opined that astute Afrikaners would be infuriated by this incident.

'To them (Cronjé) is no icon, but a fool who harms the interests of his tribe. It means that the ethos of apartheid lives on.'

I doubt whether Calland does – or even can – read *Rapport*, but had he read the issue of August 31 2003, he would have discovered that its editor, the normally diplomatic Tim du Plessis, had taken the unusual step of placing an editorial comment on the front page that completely contradicts Calland's assertion of what views enlightened Afrikaners hold on the Cronjé debacle.

Under the banner headline 'Rage Over Cronjé', *Rapport* said there was anger across the country about the fact that Cronjé had not been cleared in Sarfu's first investigation of the racism charges.

The editorial says: 'Two young players have been cruelly denied their life's dream – to play for South Africa in the World Cup tournament. Not because they were not good enough, but because of the stupidity and malice of fools.'

There will be many who will consider this sentence to be an extraordinarily apt description of Calland's article and a far more accurate reflection of the views of enlightened Afrikaners.

If anyone were to write an article stigmatising blacks by the use of pejorative terms like 'bigoted' and 'racist', all hell would break loose, Barney Pityana would have a stroke and Marthinus van Schalkwyk would report the matter to the Human Rights Commission.

This point was well made by a reader responding to Calland's article: 'The attempt was made to stereotype Afrikaners as all being like that. When somebody rapes, mutilates children or embezzles public funds they are not referred to as Xhosa/ Zulu/ English/ Sotho but if an Afrikaner steps over the line (as if choosing your roommate is such a hideous crime) a stereotype is made of them. (*Cape Argus* September 1 2003.)

Calland, quick to target the one group so historically vulnerable to the charge of 'racism', has never had the courage to criticise blacks who target whites on the basis of skin colour. Or to express sympathy for the victims of appallingly cruel treatment as has been witnessed in some of the more than 1 500 white farmers or family members murdered in their homes.

A fundamental requirement of honest, professional conduct in academia and journalism is to check your facts before rushing into print. If you don't, then, very clearly, you are anxious to prevent facts from interfering with a good story.

Unlike Calland, *Die Burger* did do some investigating and reported that Quinton Davids, Cronje's rival for the position of lock forward in the World Cup squad and thus someone with a vested interest in the matter, has played the race card before.

But even if that did not play a role and even if new facts emerge to show that Cronje was guilty of racially insensitive behaviour, that in no way justifies Calland's vicious smear against white Afrikaners.

Ironically, those who seek to divide us by using such tactics are failing.

This was manifest in the study of racism in post-apartheid South Africa commissioned by the Institute of Race Relations and conducted by sociologist Laurence Schlemmer and the strategic research company, MarkData. The findings were released in August 2001.

Commenting on the findings, Patrick Laurence wrote in the *Financial Mail* August 24 2003: 'Racism figures far less conspicuously in the everyday experience of South Africans than the prominence accorded it by politicians and the media.

'Based on face-to-face interviews with a demographically representative sample of 2 144 adult South Africans, the results show a marked level of optimism on the question of whether race relations had improved.

'The implication is that "consciousness of racism" may in part be the product of the importance attached to racism in the pronouncements of politicians and the high profile reporting of it in the media.'

☛ The racism debate obscures other issues
Mail & Guardian September 1 to 7 2000

IS PRESIDENT Thabo Mbeki playing the race fiddle while Rome is burning? Has he not learned that when one uses race as a political rallying point, racial conflict gains a momentum of its own that is often difficult to reverse in times of crisis? Has ethnic conflict in Bosnia, Rwanda, Burundi and Serbia not taught him anything?

Is the lesson of Zimbabwe not imminent enough? Or is Mbeki following Robert Mugabe's example to achieve his not-so-hidden agenda? Mugabe also used race as a political rallying point before his country's election to intimidate his opposition. Now that the dust has settled and the economy needs rebuilding he is not able to reverse the damage done and the divisions sown as a result of this election strategy.

More worrying and equally astounding is the support Mbeki gets for his political agenda from his forever-faithful handmaidens, the Human Rights Commission and the SABC – institutions that should be independent of the government and whose duty it is to serve the entire public without fear or favour.

This obsession with race and racism is nothing but a cover-up for non-delivery in the public sector and a means of obscuring issues of national importance. While the public is clamouring for solutions to crime, sexual violence, AIDS, poverty, corruption and job creation, the government is dabbling with race and racism.

What's more, money is made available for these futile exercises while there is virtually no money for development. While the role of the commission is to monitor socioeconomic rights, it has decided to prioritise racism. The focus on race and not discrimination is very telling.

Should the commission focus on investigating discrimination and take such matters to court, it would be able to set precedents that would set human rights standards and prevent such violations from taking place again.

It would also discover that the state and its institutions are often the biggest violators of human rights – as I discovered in my job as human rights commissioner. For example, by investigating a complaint of racism against the ambulance services in Cape Town, we discovered that they were routinely racist in denying services to black areas.

What our investigation enabled us to do, with the cooperation of the ambulance authorities, was to conduct training workshops in human rights with the ambulance personnel who operated the telephones.

Similarly, a complaint of discrimination against an HIV-positive woman, who applied for a job in correctional services, indicated that the department did pre-employment testing on the woman without her consent.

I can cite many examples of discrimination that were lodged before the commission that they often failed to investigate properly and successfully because of incompetence. My reports on racism on the farms in the Northern Cape were simply not followed up.

These investigations indicated that discrimination was not only a black and white issue but also had to do with inequalities in the areas of gender ethnicity, class and religion. But race has become central to our discussion because one can always point a finger at the white oppressor, while the focus on gender and racial discrimination points to the oppressor in one's bed, who might be of the same race.

It would be foolish to deny that racism exists. We all know that. Apartheid has left its mark on all of us, more profoundly on blacks than whites, and it will take a long time before we are truly a non-racial society.

The victory over apartheid was a victory over white minority domination, but the government under Mbeki behaves as though it regrets its negotiated settlement with its former oppressors, and now wants to punish white South Africa for this compromise by harping constantly on the race issue.

Legitimate opposition is racialised and Tony Leon, the leader of the opposition, is demonised as an unreconstructed racist. The media is accused of racism. Editors who are critical are nothing but racist. Judge Willem Heath is silenced as a white judge. The list is endless.

Nelson Mandela wasted no time in trying to reconcile a racially polarised society. He is admired, and reviled at times, for having brought the strangest of people together. When Mandela was called a 'kaffir' by a coloured woman in Mitchells Plain, he completely immobilised his abuser by going to talk to her.

Many of his gestures across racial lines, not least his visit to Betsie Verwoerd, left many of us puzzled, even annoyed – but therein lies the lesson for all of us. Racism flourishes in contexts where it has been internalised to such an extent that the victim begins to miss it when it begins to disappear.

Barney Pityana and his colleagues have reduced the Human Rights Commission to a race industry where his 'black consciousness' hang-ups seem to play themselves out in public.

These never-ending conferences on race and racism are used to legitimise this obsession, by inviting reputable speakers to participate in promoting the political agenda of the president.

I am glad the public is beginning to see right through this exercise and is resisting the attempts by the government to further divide us.

☛ Is the Native Club another Broederbond or will it plug intellectual vacuum?

Business Day June 12 2006 with Julia Bertelsmann

THE FORMATION of the Native Club ten years into our democracy is an astoundingly backward move given our triumph over apartheid. For all the advances we have made, there are some who hark back to the past under the guise of progress.

With the new constitution came the removal of legal obstacles to freedom of association. We now have the right to associate with any party, any group, any organisation, and we now enjoy freedom of association that we did not have under apartheid. The apartheid state sacrificed the individual to conformity and the State Security Council under PW Botha tried to create a conformist nation.

The new constitution has restored the freedom of the individual, of association, and of choice. That means we now take responsibility for the success or failure of our democracy. The value of the constitution is the restoration of this personal sense of responsibility. We are now free even to destroy ourselves.

What the past should alert us to are the dangers of conformism, of centralised control, and of the adulation of politicians. Why then have critics lambasted the formation of the Native Club?

Some of the club's opponents have been over-hasty in dismissing it as racist and ridiculous. An examination of the club shows that it has several good features, but also some discreditable ones. Critics should distinguish between the two and identify and challenge those elements that are truly objectionable.

According to its list of objectives, the Native Club aims to create an environment in which ideas can be disseminated, debated and discussed by inquiring minds; create a congenial climate for reflection and self-examination; assert itself in the realm of arts, culture, politics and the economy; and give a voice to the voiceless.

Several of its members were attracted to it precisely because they believe it will enliven political debate among black intellectuals and take us out of the post-1994 intellectual vacuum President Thabo Mbeki has complained about.

What the club has failed to address is the reasons for this vacuum, which I believe include self-censorship; using the race card to discredit people who raise debates; and the tyranny of political correctness that has come to characterise political culture.

The club steps into this vacuum, claiming to reinvigorate it with intellectual debate. However, some of its aims are questionable. If the club remains in its current state, I would not count on its commitment to unbiased and unfettered debate. Such a commitment can only be credible if the club insists on political independence.

Currently, its chairman Titus Mafolo is Mbeki's adviser, and its funding comes from the Department of Arts and Culture with additional support from Accord, the Africa Institute, and the Centre for Global Dialogue, organisations all close to the government.

A second noble aim of the club is to encourage reflection, self-examination and critical consciousness. It must, however, heed the warning attributed to Socrates in Plato's *Republic* that people are likely to resist critical self-examination unless they surround themselves with those who dare challenge their thoughts.

As it stands, the club can never be fully self-critical because it is racially, and therefore also politically and ideologically, exclusive. We cannot afford this, given South Africa's history of racial polarisation.

Democracy is the acknowledgement that the truth can only be derived by considering different points of view, no matter what the race or ideological bent of the proponent. The club's exclusivity is problematic because it contradicts ANC policy of non-racialism, non-sexism and democracy.

Between the Native Club's good, albeit imperilled, aims, lurk more sinister intentions that the club should reconsider.

First, according to Mafolo, the club was set up to counter liberalism, which it believes is the preserve of the unpatriotic white intellectual and pits the Natives against the Settlers, whatever that might mean.

This is nothing other than racial nationalism, where natives become the *imbongis* of the government. By nationalist logic à la Hugo Chávez and Evo Morales, the club plans to move away from American and European influences and look within for its bright ideas.

Both of these ambitions are deeply troubling. The club is wrong to demonise, and see its objectives as inimical to, liberalism, which they claim is anti-transformation. The Native Club is seen as a counter to neo-liberals, who are considered small but well-resourced, visible and vocal, and who shape the content of transformation through public discourse.

This accusation against the neo-liberals (whatever that may be) smacks of a deep inferiority complex. There is nothing that stops the Natives from being equally well-resourced given the rapid rise of BEE (black economic empowerment) dollar millionaires.

The club may contest liberalism, but to make it an enemy is plain stupid. The constitution is liberal and South Africa's macro-economic policy is liberal and the BEE-ites benefit from this form of unbridled economic capitalism.

Liberalism respects individual rights and freedom, favours the separation of party and state, heeds the rule of law, and encourages the formation of independent courts, strong civil society, and free markets.

There are many ideologies that counter liberalism, and if the Native Club is against it, it should clearly state where its ideologies lie.

It is also wrong to want to shun all foreign influences. If the club is serious about this, I would suggest it get rid of cellphones, BMWs, and all the paraphernalia adherents of BEE strive for.

The Native Club seems oblivious to the fact that no culture is static and that all strong civilisations have evolved by assimilating the strongest elements of foreign cultures.

True intellectuals look to a wide range of influences and adopt or develop the best ones. Nationalist self-obsession leads to the kinds of delusions suffered by Adolf Hitler, Joseph Stalin and Robert Mugabe.

Mafolo's strong connection with the presidency raises questions about the club's independence. His dubious political past also does not bode well for those who might want to be part of an organisation that upholds values of honesty, integrity and transparency.

So let us be clear on what is wrong and what is good about the Native Club.

If its main objectives are to create a national environment open to debate, and to develop a critical consciousness that will save us from a life of cultural limbo, then fostering a South Africanness that is isolated from advancements in the global world will only set us back.

If it is about opening our minds to the developments in the progressive world and is indeed about self-examination and self-reflection, then we are on our way to a truly open society.

Given its contradictory objectives, where some undermine others, I am not sure how one becomes a member, given that some members raised questions about the presence of Indians and coloureds who attended.

So, how native is the Native Club? If the adoption of the term 'native' is to invert a once pejorative title and use it for subversive means to liberate all its black members, then the title may signify progress.

If it is meant to be exclusive, then it needs to be condemned in the strongest of terms.

If it is anti-white, then it needs to say so unequivocally, so that those committed to an equal society are clear where they stand in relation to the club.

If the club is another Broederbond with some sisters hanging on, or a South African Bureau of Racial Affairs, then we can give it a big miss.

If it is an honest attempt to stimulate debate around issues that concern us collectively as a nation, then we might consider giving it a go.

☛ Video uproar betrays culture of double standards
Business Day March 13 2008

SA IS THE COUNTRY of double standards. It charges Jacob Zuma but protects Interpol chief Jackie Selebi; some criminals get off lightly while others rot in jail; it condemns Israel but supports the tyranny of Robert Mugabe; it opposes United Nations Security Council resolutions on Darfur and Burma but waxes lyrical about Bush's war in Iraq. This hypocrisy, I fear, has filtered down into the body politic of South African society and poisoned the wells of goodwill ushered in in 1994.

The video saga at the University of the Free State epitomises much of what is dangerous about these double standards. Four students are responsible for a video that is reprehensible, but the whole of white SA, and the Free State University in particular, gets daubed as racist. White journalists and columnists go haywire, beating their breasts, shouting 'O mea maxima culpa'; billboards shout 'racist campus', 'racist residence'; and we forget that sexual violence and rape are prevalent and covered up on so many campuses. Ask me, I know about sexual violations at so-called progressive universities, where student leaders were involved in the sexual harassment and rape of fellow students. These campuses were not billed as 'campuses of rape', and whole campuses are not painted with the same brush because of those who routinely perpetrate such acts of violence against female students at only one.

Equally, at many predominantly black universities, racial segregation at residences is the order of the day, but nobody speaks about that because it is assumed here that freedom of association is a right. Do you remember the coloured man who moved into Khayelitsha and was hounded out by blacks for daring to go and live in a black area? And how many hundreds of Somalis in Western Cape have been killed by other black people for simply being successful business people? Where are the headlines about this? Where is the Human Rights Commission when it comes to taking up these plights? It shouts sanctimoniously from the rooftops that whites should apologise for apartheid 14 years into our democracy, as though this video has once again given it a reason for existing.

Are these things happening perhaps because the commission has fundamentally failed in one of its key missions, to protect and promote human rights in SA and educate members of the public about it?

Remember the Native Club and all the lofty justification for setting up a race-based club. It was nothing but a safe space for black intellectuals to deal with their collective 'woundedness'. And so the Forum of Black Journalists follows suit, meeting African National Congress president Jacob Zuma behind closed doors. That black journalists even respond to such an invitation confirms my worst suspicions that, like politicians, they are prepared to defy their own ethics when power is paraded before them. Many, of course, get noticed not so much by their high standards of journalism, as by the enormous racial chips they have on their shoulders.

Notwithstanding the columns by Sipho Seepe and Steven Friedman on this page this week, arguing that racism indeed warrants attention, it is an indictment on this government and all its institutions that should be building democracy that such racial incidents still occur in this country. And the only time the Human Rights Commission seems to find its *raison d'être* is when racism rears its ugly head. Remember the gusto with which then commission chairman Barney Pityana took on Judge Dennis Davis and those guilt-ridden editors who actually gave evidence before the commission's hearings into subliminal racism in the media, when in fact they should have boycotted it.

It is this cowardice laced with white guilt and black triumphalism that perpetuates apartheid and inspires universities and the high priests of political correctness to condemn this video, but not acts of murderous racism such as the gruesome farm murders and the killing of Somalis, for example.

☛ Notion of African campuses too glib
Business Day June 19 2003

UNIVERSITIES and technikons are undergoing rapid change. The imperative for some to merge and rationalise their academic programmes has thrown some of these institutions into turmoil as battles over turf ensue.

The language of merging most of the time is incomprehensible as vice-chancellors try to make sense of what is no doubt a difficult task. Some of the confusion is captured in Prof William Makgoba's article in a *Mail & Guardian* May 2 to 8 2003 supplement 'Beyond Matric'.

As one of the heads responsible for merging the Universities of Natal and Durban Westville, he obviously gave the issue much thought. For him the merger provides the ideal opportunity to create an institution relevant to the African experience, an 'African brand' of university, that will be captured by an appropriate African logo.

He further reduces this quest for Africanness to the 'need to build and develop an African ethos within our institutions that will constructively take forward the ideals of the African Renaissance' and African development initiatives such as the New Partnership for Africa's Development (Nepad).

Makgoba assumes, like so many of his peers, a common understanding of the notion of an African university, but nowhere does he attempt to spell out what this means and how we are to take these ideals forward.

We speak glibly of being African, yet its meaning eludes us all the time. Africa encapsulates a multiplicity of peoples, cultures and voices. It is greatly divided along regional, cultural, linguistic, political and historical lines.

Makgoba's mistake is his bipolar view on the issue. He pits the concern for academic freedom and autonomy against the desire to be African, the traditional conception of a university versus a socially relevant academy, the Europeanisation versus the Africanisation of education, as though these aspects are all mutually exclusive.

For him this 'Africanness' also has to do with acknowledging government as a vital funding partner. Nowhere is Africanisation related to the academic project, the substance of scholarship and research. Where Makgoba fails, is in his tendency to dismiss the sacred tenets of academic freedom and autonomy, instead of incorporating this into his understanding of what makes universities relevant to the societies they serve.

He is clearly not able to deal with the tension that is intrinsic to the 'concept' of university – that of having universal appeal while being simultaneously culturally specific in character.

A resort to nationalism is not the answer. Nationalism inhibits the quest for a spiritual character, which is what most universities want, and as most of the universities in Europe have discovered.

It is only in re-establishing our links with the past that we will come to grips with the monastic traditions that originally shaped universities. Only then can we hope to imbue our universities with a character that will resemble all of what we are as South Africans, so ably captured by Dr Anthony Holiday, a University of the Western Cape philosopher:

'Africa's search for houses of the intellect, shaped by African identities, is in the last resort, a spiritual search, an attritional war of ethical resistance, waged in the name of treasures which are spiritual, with a spiritual homecoming as its hoped for victory. In as much as it is this, it has affinities with those battles some European educators are fighting for a recovery of the monastic spirituality which was the founding inspiration of the great universities of Europe.'

This call is no more vocal than that coming from the Association of African Universities. At its conference in March, the association called unequivocally for a recommitment to academic freedom and autonomy so that universities can once again gain public trust. While the academic community in SA is increasingly succumbing to state interference and political engineering, universities elsewhere in Africa are trying frantically to break free from state interference that has plagued them for decades.

Association members now more than ever want to do what universities are suppose to do – become part of the global community of scholarship, unfettered by state control.

Makgoba, more than anybody else, as an internationally recognised scientist, Fellow of the Royal Society no less, should know this. His task is to interrogate President Thabo Mbeki's notions of the African Renaissance and Nepad, and not accept them as givens. Heads of academic institutions should lead this debate instead of submitting uncritically.

There is no denying apartheid indelibly bedevilled the landscape of tertiary education in SA. The creation of ethnically-based universities and the alignment of some with the apartheid government were cardinal sins. The favouritism of those who openly backed the status quo has taken its toll.

Under our new democratic dispensation and facing severe fiscal constraints, many of these universities have to grapple with the challenges that academic freedom and autonomy place on them in their pursuit to be socially and politically relevant. It is something many of them have never had to agonise about.

Former right-wing universities are now trying to redeem themselves by appointing blacks considered to be politically correct into senior management positions, as their contribution to the Africanisation process, as they understand it. Honorary degrees are conferred left right and centre on senior government officials; all desperate bids to absolve themselves from their sordid pasts.

Transformation does not only mean head counts of black people, it means interrogating what we teach, how we teach and the linkages we make with international scholarship.

'What academic leaders need to realise is that the intellectual homes of the politically correct do not remain universities for very long,' as notes Holiday.

☞ Opera clicks with African students
Business Day July 31 2003

NOTHING gives me more pleasure than attending the vice-chancellor's concert at the University of Cape Town every year. On July 18 2003 the students took us on a musical tour starting with an African music demonstration directed by Dizu Plaatjies and his mates dressed in full African regalia.

They introduced us to deceptively simple-looking traditional instruments such as the Mozambican panpipes, the Zimbabwean *mbira*, and ankle beads, on which they produced the clearest sounds, transporting us for a brief moment into a rural setting.

This tranquil ambience was soon punctured by the vibrancy of the jazz band with its full-blooded renditions of student improvisations on alto saxophone, trumpet, trombone, bass and lead guitar, and piano. Just as the audience got fired up, two excellent piano and organ recitals brought us again back to earth prepared for the next round of duets, trios and sextets: spectacular arias from *Così fan Tutte, La Traviata, Pagliacci* and *Hänsel und Gretel*.

All the opera singers were black except one, and to hear them mastering Italian opera – an essentially European genre – with such finesse makes nonsense of Prof William Makgoba's assertion that our universities should become bastions of African essentialism, knowledge and experience, whatever that might mean. 'After all,' says he, 'we have African music, poetry, dance politics, philosophy, architecture, traditional medicine and so on.'

I spoke afterwards with the head of the opera school, Dr Angelo Gobbato, to ask him how he was able to transform the opera school from 98% white in the past to 90% black today. His response was enlightening. The admission of a large number of black students was not simply about increasing the head count. It was about acknowledging the strong choral tradition and rich vocal talent in the townships that can actively be incorporated into the opera tradition at UCT.

The opera school went into communities to recruit students and the response was overwhelming. At one stage more than 310 came to audition, and bursaries were made available to people with no music training but strong vocal talent.

What these students demonstrated, to echo Gobbato, was that the language of music belongs to the human soul; and that is ultimately the main objective of a university – to bring out the best in students and help them master various disciplines, whether they originate in Europe, Africa, Asia or America.

What the opera school has achieved is to get students to appreciate the rich affinities between their musical traditions and opera, and to put to use both their musical traditions and opera, utilising their already finely honed skills to master the latter.

So when Makgoba says we 'need to ask simple questions about higher education' – for example, 'where is our current higher education anchored/centred' or 'where is its identity today in Africa, Europe, Asia or Latin America?' – we need to ask him how these students fit into his African essentialist paradigm.

Gobbato believes, as I do, that there are strong affinities between Italian opera and the African aesthetic of praise poetry: vibrant song, the deeply emotional vocal connotation combined with the quality of African voices. Italian opera has deep resonance with our local African musical culture, and Gobbato's students attest to this.

As a Telkom Choral Competition member, he is often amazed at the songs that African church choirs choose for the competition. *Fidelio*, for example, which is extremely difficult, is a favourite, mastered with great finesse by African choirs. When Makgoba says that African universities should institutionalise African essentialism, knowledge, experience and existence, I should like to know what he means. All I know is that the predominantly black student audience enjoys the genre intensely and appreciates the singing as much as an Italian audience in Verona – not least when the coquettish flirtations are between the tenor, a lean white man, and the soprano, who more often than not is a buxom black woman – judging from the guffaws in the audience.

☛ Transformation minefield far from easy to negotiate
Business Day November 15 2002

SPORTS MINISTER Ngconde Balfour's admission that he does not give a damn about the white cricketers in the SA cricket team has unleashed a bitter backlash from journalists, sports lovers and the public alike.

Christine Qunta's invective blaming Balfour's gaffe on the UCB and Percy Sonn (*Business Day* November 8 2002), on the one hand; and Drew Forrest's measured analysis of the problem (*Mail & Guardian* November 8 2002), on the other hand, epitomise the political schizophrenia that has come to characterise SA society.

Qunta's column blamed Balfour's indiscretion on malcontents, a euphemism for 'white journalists' and 'opposition politicians' looking for an opportunity to 'embarrass Balfour'.

She conveniently overlooks the difficulties experienced by the UCB in their efforts to cultivate competent black cricketers and calls on Percy Sonn, whom she blames for the lack of transformation in cricket, to resign instead of the minister.

Forrest, more wisely, takes us painstakingly through the murky waters of transformation, alerting us to the complexities such a process involves.

'No purpose is served by selecting black tokens who are unable, or unready, to withstand the merciless pressures of the world game – too few black South Africans are receiving the required depth and intensity of exposure from the youngest age.

'International sport involves some of the most specialised activities known to humankind. It requires total immersion in a cricket-playing culture virtually from birth, and years of instruction and the schooling of the reflexes. Few black youngsters have the benefit of this.

'At issue is not racial bias or foot-dragging. It is the daunting development conundrum of how to create conditions for more world-class black talent to emerge,' says Forrest.

Apartheid was about denying the majority good education. Pools of skilled labour are scarce and we need to acknowledge there are not enough trained people to go around. The lack of capacity in government has caused a crisis in public sector delivery and partly explains the R2 billion spent on consultants last year.

We might have the best employment equity legislation in the world, but it will mean nothing if we do not have the wherewithal to implement it effectively.

Transformation is a long, hard process and it requires patience, endurance and the wisdom of Solomon to manage diversity successfully. Malaysia, Canada, Australia and the US provide many examples of how to avoid its pitfalls and how to succeed without reinventing the wheel.

Affirmative action has to do with the implementation of an entire range of policies and programmes geared to redress the inequalities of the past.

Such measures are necessary to make equal opportunity a reality for historically excluded groups such as black people, women and the disabled. It is a systematic means of achieving equal employment opportunity and we tend to forget that affirmative action is compatible with appointment and promotion of blacks on the basis of skills, merit and qualification.

Equally, transformation requires vital ingredients to succeed. These are: appropriate selection and recruitment policies; induction programmes for incoming members; training and development of those with potential; special training programmes; promotion from within for those who are qualified; change in the organisational culture of the broader community, to create a greater pool of formerly excluded groups; setting goals and timetables instead of quotas.

Affirmative action should take place at the selection and recruitment stage only, and thereafter all employees should be developed and promoted on merit. Top management and resources should be actively committed to implementation of its goals.

Realistic racial targets based on workforce, succession, and career plans should be developed and monitored on an annual basis. Negative racial and gender stereotypes and expectations ought to be managed. Managers should be trained in people management skills and critically evaluated on their performance in relation to the development of their subordinates.

All employees should understand the process of development and should take responsibility for self-development. A representative committee of the organisation should take responsibility for the transformation and development strategy, monitor, evaluate and update it on an annual basis.

Affirmative action is an attempt to raise standards, unlike the claims of sceptics – that it is the one sure way of reducing everything to the lowest denominator. It can work but the will for it to work must be there.

☛ Is empathy really a better gauge of aspiring doctors than high marks?

Business Day June 2 2004

THERE WAS NOTHING more disturbing to my daughter, now preparing for matric, than the headline article in the *Sunday Times* (February 1 2004), that one does not have to get straight As in order to be admitted to medicine at the top universities in SA.

Health department spokeswoman Jo-Anne Collinge blatantly declared that 'representivity' is a very important factor in the degree to which doctors serve in the public sector and rural areas. 'We don't believe academic excellence is a good predictor of who will effectively serve a diverse population,' she said.

What did she mean?

Equally senseless were the remarks of Prof Ahmed Wadee, assistant dean of students at Wits: 'Seven or eight distinctions do not necessarily make the best doctor. We want students with an interest in life. We believe empathy is important.'

'Well,' said my daughter, 'I don't need to study hard for distinctions, I have loads of empathy and an insatiable interest in life. That will surely get me into medical school. And I am black and female!'

What are we to make of these utterances?

Can anyone explain to me why an interest in life and empathy are better predictors of how a medical student will fare than academic excellence? How are these assets measured? An interest in life and empathy seem to have become euphemisms for black.

Should we infer that these qualities are lacking in white students, especially if their grades are high?

Are we abandoning academic excellence for the sake of achieving racial equity irrespective of what this will do to the health of the nation in twenty years? Are we saying to students: you are aiming for distinctions, you will therefore not be admitted into medical school?

I cannot believe Education Minister Kader Asmal would approve of such drivel!

I am amazed at the lack of nuance, even desperation, of university authorities to demonstrate racial representation without spelling out clearly what they aim to achieve and how. No one is explaining how universities hope to provide equal opportunities for those who are being denied them, giving due regard to merit and skills.

Once we allow nebulous qualities like empathy and an interest in life to trump academic excellence we are going fast down the slippery slope of mediocrity that will be hard to reverse in years to come. The assumption that most riles is that academic excellence is incompatible with equity.

If the argument is that the best students will be considered taking into account other qualities like life skills, extramural activities such as first aid, community involvement, in addition to race then that is a different matter. But often race is the key ingredient, and that is what angers parents and students alike. To quote one of the equality advocates, 'the claim that race has merely been a "plus factor" in admissions to public universities does not withstand factual scrutiny – which is why universities have long tried to keep these policies under wraps'.

Unless universities spell out very clearly how they plan to manage affirmative action and equal opportunities, I fear court action will soon follow the US legal precedent set in 2001 by Gratz and Grutter in their case against the University of Michigan.

The case went to the US Supreme Court, and in a ruling last year it struck down the use of mechanical racial preferences in admissions policy. It ruled 'universities may consider race only if they conduct a highly individualised review of each applicant's file. (Also) schools must periodically review the continued need for race preferences in light of race-neutral admissions policies now in use in five states that have proven to achieve diversity without discrimination.'

As a member of the Rhodes Scholarship selection committee, we require applicants to demonstrate, in addition to an excellent academic record, strong community involvement, an interest in sport or outdoor activity and other extramural engagements. A personal statement about their academic and sociocultural pursuits and referees' reports provide further insights into a student's potential to be a good all-rounder. This is followed up by rigorous interviews of the selected candidates.

Unless universities use such thorough and rigorous assessments of candidates on all of these grounds, and not just race, public mistrust in the differential application of admission policies will not abate.

Selection criteria that are broadly racial and very little else will open universities up to litigation in future. And I hope soon.

'Contrary' rulings explain ANC assault on judges

Business Day May 12 2005

THE IMPLICATIONS of government's proposals to transform the judiciary are worrying. George Devenish, a senior law professor, warns that the five bills are nothing more than an attempt to control the judiciary and rob it of its independence, making it subservient to the masses.

The African National Congress (ANC), naturally, denies all this as rubbish and presents its proposals as honest attempts to make the judiciary representative of race and gender, and 'acceptable to ordinary people where they live in all parts of our country,' to quote Safety and Security Minister Charles Nqakula.

He said: 'What we are concerned about is matters of policy, on which we are not going to yield any ground to anyone because it relates to our programme of democratic action.' What does he mean by 'our programme of democratic action'?

In the light of this, the intention of the five bills is rather transparent. Why is the ANC so desperate to push them through against widespread opposition, including from the judiciary itself? The answer lies in government's frustration with the many court rulings that went against it over the past years, particularly in the Grootboom and Treatment Action Campaign challenges.

In June 2002 the health minister lost an appeal against a Pretoria High Court ruling that the provision of nevirapine at only a few selected hospitals and clinics was unlawful.

In July 2002 the state challenged a high court ruling that invalidated discriminatory provisions in the Judges' Remuneration and Conditions of Employment Act for same-sex partners, and lost.

In October 2003 the Constitutional Court dismissed an appeal by the state and parastatal Alexkor against a Supreme Court of Appeals ruling to return mineral rights to a community which was forcibly relocated.

In March last year, the social development minister unsuccessfully attempted to prevent the extension of social welfare grants to all permanent residents.

In the Grootboom case, the Constitutional Court ruled that government should consider the informal settlement of Wallacedene a priority in the development of a valid housing policy and provide it with interim relief. This was considered a landmark ruling in terms of the socioeconomic rights in the constitution.

The ANC government was fed up with these rulings for reasons that need emphasising. While the transformation it espouses is necessary to make the courts accountable to the masses, it opposed court challenges made on behalf of the masses. The state's court challenges also went against the mandate the electorate gave the ANC when it voted for the party in 1994.

In this context, the language of transformation is duplicitous. It purports to make the judiciary more sympathetic to the will of the people, but it is in fact counterintuitive. Through its national democratic revolution, the ANC is more concerned with extending its tentacles over all levers of power than with empowering citizens. Mass mobilisation and social engineering will keep up the facade of democracy, while the ANC's priorities lie elsewhere.

Escalating unemployment, poverty, HIV/AIDS and the housing crisis can always be blamed on racism and an untransformed judiciary. When government prioritises arms purchases over AIDS, black economic enrichment over poor economic empowerment, then a constitution that ensures access to socioeconomic rights is a direct threat.

In a context of dire poverty, the constitution becomes a threatening document to the ANC's broader goal of entrenched control. Other than populating the institution with people who will do the ruling party's bidding, the transformation of the judiciary is nothing but a reaction to a constitution that can thwart the ANC's agenda.

The new judicial structure proposed by the bills can easily be manipulated to influence the outcome of court decisions. Under the pretext of transformation, the bills would enable government to appoint judges sympathetic to its ideology. Independence matters little.

Helen Suzman always opposed the inclusion of socioeconomic rights in the Bill of Rights, not because she was against these rights, but because she knew it would come to haunt the ANC when its own voters started rebelling against government's failure to deliver services. Citizens who use the constitution to challenge the state do so because they know that it not only guarantees rights, but places obligations on the state for the progressive realisation of those rights.

President Robert Mugabe has taught us that a compliant judiciary will fail to protect us from a hostile government.

👉 Brave judge won't slide on the Hlippery Hlophe
Business Day October 18 2007

THANK GOD for Judge Johann Kriegler – the only judge, albeit retired, who dared speak out against the Judicial Services Commission's (JSC's) decision not to impeach Western Cape Judge President John Hlophe, in spite of a long list of misdemeanours that should have disqualified him from high office long ago.

Many have commended Kriegler for his boldness, but when race is perceived to be the object of one's courage, the message loses its punch. Kriegler's mission is to save the bench from colleagues intent on bringing it into disrepute for their own vested interests. It has nothing to do with the fact that he is white. It has everything to do with the fact that he is a judge, inspired by the sacred 'oath' judges have a duty to uphold. And as for the Black Lawyers' Association calling on the JSC to sanction Kriegler for his 'improper' and 'uncollegial' show of disrespect to the JSC, they have nailed their colours of racial solidarity so solidly to the mast as to have lost all credibility. To question Kriegler's integrity for raising legitimate concerns about the JSC's lily-livered ruling exposes their professional laxity.

Equally lamentable is the lofty condemnation by advocates Dumisa Ntsebeza and Ishmael Semenya, who patronisingly accused Kriegler of failing to accept a ruling he did not like. For Ntsebeza to call Kriegler's comments unsolicited, gratuitous, intemperate, self-indulgent and unprofessional, says more about him than the judge and is a revelation of how deep the racial animosity is on the bench.

The fact that the JSC failed to divulge why a mere slap on the wrist is good enough in a case that is so public and so blatantly questionable is a serious indictment.

This same rationale applies to Parliament and the public protector, which have on several occasions besmirched their own good names by the highly irregular decisions taken in serious cases such as the Travelgate scandal. To say we should accept the ruling of the JSC as the highest judicial authority is to ask us to abandon our common sense understanding of right and wrong, especially in a case as transparent as the Oasis-Desai saga, in which Hlophe was involved.

Many previously respected black people in high places have tainted our watchdog institutions to such an extent that the institutions have become suspect and have lost their constitutional chastity. The heads of these agencies have gotten away with murder simply because they are black. A combination of patronage, race and vested interests have become the deadly cocktail by which this country is governed and have become the hallmark of Thabo Mbeki's governance. And, I fear this will determine Mbeki's re-election as president of the African National Congress, as everyone is scrambling to rearrange the deck chairs on the Titanic in the ocean of greed that has engulfed this country.

In the same vein, this cocktail is the reason why so many of our august bodies have lost their constitutional teeth. The public protector, the National Development Agency, Parliament's public accounts committee, Parliament itself, the human rights and gender commissions, the Pan African Parliament, the Land Bank, the National Council of Provinces, to name a few, have become 'whited sepulchres full of dead men's bones'.

Judges are obliged to uphold our constitutional democracy, based on equality for all, the rule of law, the independence of the judiciary and the separation of powers and, as such, Kriegler has done his duty by condemning Hlophe's unbecoming behaviour against a profession that should be beyond reproach.

Not only was he on the payroll of a very controversial company, Oasis, but he lied; and he crossed the conflict of interest barrier by failing to recuse himself in the Judge Siraj Desai-Oasis defamation suit. Hlophe has been let off the hook because he is black. It is as simple as that. It will take a lot more than Semenya's and Ntsebeza's diatribe about the 'sanctity' of the JSC to convince us otherwise.

We are indeed on a 'Hlippery Hlophe', so cleverly depicted by Chip's cartoon in the *Cape Times*, when racial solidarity trumps issues of justice and integrity in an institution that should be the embodiment of these values.

Sorry, this is just another divisive fad

Mail & Guardian January 5 to 11 2001

IN AN OPINION POLL conducted three weeks ago, 80% of the 1 000 people called, said they would not support the Declaration of Commitment signed by a group of prominent white South Africans. Do we have the right to dismiss them as racists, as upholders of white privilege, not supportive of change and reconciliation? I think not – even though some are.

The letters pages of the newspapers indicate that many people, unlike the apologists, have given sober thought to why they are refusing to say 'sorry'. They are simply tired of the double standards that characterise our democracy. And these double standards are inherent in the declaration itself.

The declaration simplistically blames the deprivation experienced by most black people mainly on racist attitudes, internalised inferiority, and the failure of white people to take responsibility for the past. The apologists, therefore, call upon their white compatriots to seek absolution and contribute towards a fund that will help empower disadvantaged people.

If a development fund is of such concern to them, why have they been silent on the failure of government to spend its poverty alleviation fund? Why are they silent about the myriad corruption scandals that are draining the financial coffers of the state? Why have they been silent about the misappropriation of taxpayers' money and actions that have exacerbated the problems of poverty and racial discrimination? Why should there be any confidence that yet another fund will be wisely spent, given that the lottery has yielded nothing thus far?

Secondly, to blame everything on race and racism is to fail to acknowledge that this government has done little for the development of black South Africa. To spend R44 billion on arms as a priority when there are much more urgent development needs, is something this so-called concerned group should have been more vocal about. But this group does not want to be seen to be criticising this government as their access to power and resources is dependent on supporting the agenda of this government – a perceptive point made by Tony Holiday of the University of the Western Cape and Helen Zille, Western Cape MEC for Education, in recent newspaper columns.

Far be it from me to question the credentials of the signatories. Some of them are, indeed, very sincere. But the agenda of the instigators is nauseatingly transparent. They, least of all, need to say sorry because they were opposed to apartheid anyway.

I can only conclude that one of their concerns stems from the overwhelming vote the Democratic Alliance got in the recent elections. The timing of the declaration, its focus on the Western Cape and its campaign slogan, a 'Home for All' – as a counter to the implicit assumptions that the Western Cape is not a home for all – explain the disquiet of some who attended the ceremony in Cape Town's St. George's Cathedral on December 16 2000. Instead of welcoming the DA's advance as a sign of a vibrant and healthy democracy, the declaration is used to put whites on a guilt trip for having chosen to vote the way they did.

Blaming the current disillusionment of blacks mainly on racism and racist attitudes is to feed into the racial stereotyping of whites and to absolve government of all responsibility. If race and racism are of such a concern to this group, why did they not condemn the racist post-election utterances that came from senior African National Congress leaders? Where was the chair of the Human Rights Commission, Barney Pityana? Imagine the furore had Tony Leon and his cronies made similar utterances. By constantly targeting white South Africans, the underlying message seems to be: 'Say sorry, be grateful and shut up. Those who are guilty have no right to criticise.'

The proponents of the Truth and Reconciliation Commission, amongst them the adherents of the declaration, are implicitly acknowledging that the TRC amnesty process was deeply flawed. Reparations have failed. And the apartheid villains like PW Botha, FW de Klerk, the Wit Wolwe, the Civil Cooperation Bureau, Magnus Malan, Craig Kotze, Craig Williamson and others – who should have said sorry – have been released into the wilds to enjoy their retirement packages in the comfort of their own homes. The apologists are saying sorry on their behalf. Bizarre, is it not?

If only the drafters of this silly idea gave thought to what they were doing we would not now be sitting with yet another fad that contributes nothing except further division. The events in Zimbabwe are instructive here. If we continue to stereotype whites, we effectively silence their right to democratic citizenship. Secondly, the declaration instils the idea that whites are to blame for the lack of economic growth and development. We should not then be alarmed when they are driven out of this country should the government fail to deliver. This is exactly what Robert Mugabe has done with the support of government. Supporters of the sorry industry may very well be sowing the seeds of their own destruction as legitimate citizens of democracy by furthering this agenda.

We must learn to live with the gory side of the negotiations deal struck between former oppressors and the ANC. Either we (meaning black and white) accept all the compromises forged at Codesa and get on with our lives. Or we exclude whites from becoming part of this vibrant democratic civil society, and take responsibility for the consequences.

☞ Patriotism soured by dashed expectations
Business Day October 4 2002

WHEN I STUDIED at the Institute for Social Studies in the Netherlands in the mid-1980s, cultural events were the order of the day.

A Middle Eastern, Asian, West African, or Latin American evening would bring out some of the most flamboyant cultural outfits, unusual foods, and exotic dances to an audience eager to compete in displays of culinary largesse and acts of patriotism to assuage their longing for home.

The South Africans, on the other hand, had nothing to be patriotic about as the television serially transmitted images of apartheid atrocities at home.

We were the pariahs of the world and I envied the spontaneous flag-waving of my fellow students, feelings that so often eluded me in my young adult life.

My first pangs of patriotism surged forth in February 1990 when Nelson Mandela regally and victoriously walked out of prison to a jubilant crowd, all wanting to own a part of him.

The second such experience was after April 1994 – when voters flocked to the first SA general election open to all – at a conference I addressed in the US as a free South African. Basking in the reflected glory of Madiba abroad was the feeling I so longed for when fellow institute students proudly regaled us with their cultural practices.

The third burst of pride was the day in 1996 when the constitution was adopted, and Deputy President Thabo Mbeki made his 'I am an African' speech.

My patriotism, regrettably, has been short-lived.

The burgeoning poverty, the rapid increase in HIV infection rates, escalating crime, widespread abuse of children and women, unacceptably high unemployment rates, and endless cash-in-transit heists leave very little to be proud of despite statements claiming that crime has stabilised – a new government euphemism for minimal improvement.

Government is fast extinguishing the pride most of us had due to its failure to deliver in the areas that matter. Public resentment has never been as palpable as it is today. Calls for the return of the death penalty are nothing but a public outcry against the failures of the criminal justice system to protect citizens' lives.

Doctors' protests have to do with gross underfunding of hospitals and the failure to prioritise spending in accordance with the health needs of the population. The court actions of the Treatment Action Campaign are more to do with outrage against state inertia about a pandemic decimating our youth than with trying to humiliate government.

Government should create the conditions for us to be proud.

In this context of such profound discontent, the Proudly South African Campaign really bugs me. It encourages a nationalism that is vacuous and part of the myth-making that has come to characterise the discourse of the spindoctors. The resurgence of government-inspired cultural nationalism detracts from the need to bolster our democratic institutions. Instead of cultivating a viable democratic culture, there is an obsession with nation building.

We have become virtual prisoners in our own homes. Living behind high walls, electronic gates, and burglar alarms has come to be considered normal. Those who do not have these facilities are thrown to the wolves.

'Born Free but Taxed to Death' is a bumper sticker that epitomises how the ordinary South African feels today. It sticks in my craw having to pay tax, VAT, rates, petrol levies, and high interest rates when as a taxpayer one gets little in return.

Provision of effective basic services to the public is what should make us Proudly South African. I will feel proud of my country when trains and buses arrive on time. I will feel proud if I can walk the streets at night. I will feel proud if the hospitals are equipped to deal with the illnesses of the majority.

As I write this, a report flashes across my television screen of six armed robbers invading a church and threatening the worshippers.

A Proudly South African campaign that mobilises relevant government departments to deliver effective public services would be more palatable than one that encourages a narrow parochialism. Endless summits, bosberaads and conferences will not deliver the goods. Implementation, enforcement and actual monitoring of policies and plans of action are what will make South Africa a country to be proud of.

Our pride should be earned. A government that manages to revitalise the all too transient feelings of patriotism I experienced on April 1994 will get my vote.

Government is fast extinguishing the pride most of us had, because of its failure to deliver in the areas that matter.

Women (Abandoned Sisters)

☛ **Sisters in power give ordinary SA women little joy**
Business Day July 12 2007

SOON we'll be celebrating National Women's Day and the country will be in a flurry of 16 days of activism against violence against women.

Women will be on every agenda and the deputy president, with her chorus of women MPs, will mouth platitudes and sing the same old refrain about what should be done to eliminate violence against women.

Remember 1995, and the Beijing Conference? The acrimonious bun fight between women MPs who wanted to stop Winnie Mandela from attending, and the feminist activists in favour of her delegate status at the conference, is now a distant memory.

Predictably, the extremely wide-ranging and all-encompassing Beijing Platform for Action proposed was far too ambitious, particularly the attempt to address the unequal status of women and the girl child in developing countries and Africa. The immediate ratification of The United Nations Convention on the Elimination of All Forms of Discrimination Against Women (Cedaw) by SA on December 15 1995, while well meaning, exacerbated the totalising discourse that often prevents feminists from achieving anything.

I went back to the documents issued at the time to assess what achievements had been made in this regard, and it was none other than Public Service Minister Geraldine Fraser-Moleketi who made the greatest promises of all that 1996 would be the year of implementation. Cedaw, she said, would help us speed up implementation given that our constitutional blocks had been laid.

More than ten years on, we can justifiably ask what the significance was of convening 40 000 delegates to adopt a global platform for action, when conditions for women have since deteriorated and when women in government and Parliament have become as self-serving as the men who govern us; when the maternal mortality rate in sub-Saharan Africa is the equivalent of three jumbo jets going down every day?

Have the strategies advanced in Beijing to improve the status of women had any effect in this country? A critical review of twelve areas of concern discussed at Beijing lamentably show that no such thing has happened. The intention to address certain focal areas needed not only substantial resources but political will, which is a commodity feminists always claim they have in vast amounts.

The 2006 Human Development Index ranks SA at 121 out of 177 countries. Its low ranking relative to its high gross domestic product per capita and Human Poverty Index, which puts it at 53 out of 102 developing countries, is due to the catastrophic effects of HIV/AIDS on life expectancy, which has dropped to 47; infant mortality; and maternal health. When SA is being depopulated of its young women (HIV affects young women three times more than men); when young men infect more than ten women on average at a time with their insistence on multiple partners; and when intergenerational sex between young girls and sugar daddies compounds the problem, surely all women in the cabinet are culpable?

With our large, critical mass of women in leadership positions in Parliament, government and big business, this is an area in which they could have made a real difference. Instead Health Minister Manto Tshabalala-Msimang is back on the front pages of *Independent* newspapers looking like a warmed-up cadaver when she should be in jail for perpetuating the spread of a pandemic that should have been on the decline during her term of office.

With regards to crime, it took more than eight years to get the Sexual Offences Act through Parliament, with violence against women and children at a record high. I came back from peaceful Vienna a week ago, having enjoyed the freedom of public spaces until late at night, to continual headlines of the abduction and murder of young girls. In a country where 23 000 children are raped a year and there are around 36 000 reported rapes a year, I wonder why we should keep on arguing for the representation of women in positions of power when the women in the cabinet have had the power to use their substantial clout to make a difference, but have failed to do so.

Just last Thursday, *Top Billing* nauseatingly featured the Queen BEE kugels giving a party in honour of President Thabo Mbeki's birthday and repeatedly thanking him, with no irony, for what he'd done for them and for his inclusion of women in the power echelons of society. And they were right – Mbeki did much to empower a small sector of women through black economic empowerment, through access to Parliament through the proportional representative electoral system and through their cooption on the grounds of vested interests. This image is wonderfully captured in the phrase coined by feminists Amina Mama and Pumla Gqola 'submitting to the patriarchal *cult of femininity*'.

Academic theorist Shireen Hassim notes: 'Changing inequities in social and economic power will require not just the increased representation of women within the state, but also the increased and assertive representation of poor women within the state, as well as a strong feminist movement outside the state.'

For as long as we have the schism between female protest action outside of the state by communities *gatvol* with poor service delivery, and female inaction in Parliament and government where it matters, the gender question will remain that, a question, and the seizure of power, rather than empowerment, a more promising option.

☛ SA's women leaders leave their sisters in the lurch
Business Day August 10 2006

I AM AS allergic to National Women's Day as I am to male chauvinist pigs.

A day that has its origins in the noble Defiance Campaign of August 9 1956 is being desecrated by the consumer industry, which sees women as nothing more than the primary consumers of their goods, sexily draped around the latest 4x4. Accordingly, National Women's Day has been transmogrified into Women's Month for those of us who need more than a day to shop. True to form, our sisters in the African National Congress are launching yet another women's movement, the Progressive Women's Movement (PWM), in commemoration of its 50th Anniversary. The more the situation deteriorates for women, the more they think a broad alliance of organisations will do the trick. The moribund

Gender Commission and the Office on the Status of Women have proven useless, but somehow the sisters think the PWM will do the trick.

It will work only if our sisters rise above party politics and prioritise women's issues above their own sectional interests. On a number of occasions, women parliamentarians have acquiesced to being the gatekeepers of the most sexist policies espoused by the leadership of the party. Their silence around Zimbabwe and Robert Mugabe's tyrannical hold on power; Operation Remove Trash and its effects on women; the HIV pandemic; and the sexual harassment case of Norman Mashabane – to name only a few examples – speak volumes.

I have yet to be convinced that this movement will call the safety and security minister, the home affairs minister, the foreign affairs minister or the health minister to account for failing to implement policies and laws that affect women directly. All the rah-rah at the launch means nothing when women continue to be at the bottom of the scale in SA.

With 40% unemployment, the feminisation of poverty continues apace. With epidemic proportions of rape, sexual abuse, femicide and HIV, women bear the brunt of these scourges. The slow pace or lack of delivery of sanitation, electricity and water cripples the livelihoods of women who remain the primary nurturers of their families, locked into overcrowded informal settlements and dismal rural areas. Our grand constitution means zilch to women who will never know what it means to be equal. Our public representatives have done nothing, absolutely nothing, for the plight of women in SA. In fact, so obsessed are they with their titles, that they forget they are public servants.

Two recent incidents reported in the media prove my point. Deputy Minerals and Energy Minister Lulu Xingwana turfed a business-class passenger out of her seat, simply because her flight bookings had been botched up. This violation was aided and abetted by South African Airways, who instead of telling the deputy minister that all passengers are equal, tried to make up for it by giving the affected passenger a travel voucher as compensation and relegated her to the back of the plane in a crew seat.

A second incident is more unsavoury. The *City Press* reported that Deputy President Phumzile Mlambo-Ngcuka went shopping for furniture and her security guards allegedly demanded that the shop be closed as the lady in question wanted to shop in private. When the salesman refused, he was duly disciplined with a written warning. Of course, all of this was furiously denied in the paper but we now know who to believe. 'Just who do these ministers think they are?' are the words on everybody's lips.

Many of our sisters are an embarrassment to the memory and meaning of August 9 1956. The Defiance Campaign was the definitive demonstration against the laws that controlled the mobility of black women and reduced them to chattel and legal minors. Our female elected officials, who got into high office on the backs of those who marched, picketed and demonstrated against unjust laws since 1913, have forgotten the people who put them there. What we see are vain and self-aggrandising MPs bloated by their own self-importance, suffering from the chronic disease of entitlement.

The recent documentary on *Special Assignment* on the take-up of child support grants by schoolgirls who increasingly fall pregnant in order to qualify for the grant is one of the greatest indictments against our public representatives in Parliament. I listened with horror as young girls facetiously talked about why the child support grant was an incentive to fall pregnant. The consequences of unprotected sex, in the form of HIV/AIDS, sexually transmitted diseases and babies, were not deterrents enough. The fearlessness with which these young women talked about sex as equal to being loved, as attention from young men, and never as a death sentence, indicated that government's attempts at spreading the prevention message have failed spectacularly.

The young men were equally frightening. Sex meant access to any number of girls on their arms and in their beds. Condoms just spoilt the fun of having sex skin to skin. 'One cannot enjoy sweets in a wrapper' – and so there seems to be no choice between pleasure and death. Early on in their lives, these young men have learnt the tricks of a patriarchal narcissism that predates colonialism, the consequences of which have become fatal for many young adults, particularly women.

While SA is being depopulated of its young women, our women ministers prance about as though we owe them. No Progressive Women's Movement (PWM) is going to save the young women of SA. If they really want to make a difference, they should start by holding themselves accountable. Second, if they want to avoid hot air becoming the

PWM trademark, and if they are serious about real transformation for women, I suggest they start implementing and monitoring the Human Rights Watch recommendations in the book, *Violence Against Women in SA: State Response to Domestic Violence and Rape*. That would be a good start – but it means shelving the rhetoric and knuckling down to some hard work.

What we black women ought to tell this president
Business Day October 28 2004

NOTHING gets President Thabo Mbeki's knickers in a knot as much as utterances he construes to be racist. More frighteningly, he lashes out histrionically at those he thinks guilty of the sin.

A recent target, among others, is an 'anonymous' white woman, whom we all know is Charlene Smith, a feminist African National Congress (ANC) activist whose loyalty to issues of justice has always preceded that of loyalty to the party.

She has the knack of sending our president into an apoplectic rage over a seemingly innocent statement that still offends him after four years! It reads: 'Here (in Africa), (AIDS) is spread primarily by heterosexual sex – spurred by men's attitudes towards women. We won't end this epidemic until we understand the role of tradition and religion – and of a culture in which rape is endemic and has become a prime means of transmitting disease, to young women as well as children.'

Whether Mbeki likes it or not, this view underpins the high rates of sexual and domestic violence, HIV infections, femicide and family murders experienced by South African women on a daily basis. The scourge of violence against women is not the prerogative of any ethnic group. In all groups men rely on patriarchal culture, religion and tradition to justify treating women as chattels and second-class citizens. This attitude has come a long way.

Even the great philosophers of our time believed women were genetically inferior, legally and politically incompetent. The radical Proudhon believed women had two functions in life: housewife and prostitute.

So what Smith says is unmitigated fact. To accuse her of saying, 'African traditions, indigenous religions and culture prescribe and institutionalise rape' and implying that 'African men are inherently potential rapists and barbaric savages' when no such evidence exists is libellous and irresponsible.

Such far-fetched rubbish I have not heard in a long time. Racist interpretations of innocent statements such as hers smack of obsession at best and paranoia at worst. They resemble the incantations of a rabid African nationalist, not of someone described by the media as an intellectual.

Surely this kind of response is out of kilter with the office of the president and enough to strike the fear of God into the hearts of any ordinary citizens who dare to voice their opinions? If a puny little white activist is capable of sending the president into continual fits of rage, what does this say of Mbeki?

Maybe the time has come to call a spade a shovel.

Maybe we black women should start telling the president most black men treat black women badly, as borne out by the startling evidence of domestic violence, default on maintenance, sexual offences and the criminal courts of the land.

Maybe we should tell the president sexual autonomy for women is a myth, men do not accept 'NO' for an answer, and many think women are their property.

Maybe we should tell the president the reason more young women than men are infected with the AIDS virus is because most men sleep around with more than one woman and refuse to use condoms.

Maybe we should tell the president girl children on school benches are sexually abused by teachers when they should be learning, according to a report of the education department.

Yes, Mr President, most of these men are black – they violate not because they are black but because the majority of men in this country are black.

Mr President, I suggest you undergo some serious antiracism training so that you can identify the sin when you see it. Lashing out at activists who dare to call abuse by its regular name weakens you and not them. Why are you selectively vociferous about some matters and not others? Why do you not similarly trumpet the promotion of safe sex, antiretroviral medicines and sympathy for those infected with HIV?

Why do the HIV/AIDS pandemic and gross human rights violations in Zimbabwe not similarly move you? Why do you not condemn men for infecting multiples of women at the same time?

Your presidential letters are obsessed with your own notions of race and what it means to be African and how others, mainly whites, misinterpret this 'sacrosanct idea' that only you, Thabo Mbeki, understand. Even your congratulatory letter to Wangari Maathai is misdirected.

After reading it, all I can say to you, Mr President, is get a life!

Abuse of women a blot on 'new SA'
Business Day March 27 2003

TWO WEEKS ago I addressed a group of middle-class coloured women in Cape Town who came together a few years ago to form a hospice movement that provides food parcels to people living with HIV/AIDS.

Apropos International Woman's Day (March 8) and Human Rights Day (March 21) they asked me to speak about women's human rights. Having done this for the past twenty years, I focused instead on a topic which always gets women into a tizz: what conditions are necessary to end the subordination of women.

It struck an instant chord with the women who recognised themselves in what I proposed.

They did not argue with the view of leading socialist feminists that the subordination of women would end with: the abolition of the sexual division of labour; the alleviation of the burden of domestic labour and child-care; the removal of all kinds of institutionalised forms of discrimination; the attainment of political equality; the establishment of freedom of choice over child-bearing; the adoption of adequate measures against male violence and control over women.

These women identified wholeheartedly with the examples of overt and subtle forms of discrimination I cited, and as I took them through the Bill of Rights they were surprised to discover the extent to which the constitution is gender-sensitive.

After my speech the chairwoman, full of the joys of Germaine Greer, thanked me and said how much my speech had reminded her of her 80-year-old mother, who had been a feminist way before her time. She rounded off the evening exclaiming: If only women like Patricia de Lille and I would run SA, we would be sure to bring back the death penalty in an instant because women like us would not mess around with criminals.

Needless to say, as a strong abolitionist, I left feeling very depressed that my speech had been counterproductive and aroused sentiments contrary to the human rights culture I had tried to instil.

This attitude, of course, had more to do with the fact that violence against women is out of control, than it had to do with the death penalty. The call for this penalty is obviously one of desperation, in a climate where men use sex and power to keep women in subordination.

A recent book – *Violence Against Women: A National Survey* – published by the Institute for Security Studies, is a serious indictment of our society for tolerating what could be seen as epidemic proportions of violence against women.

Of the 1 000 women interviewed, 80% claimed to have experienced emotional abuse, 76% physical abuse, 63% sexual abuse and 62% economic abuse. The home, instead of being a safe haven, was where most of the abuse occurred, and children frequently witnessed violence.

This report concurs with the report by the Medical Research Council in early 2000, and a study conducted by Human Rights Watch in 1999, and shows that not much has improved since then.

In more than half of the cases the perpetrator was the spouse or partner, indicating that abuse has become part of domestic life, affecting how women live, work, and sleep in their daily lives. Responses from the police and courts were less than satisfactory.

Abused women generally were ignorant of their rights and police rarely explained the interdict, or access to the other medico-legal services available. More disheartening were the exceptionally low conviction rates for sexual and domestic violence.

What the '16-day public awareness campaign' achieved we will never know. However, much needs to be done. The Gender Commission can help by vigorously monitoring the police stations, courts, and district surgeons' offices to remove obstacles to effective prosecution. The media should consistently highlight test cases and expose the criminal justice system where it is weak.

It is the state's duty to take adequate measures against male violence and control over women. Unless we begin to see real progress on this front, feisty women such as the ones I addressed, will continue to call for the death penalty and roll back the substantial democratic gains we have made with the advent of 1994.

🙾 Let's get real about improving the lives of women
Business Day August 5 2004

WOMEN of Worth, Shoprite Checkers Women of the Year, MTN-Women in the Media – like postindependent Nigeria, this country is awash with facile celebrations in honour of women pretending that all is well on the women's empowerment front.

Not to mention the designer dresses, and competing designers who transform our ugly ducklings into Snow Queens in time for Gwen Gill's pages in the *Sunday Times*. As far as I am concerned, the empresses have no clothes.

With William Kekana having just received six life sentences for the hijacking and murder of baby Kayla, her mother Drennen and Drennen's mother-in-law; with the recent kidnap of Leigh Williams, and the not-so-recent kidnap and murder of Sasha-Leigh Crook, the position of women is dismal to say the least.

High-profile crimes against women and children such as these bring into sharp relief the thousands of low-profile violations against women daily in SA.

Suddenly we heard that about 4 000 kidnappings occur annually, a phenomenon most of us had been ignorant of to date.

Femicide is as common, with one in six women who are murdered regularly by either their partner or husband, according to the Medical Research Council.

Sexual and domestic violence is not abating.

And all of this is compounded by scary statistics of HIV/AIDS among young women. The National Youth Survey conducted by the Wits University reproductive health research unit and *LoveLife* found that 77% of young South Africans infected with HIV were women. Nearly one in four women aged twenty to 24 was HIV-positive as against one in fourteen men of that age.

This scenario paints a picture that should jolt women into organised action. Surely a government complicit in depopulating SA of women provides us with no cause for celebration? Media hype about the appointment of women as premiers and to key cabinet posts, and the gender-sensitivity of the president, was much ado about nothing.

The usual suspect feminists wrote at length how wonderful it was. Yet political analyst Steven Friedman exposed this charade. He argued that appointing women to some of these posts was not necessarily a victory for women or democracy. Not one of the four women made premier topped her provincial electoral list. This means that they owe their support and loyalty to the African National Congress national executive, not their provincial party. 'It seems unlikely placing women in office because they are beholden to the centre will produce a gain for women's political empowerment,' says Friedman.

As we fête ten years of democracy, whom do we look to for inspiration? Lest we forget, August 9 is the celebration of 20 000 women of all races, classes, organisations and religions, marching to the Union Buildings in 1956 to challenge government pass laws.

They came from a noble lineage of women in Europe, England and the US who had gone before and who literally fought tooth and nail for a just dispensation in their respective nations. In the 19th and early-20th centuries, women like Emmeline Pankhurst and Harriet Taylor Mills waged bitter struggles over the legal status of women. At one stage Pankhurst advocated destruction of property, as it was through property, she argued, that women were most discriminated against.

In 1907, when women marched with petitions to the House of Commons in London, riots ensued. Police imprisoned 57 women. Riots at Trafalgar Square and Hyde Park were met by vicious police action. Women organised window-smashing raids on shops and fashionable men's clubs in the West End of London. Street lamps were broken. Train seats, flower beds and golf greens were damaged. Telephone wires were cut. Fuse boxes were blown up. Sports pavilions and grandstands at races were burnt down. Several empty houses and stately homes and church property were destroyed. And bombs were placed near the Bank of England. Suffragists interrupted House of Commons debates.

At the 1913 Derby, a suffragette ran on to the track and tried to grab the bridle of a horse owned by the king. The impact fractured her skull and she died.

These women were treated with much brutality, beatings, arrests, imprisonment, forced feeding in jail, and death.

Such militancy was unusual for these middle-class women. Yet they knew nothing less would bring them nearer emancipation. And lest you think I am advocating civil disobedience, let me reassure readers I am too much of a pacifist to go that route.

Yet the time has come for us to cease our facile celebrations, and use our considerable influence and power to hold institutions specifically tasked with improving women's status accountable.

Constitutional equality is no guarantee that the lives of women will improve.

Double standards muddy the waters of Zuma trial
Business Day April 6 2006

I WRITE this column with trepidation lest it be misconstrued.

The Jacob Zuma (JZ) trial has provoked both his supporters and his detractors into a frenzy because both sides feel aggrieved.

Let me start with his critics. Because JZ was found to have had a corrupt relationship with Schabir Shaik, and because he is a polygamist and womaniser, his detractors assume him guilty before they have even heard the evidence. That he slept with someone who is HIV-positive, as reprehensible as that might be, does not mean that we have a right to assume that he has raped the woman and therefore has no right to a fair trial.

Second, JZ is fighting for his political life and I doubt that he would have been so stupid as to rape someone. If he did then he is really stupid.

Third, every rape happens in certain circumstances and because it is often between two people where no or few witnesses are about, it is important to hear all the evidence, even the personal sexual histories of the complainant and the accused when it is deemed necessary.

This trial is more about sexual politics and gender relations than it is about rape and epitomises the lifestyle of so many cadres in exile and in the camps, which continues much in the same vein post-1994. And that is why there is a lid on the report on sexual violence in the ANC camps and could partly explain why the HIV/AIDS pandemic is not declining. The leaders at the top live by example.

Fourth, not all women who shout rape or sexual harassment are victims. The feminists unfortunately have used the word victim and the word rape (rarely alleged rape) throughout this sordid saga, denying their own paradigm that women have agency too; that they can say no to sex; that they are sexual beings too; and that they too can be wily about ensnaring men.

At the University of the Western Cape where I was the gender equity officer I dealt with enough cases where women used claims of rape and sexual harassment claims to get even with their partners. I was called the 'gender police' and I feminised our courts substantially.

This does not preclude the fact that in most circumstances of rape women have no protection or defence and that it often happens under violent conditions that are life threatening.

The fact is this alleged rape by JZ of the complainant did not happen under violent circumstances. It happened between two people who know each other. At no stage did the complainant say no and she admitted that JZ might have thought it okay to have sex. There was a policeman on the premises and other people. This complicates the matter even further. Date rape is always difficult to prove, which is why all evidence must be led.

As for JZ's supporters, I can fully understand why they are angry.

They know that there are many politicians who are equally if not more corrupt than JZ and that JZ's sins are minuscule in comparison with the biggies. His successor was appointed deputy president with big question marks over her involvement in the oil scandal, not to speak of the diamond tiara and undisclosed directorships.

Parliament's travel scandal, which allegedly involves more than a hundred MPs, ministers and others, is being smothered, and no court case or commission of inquiry is being set up to investigate that. In fact, Harry Charlton has been fired for blowing the whistle.

The current exposé by auditor general Shauket Fakie of hundreds of undisclosed directorships shows how endemically corrupt politicians are – from the top to the bottom – yet President Mbeki refuses to set up inquiries into these.

JZ's supporters have a right to feel that he has been set up. The linkage with the intelligence ministry is not coincidental. All this does not excuse their behaviour or their harassment of the complainant. But what this whole sorry saga points to is contempt for the rule of law when President Mbeki applies double standards. Mbeki is weakening the constitutional state with his inconsistencies around what gets investigated and what doesn't. Can we blame the masses when they become deeply suspicious of the rule of law? Judge Willem van der Merwe is under enormous pressure to do the politically correct thing. As a white Afrikaner male, he will not escape the racist prejudices Judge Hilary Squires was subjected to.

What we all should remember is this: we are sitting with the consequences of a Judicial Services Commission that appoints people on the basis of colour rather than expertise first and that even their own black appointees have had to recuse themselves on the basis of some or other linkage with the defendant. Judgments therefore will continually be questioned with reference to the judge's race rather than sound judicial logic and jurisprudence.

We will rue the day our judges and their judgments became viewed as untrustworthy.

And, by the way, no, I do not want Jacob Zuma to be my president.

☛ Tshabalala-Msimang gives women a bad name
Business Day July 26 2002

A RECENT CARTOON in the *Cape Argus* depicts Manto Tshabalala-Msimang's head as the skull with crossbones, aptly entitled: 'POISON – keep far away from HIV/AIDS Treatment Decision Making.' This is one of many cartoons caricaturing our misdirected health minister.

The butt of constant ridicule, how many more cartoons of similar ilk are we going to see before we see her go. She even topped the *Sunday Times* list as *Mampara* of the week, a second time since taking office.

The deluge of calls and articles in the papers supporting Archbishop Njongonkulu Ndungane's call on her to resign, as I did also a year ago, remains unheeded simply because what the electorate wants is of no consequence.

It has become abundantly clear now, that Tshabalala-Msimang should not resign. She should be fired! Unfortunately with a president that has full confidence in her ability to do her job, she virtually has carte blanche to remain reckless.

And that is the problem with our democracy.

We have yet to see cabinet ministers fired for being useless. Not one cabinet minister has been discharged for incompetence, non-delivery, corruption and the like since 1994.

On the contrary, these attributes seem to be the criteria that qualify one for higher office these days. Like the nationalists of old, the more corrupt and the more useless, the higher the office. I can name many senior state officials who now hold higher office than before despite their failure to perform satisfactorily.

What I find even more disconcerting about Tshabalala-Msimang is that she gives women a bad name. Feminist activists have argued strongly for the equal inclusion of women in government structures on the assumption they will do justice to gender equality and issues that affect women most deeply.

Well, we have been wrong. By now I would have expected the women in Parliament, in the cabinet and in senior public positions, to be convulsed by the utterances of the minister and to have called for her head.

That they are not vociferous about the AIDS pandemic, and most notably its effects on women, exemplifies how powerful the party list system is in silencing women. That is exactly what is wrong with the word empowerment in government circles.

Those with power – usually male rulers – confer power on women who are seen to be compliant and beholden to the piper that calls the tune.

After Women's Day on August 9, should we not call on women to march the health minister out of office, like women marched in 1956 against the pass laws?

Lest you think this is too dramatic, let me tell you why this is more than justified.

More than six million South Africans will be infected with HIV/AIDS by 2009. Most of them make up the economically active sector of our population. Young women in particular are most affected by the disease. HIV/AIDS burdens women in ways peculiar to their gender.

As the main nurturers and caregivers of the family the responsibility to care for the sick and dying becomes mainly theirs.

More seriously, women as citizens in their own right are directly affected by the disease themselves, with the spectre of death hanging over their heads, knowing they will leave many orphans behind, with very little prospect of care.

Many are the family's sole breadwinners and with poverty becoming increasingly feminised, the state has an extra responsibility to ease the burden of women. The health minister has not risen to the challenge.

Under such circumstances how can we tolerate a minister who denies that HIV causes AIDS? How can we allow her to persecute those who dare to follow internationally recognised scientific prescriptions for the prevention, treatment and care of the disease?

How can we tolerate a minister who unashamedly admits the Constitutional Court's judgment forces her against her will to supply nevirapine to HIV-positive pregnant women? How can we let her torpedo a United Nations Global AIDS Fund grant to KwaZulu-Natal, on the pretext government was not consulted?

Having failed, spectacularly, to be proactive about soliciting grants to combat the disease she now wants to take from those that took the initiative in a province where the pandemic is spiralling out of control.

In any civilised democracy, the health minister would have been given the boot. Why should a woman like her be thrust upon us?

She clearly commands no respect and her latest shenanigans should be the death knell of a minister who failed to be proactive when she should have been.

☞ Mother Theresas bring comfort to the needy

Business Day November 29 2002

AGNES NKOSI is an unsung hero. At 60 she has dedicated her life to working with the severely disabled in the Eerstehoek district in Mpumalanga close to the Swaziland border.

She runs one of the best community-based rehabilitation programmes in the country, an oasis in the deep rural areas called the Chief Dlamini Cheshire Home. Disabled persons and those left without care by migrant-labour relatives are provided with accommodation, nursing care and rehabilitation.

The entire family is involved in the teaching and rehabilitation of disabled members and the complex includes a cerebral palsy children's stimulation centre, an adult literacy centre, support groups for the disabled, income generation groups, women's clubs and burial self-help groups.

Agnes assists pensioners and women to obtain disability and child maintenance grants and renders an invaluable service to the community while her grant for the centre from welfare department is, ironically, often irregular.

Stephanie Kilroe and Joan Marshall run the Lifeline Counsellor Programmes in Western Cape and Eastern Cape respectively. These programmes recruit unemployed people from disadvantaged communities with high HIV prevalence rates and offer them training in relationship counselling and health education about the disease.

These lay counsellors work in clinics in Khayelitsha, Guguletu, Nyanga, Mitchells Plain and the Central Health District. They help people get HIV tests in the local clinics, and by means of the rapid test know the results in twenty minutes. In Khayelitsha alone the HIV test acceptance rate has gone up to 81%. In Buffalo City they operate in 45 primary health care clinics; 120 lay counsellors provide services to 6 689 people in the area.

These partnerships between the health department, traditional healers, local clinics and Lifeline have alleviated the health crisis considerably in their respective areas, yet they depend heavily on foreign donors.

Estelle Geldenhuys, Jocelyn Freed and a group of enterprising women initiated Warmth (War Against Malnutrition, Tuberculosis and Hunger), an innovative community-based feeding scheme that provides low cost nutritious food to poor communities in the Western Cape.

This is a feeding scheme with a difference. Kitchen operators are provided with equipment and receive food supplies to provide nutritious food to various communities in the region. The kitchens are run like businesses, developing the entrepreneurial and business skills of operators in the process. Nutritious meals are provided to the poor at very low cost and 250 workshops are run to educate unemployed women about health and nutrition for their children and families.

This innovative system is an excellent model for alleviating poverty and creating jobs for women at the same time.

Partnerships with government can achieve more when they look for new and unique ways of breaking poverty.

Mpho Sebanyoni, a multiple award winner for community service, set up the Moretele Sunrise Hospice in Temba near Hammanskraal. This hospice operates a home-based hospice movement that services 78 satellite operations in North West.

A carefully-tended demonstration garden is used to educate people living with AIDS how to cook nutritious meals and the herb garden is used for the treatment of oral thrush, for massage oils, for ointment, for health teas and the like.

These are a few of the projects out of a total of 150 submissions short-listed for the Impumelelo Innovations Award.

The panel of judges that convened at the Holiday Inn in Cape Town on November 21-22 2002 had a difficult time selecting projects for the award.

The challenge to stick to the criteria buckled under the panel's face-to-face encounters with the numerous Mother Theresas that have pioneered creative solutions to public problems of poverty, unemployment and disease.

These initiatives seldom become headlines. But they are quiet indicators of what partnerships with government can achieve when they look for new and unique ways of breaking the poverty that grips so much of this country. Remarks heard as judges left the hall after two days of presentations: 'I leave here with a deep feeling of inferiority,' and 'This exercise confronts one with moral dilemmas that are difficult to comprehend, given the R1 billion of unspent public funds'. It sums up how many of us felt after the hearings.

☛ Back to the barricades, sisters
Weekend Argus August 11 to 12 2001

ON READING in the *Mail & Guardian* (August 3 to 9 2001) that the Commission of Gender Equality is proposing to hold hearings into sexism in the advertising industry, I despaired.

South Africa is fast becoming expert at hosting one public farce after another. I speak of course of the conference on racism in 1999, the

Hearings into Racism in the Media in 2000, and now the United Nations Conference on Racism.

True to form, the gender commission is about to add another public charade to the list.

Is it planning to serve subpoenas on offending institutions? Is it going to charge them for subliminal sexism in advertisements? Just what is it planning to achieve with these hearings? Just to what lengths is the gender commission prepared to go to pretend that it is doing something of note when it is in fact clutching at straws?

Crippled by infighting, confirming the stereotype that women cannot work together, its inability to use the power that it has to advance the cause of women has been astounding.

Perhaps the time has come for the commission to be guided by women outside of these state institutions as to what its priorities should be. Has feminist literature not taught us to distinguish between practical versus strategic gender interests?

While sexism in the media is an issue, is it justified to pursue a matter of relative insignificance when there are larger issues at stake?

Tackling sexism in the media does not in any way alleviate the epidemic of domestic and sexual violence confronting women in this country.

It will not bring water and electricity to the homes of poor black women in this country.

Getting advertising agencies to refrain from wrapping a naked body around a Ferrari will not bring houses to the women of Bredell.

The lethargy of the gender commission in addressing and monitoring the enforcement of policies regarding domestic violence, AIDS, female unemployment and so on, is due to its reluctance to challenge government directly and hold it accountable. Have we seen women in Parliament, except the feisty Patricia de Lille of course, opposing government on the arms deal?

Have we seen women in government challenge the president in his incomprehensible stance on AIDS, a view he shockingly reiterated in his recent interview in *Hardtalk* with Tim Sebastian of the British Broadcasting Corporation?

Does it matter to these elected women that the AIDS epidemic is destroying the very fabric of women's lives? Women who are not only the main breadwinners and child rearers, but who also have to worry about their own lives?

More than that, many of them are dying at a rapid rate, burdened by the knowledge that they will leave orphans behind who will have no one to care for them.

Why are the gender commissioners not protesting in the streets about the need for nevirapine to prevent mother-to-child transmission? They don't because it means challenging the hand that feeds them. It means stepping on the toes of comrades who put them into positions of power. What we need in this country is some boots-on street activism like we had prior to 1994.

Charlene Smith, journalist for the *Mail & Guardian*, has singlehandedly taken on some issues that the gender commission should have taken on, on a broader scale, to make an impact on sexual violence against women. Her expert research on rape and the failure to provide antiretroviral medicine to rape survivors and the monitoring thereof, has made reading her on the need for the effective treatment and counselling of rape survivors indispensable to advising doctors, health-care workers, prosecutors and magistrates, police officers and social workers. Her pre-trial court reports have ensured stiffer sentences for offenders. Her victim impact statements for the High Court have resulted in expert judgments that have been reproduced in the *South African Law Journal*.

Smith has successfully put the issue of rape, HIV and anti-retrovirals on the agenda in South Africa and internationally – so much so that some private hospital groups have opened more rape clinics and have dispensed anti-retroviral starter packs and HIV tests freely to rape survivors. Through her dedicated and sterling work she has influenced some insurance agencies to include medical insurance for anti-retrovirals and HIV care.

Her tireless activism led to Clicks, Diskom and Musica stores launching a major anti-rape campaign in 1999, culminating in her writing a booklet for them on surviving rape. With Nathabiseng Mogale, of People Opposing Woman Abuse (Powa), they launched a million-signature campaign calling for free anti-retrovirals for those raped, better pay for prosecutors and police, and a Victims' Charter.

Powa obtained more than 900 000 signatures, probably of the biggest petitions in the history of this country. Smith's activism has led her to question the inertia of the state and has brought her into conflict with the president. Her loyalty to justice has taken precedence over her loyalty to the politicians.

National priorities seem to be eluding former activists who very clearly knew before 1994 what the main concerns were. Now they are part and parcel of government, the trappings of power and credit cards have blinded them to the realities confronting South African women.

Award ceremony upon award ceremony is held where the elite recycle awards to each other. Woman of the Year, Woman of Worth and Checkers Woman of the Year have become beauty extravaganzas for the ruling elite where they shamelessly parade their Gucci shoes and Escada designer wear to a public of women whose poverty tip the scales year in and year out.

Women, it is time to wake up and take control of our lives. The sisters in parliament are not going to do it for us. Marches, demonstrations, pickets, advocacy and the enforcement of crucial policies are tried and tested tactics that will help us achieve our goals.

These are the methods that were used by the suffragists internationally and by our very own women on August 9 1956, when en masse they defied the government to state their case.

☛ Women's rights the victim of sordid saga
The Sunday Independent June 13 2004

IN AN ARTICLE in *The Sunday Independent* Smuts Ngonyama, the head of the office of the presidency and communications in the ANC, exposes with chilling clarity the cynicism and hypocrisy that underpin the ANC's claim to support women's rights. ('Naidu's claims about Mbeki are blatant lies.' June 6 2004)

Referring to the decision by the foreign affairs minister, Nkosazana Dlamini-Zuma to exonerate Norman Mashabane, our ambassador in Indonesia, after his own department had found him guilty of 21 charges of sexual harassment, he wrote: 'Your newspaper knows that the South African Police Service conducted an investigation into the allegations made against Mashabane. It established that all of these were absolutely without foundation.'

Ngonyama was either wilfully misleading the public or negligently ignorant of the facts, because another article elsewhere in the same edition revealed that the police sent to Jakarta, by Dlamini-Zuma, chose to interview only one of seven locally-employed embassy staff who had complained of sexual harassment.

Significantly she was the only one to retract her claims against Mashabane. Equally significantly the police made not the slightest effort to interview career diplomat Lara Swart. She was transferred to our embassy in South Korea after proving her case of sexual harassment against Mashabane in a departmental disciplinary hearing.

M-Net's *Carte Blanche* team members, in a programme broadcast last Sunday revealed that they had also travelled to Jakarta. Unlike Dlamini-Zuma's plods, they found no difficulty in contacting three of the six Indonesian women who had chosen to leave the embassy's employ because of Mashabane's unwanted attentions. All were happy to testify on camera about his behaviour.

To nobody's surprise, I am sure, *Carte Blanche* ascertained that the only woman who had withdrawn her allegations against Mashabane – and the only one whose evidence Dlamini-Zuma regards as credible – now works as Mashabane's personal secretary. She was only given this promotion once she had retracted her claims! She also had previous disciplinary charges against her withdrawn.

Swart, who clearly has no prospect of promotion, was prepared to testify on camera, unlike Mashabane, who declined a similar invitation from M-Net. With her husband present, Swart told of an embassy function where Mashabane called her aside and suggested that she book a trip – just for the two of them – to one of the Indonesian provinces. She spoke about how he then forcibly embraced her and, despite her protests, fondled her and thrust his tongue into her mouth.

Distraught at his failure to desist, she fainted, gashing her head in the process, but he continued to force himself upon her until her husband arrived to collect her.

She told her interviewers that, after she had laid a complaint against Mashabane, he called a meeting of the embassy staff and stated that he would never have sex with a white woman because he found the thought disgusting.

In making such a claim, Swart is either telling the truth or extremely stupid, because if she is lying, all her colleagues would be able to deny this statement. I believe her, not least because this must have formed part of the evidence that convinced the internal investigation by the department of foreign affairs to find Mashabane guilty as charged and recommended his dismissal.

What is self-evident is that if a white male ambassador were to tell his staff that he would never have sex with a black woman because he found the notion repugnant, he would face instant dismissal.

And in this regard, Mashabane is clearly not on a par with ANC heavyweights such as Tokyo Sexwale, Valli Moosa, Essop Pahad *et al* who have bridged the racial divide without disgust.

It is difficult to come to any conclusion other than that the police who were sent to Jakarta were either instructed to be party to a cover-up or were so negligent that their work can only be described as a travesty of justice and a dereliction of duty.

Nauseating but not surprising is Ngonyama's concluding statement on this matter in the article he authored: 'We hope that the necessary disciplinary action and possible criminal prosecutions will be taken against those involved in the dirty campaign against Mashabane.'

Swart would be well advised to alert her lawyers to this sordid saga.

Ruling Alliance (Party Poopers)

► **We must shed notion that only ANC can save SA**
Business Day August 5 2008

ALEX BORAINE, at the recent launch of his autobiography, *A Life in Transition*, lamented: 'This is not what we struggled for.' He firmly believes that a realignment of politics and a moral consensus will take SA out of its morass.

Many people who today lament SA's descent into chaos, contributed towards its decline. When we should have given moral leadership on life-and-death issues, such as challenging President Thabo Mbeki's views on HIV/AIDS, or his silence about Zimbabwean President Robert Mugabe's atrocities, many came out in his defence. When MPs defrauded Parliament, we should have marched them out of office; when arms were prioritised over AIDS, we should have risen up.

This post-liberation acquiescence, described in Judith Todd's memoir, *Through the Darkness*, has led to the destruction of democracy in many countries. When Mugabe massacred 20 000 Matabele in 1983, it was viewed as an aberration by many world leaders, who kept *schtum* when it happened.

When Zimbabwean farmers were murdered, terrorised and forced to flee, leaders looked on nonchalantly, forgetting that these were the producers of food. Mugabe was a tyrant early in his presidency. Similarly, Mbeki showed worrying autocratic tendencies early in his reign. Yet greed blinded the sycophants around him to his harmful idiosyncrasies, and they just told the emperor what he wanted to hear.

When things went awry early on in our democracy, political leaders were often given the benefit of the doubt, the rationale being that since they struggled for a moral cause, they must therefore be highly moral. Hence, the escalating corruption, political intolerance, non-delivery and mismanagement were initially excused as mistakes, committed by infants of democracy. Many comrades refused to see the warning signals, covering up until the festering sores, like gangrene, became too septic and widespread to cure.

Civic leaders and the media practised the masterful art of self-censorship, and critique was silenced in subtle ways. Sympathisers of the government turned a blind eye, wanting to benefit from government's largesse, cosying up to the ruling elite through acquiescence and tacit support lest they jeopardise their vested interests. White guilt shut up many a critic. ANC supporters, understandably, found it hard to criticise a government they had voted into power. The destiny of the ANC was so deeply wrapped up with their own that they could not be seen to judge a party with which they had become synonymous.

So, Boraine's call for the politics of realignment is understandable but not feasible. Discounting the efficacy of the official opposition purely from a racial point of view, he argues that opposition must come from within.

This is unlikely, since the survival of the tripartite alliance depends on precisely that – an alliance. Should they break up and each go their separate ways, the ruling class will surely collapse. In this context of two centres of power, where the ANC has effectively become its own opposition, it is difficult for a political saviour to emerge. The conflation of Parliament, under speaker Baleka Mbete's gavel, with the Zuma centre of power has become the new political reality, as the debates around the Scorpions and the SABC so ably demonstrate.

In this climate of ruling party consolidation, leaders of Boraine's stature should unapologetically call for the strengthening of opposition parties, regardless of who leads them, and marshal all the resources to strengthen them in their myriad forms. And here, civil society and the media have a monumental role to play in strengthening political competition instead of weakening it, as they are doing in Cape Town and as happened with the Movement for Democratic Change in Zimbabwe.

The only solution is a new political party that can take us back to the constitution and start on a clean slate. We should shed this notion that only the ANC can save us.

☛ Intolerant ANC ignores biggest threat to its power
Business Day May 17 2007

OPPOSITION is good for democracy anywhere in the world. Nothing illustrates this better than Tony Blair's and George Bush's imminent departure from office, after a spell of omnipotent rule against weak opposition parties.

In SA, where one-party dominance breeds arrogance, opposition is barely tolerated. The African National Congress' (ANC's) fights against its political competitors are particularly vicious when the latter are on the verge of assuming real power, as when the United Democratic Movement was on the rise in Eastern Cape a few years ago, the Inkatha Freedom Party in KwaZulu-Natal, and the Democratic Alliance-led coalition in Western Cape.

Opposition parties do have relatively free reign in this country but a probe beneath the surface reveals it is not as good as it seems. Since Helen Zille's rise to power, the ANC has attempted seven coups against the Democratic Alliance coalition, eroding bit by bit the space needed to govern effectively. Like a rabid dog, it now threatens to redraw the provincial boundaries yet again, to further weaken the coalition. It might even be helped in its ambition to centralise control by those dwindling parties that fear attrition at the next floor-crossing period in September.

Having survived all these attempts, Zille complains that so much positive energy is being wasted that could be better channelled into service delivery and improving the quality of life of the poor. The ANC should heed John F Kennedy's advice 50 years ago, that 'without debate, without criticism, no administration and no country can succeed; and no republic can survive'.

The transition from struggle to statehood is the ANC's biggest challenge. Its obsession with power has come to override its revolutionary goal to provide services to all, even if it splits the party asunder. Its intolerance of interparty political competition and intraparty differences has had deleterious effects on governance at both provincial and municipal levels. The constant factionalism and internal feuding have led to management paralyses in more than 100 municipalities and many provinces are not doing too well either. The ANC's own strongholds, in Limpopo, Free State, Mpumalanga, Western Cape and Eastern Cape, are floundering.

At local level, the internecine fights are worse if the excellent recent Centre for Development and Enterprise (CDE) report on service delivery protests in Khutsong and Phumelela is anything to go by. Not only has the ANC expended a lot of energy trying to weaken Zille but this strategy has become commonplace at intraparty levels too, crippling the ANC's own governance at municipal level, alienating the party further from its working class and rural bases. The ANC should stop dividing and start ruling. Better still, start governing.

If the ANC wants to survive, it should take note of the CDE's research, especially the lessons tabled at the end of the report. The uprisings in Khutsong and Phumelela could have been averted had the government simply responded to the due process followed by community organisations and representatives in raising issues that affected them. The government's failure to respond timeously to their objections to the redemarcation of their municipal boundaries provoked the unrest. Their legitimate anger was compounded by the government's disregard of their complaints about poor sanitation, the lack of proper infrastructure, the failure to remove sewage and garbage, the gross incompetence of municipal staff, and their failure to deliver.

During this whole process, the cavalier disregard for citizen participation, the lack of accountability and the imposition of top-down solutions regardless of public sentiment fuelled the flames of community anger and enraged the public so much so that their white counterparts pitched in to support the black communities against the government. To add insult to injury, useless party loyalists were redeployed to jobs elsewhere, instead of being sacked for their dereliction of duty.

If the ANC is intolerant of factions within its own ranks, then how much more ruthless will it be towards opposition parties who threaten its power base?

The ruling party's obsession with absolute control has made it so intolerant of party political competition that service delivery has become the casualty of infighting. If it continues on this path, its political intolerance will eventually destroy it. The ANC should realise that a threat more worrying to its longevity than the looming succession battle is its failure to deliver basic services to the poor.

If it wants to survive, it would do well to heed former Mexican president Vincente Fox's advice on what constitutes good governance: 'One of the fundamental ingredients of the new governance is good government. A government close to society, always ready to listen to it; a government fully respectful of legality, honest, transparent and efficient; but above all, a government conscious of its mission of promoting human and social development as the basis for attaining a more just and prosperous society.'

☞ No vote of confidence for Mbeki's 'Party of Death'
Business Day December 14 2006

SOME TIME AGO I asked the London-based daughter of loyal African National Congress (ANC) supporters (returned exiles) whether she would vote for the ANC if she lived here. Her immediate response was: 'I cannot support the Party of Death.'

I was as jolted by this response as were her parents at her description of their party – once synonymous with the struggle for justice and democracy. Seen now as the instrument that has doomed many people, mostly black, to death, she failed to see why people could still be loyal to a party that has long failed to be loyal to them.

The most recent statistics – of 940 people between the ages of fifteen and 30 dying daily of AIDS – is for me the greatest indictment of President Thabo Mbeki's rule and makes the apartheid government seem humane in comparison. As horrendous as the previous regime was, 940 people did not die every day under its rule. Nor did we have 18 000 murders, 350 000 rapes against women and children, and more than 13 000 road deaths annually under apartheid.

I am ashamed of the ANC. I am ashamed to read the daily accounts of women suffering and dying from HIV/AIDS, of children orphaned and caring for their younger siblings, of babies dying of AIDS, of grandmothers burying their own children, of young women and men disappearing from the official statistics. The media has been good about writing stories of sufferers to give the disease a human face, in the hope government will act.

I am ashamed of the endless corruption that has amounted to billions since 1994, while the majority of people in this country live in abject poverty. I am ashamed that Tony Yengeni, convicted fraudster, is carried shoulder-high like a hero to prison by senior ANC officials. Many ANC supporters, who are ashamed of Mbeki's stance, condemn him quietly, but will never raise their heads above the parapet lest they lose access to resources and impede their own vested interests.

I am constantly asked by foreigners, and even local people, why we have allowed the AIDS epidemic to escalate from less than 1% in 1990 to 7,6% in 1994 when the ANC came to power, to 29% this year. With the pandemic already in the 'graveyard cycle', my answer is to point them in the direction of Mbeki's own utterances and those of his acolytes who have been vociferous in defending him.

Remember his 2001 Fort Hare speech, in which he blamed his critics for believing Africans are 'natural-born, promiscuous germ carriers' with an 'unconquerable devotion to the sin of lust'. Remember when he opened the first International AIDS conference in Durban insisting that poverty is a greater enemy than the virus, and hundreds of delegates walked out in protest and disgust. Remember how he ignored the Durban Declaration, signed by 5 000 AIDS researchers and physicians, which stated unequivocally that 'HIV causes AIDS'. Remember how he denied knowing anyone with the virus. Remember the support for Peter Mokaba's macabre document: 'Castro Hlongwane, Caravans, Cats, Geese, Foot & Mouth and Statistics – HIV/AIDS and the Struggle for the Humanisation of the African.' Remember this bout of madness culminating in the presidential vilification of Charlene Smith, who dared to call the sin by its regular name.

Fuelled by denial and inaction, we sit today with a pandemic that has become the epicentre of the disease in sub-Saharan Africa. Yet when Democratic Alliance leader Tony Leon announced his resignation, we saw reams of venom directed at him.

When thousands of black people are dying under Mbeki's rule, our so-called analysts focused on Leon's style of leadership. Some columns about him were fair, but others were quite vitriolic, the most virulent coming from the Institute for Democracy, an organisation that should be promoting democracy and respect for opposition, but has instead become an apologist for a ruling party that has lost vision and direction and has failed its citizens spectacularly.

The focus on Leon's persona rather than his policies and his feisty role in holding government accountable has become the hobbyhorse of commentators such as Richard Calland, Ken Owen, Steven Friedman, Judith February and others accusing Leon of all the things they are guilty of.

If leadership style is indeed a dismissible offence, Mbeki should be the first to go, then most of the cabinet, followed by Patricia de Lille. Embroiled in unseemly spectacles and infighting, the Independent Democrats have been treated with kid gloves by these watchdogs of democracy, which are glaringly partial in their criticism.

No wonder these commentators have not been blacklisted by the SABC.

☞ A clouded national psyche revealed after acquittal
Business Day May 18 2006

JACOB ZUMA's acquittal provoked responses that are deeply disturbing from a range of quarters.

Why he, and not the woman, is considered a villain remains puzzling but it gives us a peep into the nation's psyche. The *Sunday Times* (May 14 2006), not least, has played a leading role in feeding this psychosis, with its histrionic headline: 'Zuma divides the nation'. Had it noted the thoughtful articles published on its own pages by Robin Palmer, professor of law at the University of KwaZulu-Natal, and David Masondo, the Communist Youth League leader, its editorial would have been more measured.

Palmer brilliantly expounds Judge Willem van der Merwe's judgment in the hope that the public distinguish fact from emotional fiction. One cannot shout rape falsely against anyone, let alone a high-profile politician, and expect to get away with it. This fallacious charge has thrust Zuma's private life on to the national stage. Masondo correctly warns against blurring the lines between Zuma's right to a fair trial and his right to privacy, as problematic as that might be for feminists.

Van der Merwe's verdict was a victory of legal justice over political intrigue. Just as false accusations of racism undermine what the struggle against racial domination was all about, so too do false claims of rape undermine the struggle against violence against women. It would have helped if the media and feminist activists took note of the evidence before making insinuations about Zuma.

Zuma's supporters were jubilant, and rightly so, because they knew this was a setup. They are also angry that a huge, expensive court process was put in motion in reaction to a vexatious accuser who is allowed to shout rape falsely, and so mobilising a train of reactions that expose Zuma's private life, making him the laughing stock of the nation, when others in leadership positions live equally profligate lives.

They also know this case was prioritised over a long queue of serious rape cases that are not being fast-tracked and not given the visibility they deserve. This is what feminists should be marching about.

They also know that the state machinery is being used ruthlessly against presidential hopefuls when other scandals warrant equal urgency.

The reactions of some sections of the media were equally interesting. At a Radio 702 press conference, the media did not expect Zuma to apologise for having unprotected sex, nor did they expect him to call on his supporters not to harass the complainant. So they were quick to call it a 'charm offensive', because to them Zuma should have been found guilty, because this at least would have been one obstacle to his race for presidential power.

The feminist response was equally disappointing. As is their wont, they assumed the accused guilty before they heard the evidence and twisted the evidence to such an extent that Zuma came across as the proverbial male chauvinist swine clinging to all the stereotypes about women that feminists abhor. So when he was found not guilty, they continued to vilify him.

And why were people disappointed when he was acquitted?

Zuma, by his own admission, is an uneducated peasant who rose to power through his political involvement in the struggle over a long period. There is nothing wrong with this.

But Zuma is also a traditionalist. A known polygamist owning a traditional kraal in KwaZulu-Natal – a position incidentally allowed for in the constitution – he has also, more seriously, been portrayed as financially illiterate, hence his dependence on Schabir Shaik, his financial adviser who was found guilty of corruption.

Zuma's populist appeal is the other thing people fear. His supporters seem uncontrollable, militant and hot-headed, and the prospect of his ascending the throne with a rabble like that is too ghastly to contemplate.

All of these issues clouded the way people responded to the acquittal, and because they despise all of the above-mentioned features, they wanted Zuma to be found guilty.

It matters not to them that Zuma is likeable to the African National Congress (ANC) rank and file; or that Zuma was sincere when he said sorry about the whole sordid saga; it matters not that most men think about women the way Zuma does. They wanted to see him crucified because he represents to them the backward, primitive, rapacious black man that we cannot afford to have as president. And it is this racist perception that troubles me. There are sound reasons why I do not want Zuma to be president and those have been overlooked during this horrible saga.

When a contender like Zuma has populist appeal, it is important for his supporters to see the rule of law being applied fairly and squarely. When the lawmakers invoke the law selectively for reasons other than justice, they create opportunities for lawlessness.

Zuma's supporters are the creation of this government and it should take responsibility for the populist anger out there. The *Sunday Times* headlines are as false as the rape charge. The difference between Zuma and Thabo Mbeki is this: Mbeki denied HIV/AIDS; Zuma defied it.

The ANC's succession battle is dividing the nation and it is precisely the political intrigue around this that creates the cleavages between the Zuma supporters and the Mbeki supporters and those of us who want neither.

Now is the time for the ANC to depart from the conspiratorial, Stalinist modus operandi of presidential appointments and open the election to a democratic process where we can all have a say in who our president should be. If this prevailed, 2009 would not be as threatening as it seems.

☛ More to ANC's grassroots revolt than Zuma case
Business Day July 7 2005

NO SOONER had Marthinus van Schalkwyk sung a paean to the African National Congress' (ANC) tradition of internal democracy and its warm embrace than all hell broke loose at the ANC's national general council meeting in Pretoria.

What we witnessed was an unprecedented grassroots revolt against the party's unsuspecting leadership. This was the culmination of a host of internal grievances that reached boiling point, scalding all in sight. The 'rebels' considered the council the ideal place to let the smug and self-important leadership know what was troubling its members.

Denied such opportunities in Parliament and to the national executive committee, the foot soldiers used their critical mass to trounce President Thabo Mbeki and to let him know where to get off. To someone who is mostly surrounded by obsequious sycophants, Mbeki seemed disturbed by this unseemly spectacle.

Mbeki's plot to oust Jacob Zuma, considered fair by some, foul by others, backfired horribly. Using selective justice to expose Zuma via the corruption charges against Schabir Shaik resulted in unintended consequences that nearly split the ANC apart. Had this same justice been applied equally to those implicated in the Travelgate and Oilgate scandals, and many others before, the pro-Zuma faction would hardly have a case. Had the National Prosecuting Authority investigated others in the party with equal alacrity, this lack of urgency would not be as suspect as it is.

Moreover, Mbeki's attempts to centralise control through cooption, nepotism, cronyism, and black economic empowerment have unleashed a resistance to black minority elitism reminiscent of our opposition to white minority domination, especially when government fails to deliver services to the poor. The silence on HIV/AIDS and Zimbabwe worsens the situation. And the conspiratorial, cliquey, secretive and power-hungry style of leadership is what the rank and file will no longer tolerate.

Thus, this gentle uprising is about something more than support for Zuma – something hardly mentioned by analysts. It is a growing anger against an 'exile modus operandi' that has forgotten how the negotiated settlement happened; that has forgotten how the comrades inside SA sacrificed all to oppose the apartheid state; how they united by suspending their own ambitions and racial differences to overthrow the National Party. Some went to jail, some sacrificed their education, some lost their families, some were detained without trial, some were tortured, and gave up everything for the greater good, whereas the 'exilers' seem to reward themselves for their roles as though only their contributions matter.

This form of governance is alien to a home-grown activism borne out of focused resistance, diversity and debate as exemplified by the struggles before Sharpeville, and the grassroots movements of the 1970s and 1980s culminating in the United Democratic Front in 1983.

To add insult to injury, Mbeki's cooption of apartheid spy *Kortbroek*, to reward him for giving Western Cape to the ANC on a platter, further infuriates the comrades. Through consensus politics, Mbeki has acquired strange bedfellows while overlooking competent people who contributed much to the development of SA.

In all of this political upheaval, the ANC's allies should not be let off the hook. Supporting Zuma simply to spite Mbeki is cheap politics par excellence. The left ignores the rule of law at its peril by undermining Judge Hilary Squires' judgment. Disdain for the law will come back to haunt it should it have ambitions to govern SA, because the electorate will not forget. Labour union Cosatu and the South African Communist Party need to reinvent themselves and engage with global politics and the new world order instead of eschewing it.

A mass base cannot be sustained on strikes and demonstrations alone. It will run out of steam unless the left captures a new credible vision with clear strategies for empowering the poor, the unemployed, and the workers. It cannot just ignore the current labour regime and fight government in its quest to create jobs; it cannot pursue a Proudly South African campaign that smashes competition and increases costs.

Behaving like the labour aristocracy that it is, when unemployment and poverty levels are unusually high, will come back to bite it in the shins. It has to grapple with the labour regime, the fluctuating currency, competition, international trade and markets if it wants to play a meaningful role in the political economy of SA.

The ANC's allies have two choices: they can keep abreast of international developments to better comprehend how to deal with mass unemployment and poverty; or they can rely on the toyi-toyi for a better future. But that will not get them very far.

In this battle there are no winners. The alliance needs all its partners to make democracy work – but then they all need a new vision.

☞ Criticise the president and cross his sycophants
Business Day February 1 2005

IN HER BOOK, *A Life of One's Own*, Hilda Bernstein, a disillusioned communist, writes of Stalin that 'his strength lay in his rigid management of the party machine that controlled appointments to key posts; his approval was a sure avenue of advancement. Thus he gathered round himself a body of faithful henchmen whose political fortunes were linked with his and who owed him unquestioning personal allegiance.'

Stalin would 'permit no covert criticism, and no expression of dissent was allowed ... in the party press or journals. He became a remote and isolated figure, exalted above ordinary mortals.'

Every autocrat has his henchmen and -women. The National Party had hundreds. Many have disappeared. Others, like Pik Botha, have reinvented themselves, willing to act as spokesmen for any ruling party, as witnessed on a recent Dennis Davis programme, Judge for Yourself.

The African National Congress (ANC), too, has its flock of loyalists, prepared to defend the party and its leader, regardless. Agents provocateurs on a range of polemical concerns, playing the role of a lightning rod, come easily as the rewards for doing so are great. One such person is Thami Mazwai, a board member of that troublesome and conflict-ridden institution, the South African Broadcasting Corporation (SABC). Renowned for his many gaffes, especially his comment that objectivity is not a requirement for good journalism, he put his foot in it again in his attack on Allister Sparks in the *Cape Times* (December 23 2004).

This column was significant because it paved the way for President Thabo Mbeki's 'cold war' speech in Sudan; his subsequent reference to 'sweet birds' as the enemies of liberation; and the recent spate of presidential letters.

These veiled threats against the liberal opposition and those who dare to criticise set the tone for the new year and what we will be subjected to in the run-up to the next election.

I hold no brief for Sparks. I did not even like his column on the president, although I agreed with some of his sentiments. But for someone who sits on the SABC board, Mazwai's response is over the top. While supposedly promoting free speech, his interpretation of Sparks smacks of a Stalinist discourse that increasingly has come to characterise the president's online letters. Mazwai accuses Sparks of a number of things, most notably that in criticising the president's columns:

- 'He was disrespectful of President Mbeki and in fact insulted the person of the president.'
- 'He treated the president with irreverence.'
- 'He forgot his station. Only those who are equal to, or more than Mbeki's equal, may criticise him.'

In modern society, it is hoped, respect is earned. One is not entitled to respect simply by virtue of being old and in authority. Zimbabwean President Robert Mugabe is a prime example of an old man in authority who deserves a ticket to hell, least of all respect. Old age and one's class position are not necessary and sufficient conditions for respect. This sentiment is even more ludicrous, given that Sparks is probably older than Mbeki.

If old age is such a societal virtue, why are so many black pensioners subject to the worst forms of abuse on pension day, standing in queues for hours in scorching heat or freezing cold?

Mazwai's punch line – no one has the right to criticise Mbeki unless one is part of the lofty inner circle – is another bizarre assertion. As such, Archbishop Desmond Tutu qualifies.

But even if you are of the cleric's stature, he opines, then you had better know what you are talking about, because not even the elevated (Tutu) can compete intellectually with the chosen (Mbeki). 'Only the president of the ANC, if not one of the top five in the ANC, is able to respond to what they say and this carries weight in loftier circles.'

Sparks must be 'bitter and disrespectful', for how else are we to interpret his hate speech against the president, whose position should command reverence and respect? Did Sparks not understand that as a mere mortal he had no right to comment on the president's holy writ? But we all know, says Mazwai, his criticism of Mbeki is actually a direct attack on the person of the president, and not really his columns. Actually, it is part of a bigger plot – an attempt by white and other liberals (meaning black), to coerce government into turning this country into a liberal democracy, as though it isn't one already.

What else do we expect from a wolf, like Sparks, in sheep's clothing – intent on destroying SA with his liberal agenda?

When the ANC is in trouble – as it is with large-scale unemployment, poverty, HIV/AIDS and lack of investment – it confronts, it invokes war talk. Someone has to be portrayed as the enemy of the people when the real culprit is in fact government's failure to deliver. In the absence of any real threat but itself, the ANC has to demonise 'the liberals' as the cause of the problem, in the way the National Party conjured up communists under every bed!

As a journalist, Mazwai should know the only way to judge the president is through his writings. It is the only peephole into his aloof soul. It will be the raw material political scientists and biographers will use to deconstruct the soul of a man who shamelessly exposed his demons on the internet for generations to come. Journalists, indeed everybody, have a right to analyse, interpret or criticise, and any denial of this right contradicts the essence of what an open society is all about.

Calls for respect for the president, as an institution of reverence, are often a euphemism for wanting a compliant, docile and obeisant public. To elevate the presidency to a deity and suggest that only those 'high' enough are entitled to speak is to misunderstand fundamentally what freedom of speech – the bedrock of democracy – is all about.

☞ Political parties with a personality disorder
Business Day September 15 2005

NELSON MANDELA was a truly modern leader, despite his age. He was an architect of probably one of the first truly open societies in Africa.

His leadership was inclusive and based firmly on the constitution with its emphasis on human rights, equality and the rule of law. It was conciliatory and completely un-Machiavellian.

Under his leadership, ministers were independent, autonomous and eccentric. He respected opposition and took risks. He made mistakes, but was willing to learn from his advisers and move on. More importantly, he knew when to leave and so his legend will live on.

The same cannot be said of our current leaders. As I am writing this column, I am watching *Parliament Live* on SABC3. A most disturbing observation is the African National Congress' (ANC's) Pavlovian reaction to President Thabo Mbeki. The only time the ruling party is silent is when Mbeki speaks. And no matter what he says, they applaud idiotically. What ANC MPs have yet to learn is that the personality cult will come back to haunt them. The Mbeki cult was caught off guard at the recent national general council meeting when the rank and file took control and strongly supported Jacob Zuma.

The same scenario is playing itself out in KwaZulu-Natal with Mangosuthu Buthelezi and Ziba Jiyane. The Inkatha Freedom Party leader refuses to hand over the mantle to younger leaders, and holds on to power, no matter how alienated his members feel. To ruin a party that could play an important opposition voice in KwaZulu-Natal is beyond self-serving. Buthelezi should retire gracefully and recognise that he has done national service way beyond the call of duty.

Another party going the way of all flesh is the Independent Democrats (ID) under Patricia de Lille. The ID needed a visionary leader with clear policy directives and a programme for action, but unfortunately De Lille started her party on the hop, having given no thought to policy. Conceived in the sin of 'crosstitution', it is, ironically, fighting enormous battles trying to prevent its disgruntled members from crossing the floor to other parties.

The ID has been embattled since day one. It has not even had a honeymoon. The personality cult around De Lille is in tatters. It was predictable to those of us who knew her that once De Lille started her own party her persona would be exposed for what it is. It was easy to be a shining star in an insignificant party and, lest we forget, as chief whip De Lille was central to Pan Africanist Congress ideology, many of its policies out of kilter with modern society.

Starting off with a whopping budget of R144 548 from Parliament for having won two of the 840 seats nationwide, the ID had no reason to fail. But by May 26 2003, the ID leadership in Gauteng was hit by internal conflict. Three founding members were expelled without hearings. In June 2003, Gauteng member Cordelia Sibuyi allegedly defrauded prospective ID members of thousands of rand, falsely promising them jobs, it was reported in the *Mercury*. In June 2003, thirteen former ID employees began a case with the Commission for Conciliation, Mediation and Arbitration, on the grounds that they had not been paid.

The launch of the Gauteng branch was an embarrassing fiasco, and this became a refrain for many more meetings. A third of delegates walked out, as accusations of autocratic leadership and counter-accusations became the order of the day.

In Eastern Cape, ID justice portfolio head Mbuyiselo Jozana was asked to step down pending an investigation into allegations of fraud and embezzlement. He was later arrested on two counts of fraud involving R77 000, according to a newspaper report.

Soon thereafter, the compilation of the ID's list of national candidates exploded in controversy as claims of nepotism were hurled against De Lille for placing her sister 23rd (and ninth on the provincial list); the sister being accused by other ID members of having no prior political involvement. When one thought the situation could not get worse, up popped accusations that De Lille had taken money from gang leader Quinton Marinus. To put out that fire took another hearing against former Western Cape leader Lennit Max, her accuser. More inquiries and legal costs followed.

On Tuesday this week, The *Cape Argus* reported that an ID MPL from Northern Cape, John Gunda, had been sentenced to ten years in prison for rape. Since December last year, the ID has not been able to convene its Western Cape provincial congress and its disputes with Max and Themba Sono, and other leading members, are just more of the same and ample evidence that the ID should dissolve.

The cult of the personality has boomeranged on a party that has been mesmerised by a politician who made her name in reaction to ANC misrule rather than in response to a new political direction needed for the country.

Since the ID's ignominious start, it has deflected attention from its problems by carping at the official opposition and supporting the ANC on all major budget votes – 32 out of the 34.

The ID is rarely in Parliament when budget votes are passed, and at no stage were there more than two of the seven MPs in the National

Assembly. Under De Lille's leadership, the ID has become a lame-duck party and is everything but independent or democratic, hence its increasing flirtation with the ANC under the guise of consensus politics, whatever that might mean.

As a new kid on the block, and after just two years, it seems to have had a fair share of thugs and thieves as members, leaving those few honest souls who joined the party for noble reasons once again in the wilderness. It is an important lesson for those who chase after personalities rather than clear political policies and programmes.

☛ Use your vote to fight a one-party state
Mail & Guardian November 10 to 19 2000

GLENDA DANIELS captures very eloquently in 'Give us a good reason to vote' (*Mail & Guardian* October 27-November 2 2000) the sentiments of people on the left about voting for the African National Congress (ANC) in the next election.

She mentions her lack of confidence in her party; that to abstain from voting is to neglect one's civic duty; that she is disillusioned like everybody, but that the political landscape leaves her no alternative. Furthermore, she says that she disagrees 'on fundamental issues of principle with the ANC over far too many of the party's stances' on AIDS, Zimbabwe, and the obsession with race and racism to deflect attention from the real issues.

She accuses the president of using his views on race to deflect issues of major concern by attacking the opposition at the Congress of South African Trade Unions conference, instead of addressing their concerns. She then talks about a national depression engulfing the nation and concludes that:
- She cannot vote Democratic Party/Democratic Alliance as they protect white privilege;
- There is no viable political alternative;
- There is a desperate need for a party that will accommodate black and white, rich and poor, men and women, feminists, environmentalists, gay activists, AIDS activists, anti-gun lobbyists.

Until such time, she cannot vote and she hopes against all hope that the ANC will get back to its principles.

Given all the issues I mentioned earlier, I wish to suggest that Daniels' view, and it is the view of many on the left, is deeply flawed and highly problematic for the development of democracy in South Africa. It is based on a sentimentalism and nostalgia for the sense of common purpose that characterised the liberation movement.

Our common purpose was to overthrow apartheid, and nothing more, even though we in the liberation movement assumed common interests across class, race, ethnicity, gender and so on.

The post-apartheid era has demonstrated very vividly that even people on the left (former comrades) had very little in common with each other, exemplified by fights that soon broke out among comrades in the Independent Broadcasting Authority, the Human Rights Commission, the SABC, the Land Bank and the ANC.

Many of my friends admit that they have lost political perspective because of their loyalty to the ANC. Loyalty to the party has taken precedence over loyalty to justice.

As a liberation movement, the ANC had the moral high ground. As the majority party in government it no longer commands that moral high ground and can be found wanting on many levels, because it has reneged on many of its own very noble policies.

The challenge is to grow and consolidate democracy in South Africa by looking very closely at other post-independent countries in Africa, Latin America and Eastern Europe. And this requires respect from both government and civil society for the development of a democratic culture that, at times, requires precedence over party loyalties.

Unfortunately the donor community withdrew a lot of their funding from NGOs after 1994, preferring to pump money into government thereby weakening civil society quite dramatically. There is an acknowledgement that this was the wrong decision, and attempts are being made to redress the situation.

The culture of political correctness has also contributed very seriously to the silence of civic organisations who did not want to be seen criticising a democratic government and a black one at that. In addition to this silence these organisations failed to reposition themselves strategically vis-à-vis the new state.

A vibrant multiparty democracy needs a multiplicity of voices and Tim Modise's programme, *The Tim Modise Show*, is an example of how one grows tolerance and respect for a diversity of views. Patricia de Lille has played a crucial role in holding the government accountable on the arms deal, children in detention, AIDS and so on.

The proliferation of one-party states in Africa demonstrates the importance of encouraging multi-party views, however unpalatable some of them are. Respect for the concept of loyal opposition is a very alien concept in post-independent countries in general and in the ANC in particular!

The AIDS debacle and the conference on racism in the media are indications that internal democracy is not alive and well in the ANC. Opposition parties, too, can be loyal to democracy, even should they differ on matters of policy. To dismiss them by constantly racialising them is to fail to assess them on merit.

Developing opposition requires that we look past race and look at how opposition as an institution needs to be cultivated and developed. It is customary for the left, after independence, to dismiss opposition and wait for the fateful day until a social democratic/socialist movement is formed to oppose the new government in power. And what happens when nobody is looking is that people vote again and again for the ANC, for sentimental reasons, entrenching their majority and so eroding the possibility of a real opposition developing.

The all-inclusive opposition that Daniels is looking for only happens in twenty years' time, as in Zimbabwe, when it is far too late.

There is a growing alliance between the trade union movement, the South African Communist Party and the South African NGO Coalition. No real democratic centre is developing that will keep the country on track in terms of its accountability to the citizens. Hence the proliferation of litigation on issues of socioeconomic rights.

The public will increasingly use the Constitutional Court to challenge the non-delivery of services. The Grootboom community housing case, the AIDS lobby, pensions by the Black Sash, are examples of how people are going to use other institutions to hold the government accountable as they increasingly lose faith in the government to prioritise their concerns.

Social and political scientists have studied this for years and, true to form, this is what happens in most post-independent countries, to the detriment of the development of truly democratic states.

The role of Parliament is steadily being marginalised as decision making shifts more and more to the executive. Question time has been restricted and increasingly Parliament has become a rubber stamp for the government, as exemplified by their support for the presidential view on AIDS, the serving of subpoenas on the media editors, the Zimbabwe issue, Minister of Justice and Constitutional Development Penuell Maduna's utterances and so on.

MPs are not engaging with issues as they should. They seem to be more in recess than in office, except for a few. The key question is how parliamentary oversight should interact with executive authority. To quote a Centre for Development and Enterprise report: 'This unfortunate disjuncture between Members of Parliament and voters weakens MPs within their parties and in Parliament as a whole. It adds to a feeling of isolation between "leaders and the led" and strengthens the hand of the party leadership.'

But just recently we had a brief glimpse of what Parliament could be like with the public disciplining of an MP. But he is a small fry, so it is easy to make a public example of him. What about Winnie Mandela, Maduna and many others who have not been called to order?

The public accounts standing committee's handling of the arms deal is another good example. It is rare that an ANC MP challenges the executive on their performance or lack of it.

Due to its dominance in Parliament, the ANC dominates the committee system, and even outvotes the opposition wherever it can. Yet many ANC MPs are reluctant to use their powers to hold the executive accountable. It is easy to expose soft targets, and not those within the ranks. The two-thirds majority is therefore detrimental to growing a vibrant democracy.

Furthermore, the independence of media should be guarded at all costs. The persecution of the media under the guise of the accusation of racism was as blatant an attempt to control it, as it was to undermine it. Even the HRC acted as a willing agent to carry out the government's agenda sideways. By racialising the media, government has been consistently guilty of trying to weaken it as an institution.

Then there are those journalists and others who have given their fair share towards contributing to compromising media independence: by becoming the mouthpiece of the government, by avoiding criticism of government and by suffering from the disease of political correctness because of white guilt. The recent Shaun Johnson fiasco over advertising given to the government is a case in point. Independent media institutions such as the IBA, the SABC, and even certain editors, have been complicit in eroding the freedom of independence of the press because of white guilt.

In conclusion, a two-thirds majority government is detrimental to democracy in South Africa, because then Parliament and government are very much one and the same thing.

We constantly hear that there is no money to address issues of national concern, but there is money for a 15% increase, above the inflation rate, to MPs and ministers; R78 million has been found to revamp the civic centre, the Cape Town Unicity. Money was found to put together an AIDS Council that was not needed. Money was found to mount a racism conference in Sandton.

We have been rocked by our fair share of corruption scandals and in many instances money has still not been recovered. I am convinced that there is enough money to do what is doable, but somehow we have failed to hold government accountable.

For all the money that has been wasted, Crossroads and Alexandra, by now, could have been redeveloped to give hope to the poor. The government's priority is clearly not the poor. The solution is to challenge and decrease ANC's majority in the local government election, as a majority government is not good for any democracy.

☞ Supine MPs blow chance for people's Parliament
Business Day November 25 2004

IN THE heady days of apartheid, our African National Congress Woodstock branch was quite active. It was a motley crowd of ANC hacks, old unity movement types, Trotskyites, and so on. The one thing we all had in common, was our abhorrence of apartheid.

On one occasion, we were asked to elect a delegate to represent our branch at an impending ANC national conference. A very loyal activist was elected. At a subsequent meeting some who considered him too much of a renegade ('workerist', 'Trot' – epithets hurled at those who dared to question the conventional wisdom of the party) objected to his election and proposed reversing the vote. The hacks invoked, against all logic, an array of Stalinist ploys to overturn the decision. After two hours of fierce debate, I left the meeting in protest.

A creeping sense of déjà vu came over me as I witnessed the recent fiasco in the National Council of Provinces (NCOP). After the controversial encounter between President Thabo Mbeki and Democratic Alliance (DA) MP Ryan Coetzee, the DA's Juanita Terblanche proposed a motion condemning Mbeki's reluctance to address the crime of rape against women and children; it was adopted unanimously by the dozy MPs. Subsequent attempts to reverse the decision once again reduced Parliament to the circus it has become. Days later, when they realised what they had done, and under great pressure allegedly from the executive, the NCOP reversed this decision.

This incident is one of many that herald the decline of an institution that had the hope of being a real people's Parliament.

Before 1994, it was a much-shunned institution, and it was fascinating to see transformation at the coal face, with portfolio committees getting to grips with legislative and policy reforms peculiar to their ministries.

The debates around abortion, sexual violence, children's rights and justice, and so on, generated real exchanges between civil society and government. The new Parliament inspired hope and represented a living testimony of conversations between a diverse public and the legislature, symbolised by Frene Ginwala's stylish saris to Baleka Mbete's chic African dress. This window of opportunity, alas, was short lived.

The rot set in with the exposé of the arms deal by the standing committee on public accounts, the conviction of Tony Yengeni after protracted denials that he received kickbacks, and the subsequent resignation of Andrew Feinstein and Gavin Woods. Truly honourable, these MPs decided they would sooner commit political suicide than betray the public and the principles of Parliament.

Scarcely having recovered from the Maduna versus Kluever affair, the De Lille versus Ginwala affair and the many ethics committee transgressions, Parliament remained bugged by controversy.

These transgressions continue today, and the never-ending arms deal and now the alleged travel voucher cover-up, are part of a litany of sagas that demonstrate a rapid descent into an irreversible morass, akin to Zimbabwe's parliament when it began its decline.

Statutory bodies like the public protector, the National Prosecuting Authority, the Scorpions, and the auditor general have done very little to keep Parliament on the straight and narrow. Adept at exposing Mark Thatcher in a case infinitely more complex than Travelgate, the Scorpions have been unable to apply their robust investigative skills to prosecute corrupt MPs accused of defrauding the taxpayer of millions.

The Scorpions and PricewaterhouseCoopers, have failed to disclose to the public what is really going on. Why do those implicated investigate themselves? Why has an independent commission of inquiry not been appointed to investigate the scandal publicly? Why has the Bathong Travel Agency not been liquidated? Why are the courts failing to bring implicated MPs to book?

That MPs are made to pay back what they have stolen is not good enough. They should be fired for living the high life with taxpayer's money and besmirching a body that should be the embodiment of the rule of law.

Under Mbeki's leadership, Parliament has become a lame duck and a rubber stamp for the executive, to whom it has become beholden on most matters. Reduction of question time and the president's occasional visits have hurt the quality of debate.

Ruling-party dominance in all parliamentary committees makes oversight a very difficult task. Transparency and accountability are no longer sacred values striven for, and independence has become a rare gift among ANC politicians.

Not once has any ANC MP posed a critical question to a cabinet minister, not even on matters of conscience such as HIV/AIDS, abortion or the death penalty, as noted by Tim Hughes, Director of South African Institute of International Affairs.

The custom of posing sweetheart questions to the executive perpetuates a tradition within the ANC, as one observer crassly put it – of farting each other warm.

It has taken its toll on those MPs who work hard and who take their jobs seriously. They no longer can afford to be considered along with the corrupt, the laughing stock of the nation, and leave in despair as Raenette

Taljaard and Andrew Feinstein and others have done. Parliament should be attracting rather than repelling career politicians.

☛ ANC compounds porcine heritage of ally NNP
Business Day July 8 2004

MORALLY degenerate is an apt description for how an apartheid-era practice of 'baantjies vir boeties' and the gravy-train ethos of the 'new, ten years of democracy SA' have been seamlessly melded by the African National Congress (ANC)-New National Party (NNP) partnership in the Western Cape.

The last two issues of *Noseweek*, and local newspapers such as the *Cape Times*, have documented the extraordinarily cynical way in which leading members of the ANC, a party which claims to champion the poor, have targeted the poor in their financial depredations.

And, clinging grimly to the ANC's nipple of patronage, the NNP, true to its disreputable porcine heritage, has been happy to join them at the trough.

The June 2004 issue of *Noseweek*, in an article headlined 'ANC Fat-cats in Feeding Frenzy', provided a lengthy exposé of how the poor in Hout Bay were conned out of their fishing quotas by unscrupulous party activists, among them some prominent names.

Details are also provided of how fraudulently-altered documents have given them development rights in Hout Bay that will increase their already obscenely inflated fortunes.

Implicated in all of this, alleges *Noseweek*, is our Public Works Minister Stella Sigcau. It is a matter of historic record that Sigcau was the recipient of a gambling casino bribe in the homeland days, but such trivialities 'like misleading Parliament' seem to enhance rather than detract from one's CV these days.

And, if the evidence provided in the current issue of *Noseweek* is correct, misleading Parliament is precisely what she did when questioned by the Democratic Alliance (DA) on *Noseweek*'s Hout Bay exposé.

As the sordid musical chairs of Western Cape premiers played itself out, we were assured by the ANC that things would change for the better under Ebrahim Rasool. Now the new premier is alleged by *Noseweek* to have deprived the provincial fiscus of R40 million to provide a tax break for ANC and homeland-era cronies in the gambling business – a business that targets the poor.

Last year Marthinus van Schalkwyk is alleged to have lied to the provincial legislature about the Roodefontein Golf Estate development in Plettenberg Bay, a telling portent of the currently snowballing series of local ANC-NNP land deal scandals.

(Would that the *Cape Times* pursue and demand with equal vigour an inquiry as they did with Harksen and the DA!)

I refer firstly to the prime piece of sea front, Big Bay real estate at Bloubergstrand, gifted by the ANC-NNP alliance that now rules the cash-strapped Cape Town municipality – usually from behind closed doors and without the benefit of minutes – to Tokyo Sexwale. Sexwale offered R36 million less than the highest tender but won (against the recommendations of the committee) as a 'previously disadvantaged' entity with a stronger 'black empowerment' component to his bid.

It is difficult to see Sexwale as 'disempowered'. This deal, however, gives us an understanding of why, in less than a decade, he has vaulted, with unprecedented speed and ease, from what he now probably regards as a politician's pathetic tithe, to a fortune estimated to exceed R1.5 billion.

And, in a similar deal in the ANC-NNP-controlled Stellenbosch municipality, their business cronies have paid just R35 million for the 247ha Paradyskloof site – valued by the Wildlife and Environment Society of SA at more than R100 million.

Furthermore, as South African Rugby Football Union president Brian van Rooyen has indicated, cash-strapped sports unions have been coerced into parting with probably millions to create a trust fund for the widow of Steve Tshwete – who was not even sports minister when he died.

In a macabre world first, the ANC has created a gravy train beyond the grave! Questions in Parliament, please!

As the stench of ANC-NNP corruption becomes ever more pervasive, I, like many others, am fast losing faith in the noble ideals of the Freedom Charter, and the ANC's commitment to the struggle for justice and equality.

An unhealthy symbiotic relationship, in an increasingly sinister and evil way, symbolises the ANC-NNP alliance.

It also contributes a saddening epitaph to the gravestone of our still-born ambitions to be respected as a country that falls outside the mainstream of Africa's endemic corruption.

☛ SA's big-mouth communists offer no real solutions
Business Day July 26 2007

LAST WEEK I went to work wearing red and black. The security guard at reception asked me why I was dressed like a member of the South African Communist Party (SACP).

I jokingly replied that I was a member, provoking the following response: 'Communism is outdated. It did not work anywhere in the world so why does the SACP want to pretend it is an alternative for the poor in SA? This is the ideology Mugabe preached and look where his people are running to for survival – to SA. Only when you generate growth can you create jobs.'

I was astounded at the guard's emphatic denunciation of an ideology he felt was being forced on the poor. And this is the nub of the matter. While the SACP invokes a language that is sympathetic to poverty, unemployment and job creation, communism is not a solution for the world's poor, nor has it been anywhere it has been practised.

It is true that the SACP has, since its inception in SA, played a significant role in opposing colonialism, fighting for the poor and undermining apartheid. South African communists have also been some of SA's most principled and committed fighters of exploitation, oppression and racial domination, but many did so within an ideological framework they knew was highly questionable, at least since the 1970s.

The brinkmanship between the African National Congress (ANC) and SACP leadership before the recent SACP conference – the SACP's threats of going it alone; the discourse of the national democratic revolution, of colonialism of a special type, of the developmental state; and threats to expel members who do not toe the line – was all very intriguing, but the SACP did not come close to presenting a viable alternative economic policy to the ANC's macroeconomic policy.

Discussing the Democratic Alliance's (DA's) economic policy recently, Prof Anthony Butler presented the SACP's alternative as a viable counterweight to the DA's and the ANC's macroeconomic policy, based on communism's sympathies for the poor, the working class and those living with HIV/AIDS. He argued that the SACP was 'not really ruinously leftist' while ignoring the fundamental question – which economic model is the SACP really advancing?

Surfing the internet to investigate whether the SACP is indeed 'not really ruinously leftist', as Butler claimed, I found the SACP newsletter (volume 6, number 12, July 4 2007). I was astounded to find the language of my sociology classes of 30 years ago still ideologically intact, and used with great gusto by respected sociologist and SACP general secretary Blade Nzimande: '(We will) embark on concrete joint programmes of action to deepen and consolidate our national democratic revolution. Congress will focus on building the capacity of the SACP to lead the overall offensive of building working-class hegemony in society in order to deepen and consolidate a socialist-oriented national democratic revolution as the only road to socialism. Our congress will ... place colonialism of a special type (CST) at the centre of our debates.'

All this language is anathema to postmodern societies in which constitutional democracy and some form of capitalism are the only viable ways to lift the poor out of their misery. This anachronistic communist discourse obfuscates how the SACP hopes to deepen the national democratic revolution, or a developmental state, or build the hegemony of the working class, when the world has moved on.

Year in and year out, the SACP continues in this vein and, with a declining membership, clings to its alliance partners for its survival. Refusing to become an autonomous political party, it knows instinctively that it may not survive on its own with an ideology that has been discredited the world over.

The African poor and working classes look at China's embrace of capitalism, the transformation of former east European socialist countries and the economic rise of southeast Asia and many Latin American countries, and they just know that communism is no solution. When the poor in SA see the poor from Zimbabwe, Angola, Ethiopia, Eritrea, the Democratic Republic of Congo and Somalia flooding over our borders, they increasingly question the legacies left by ideologues such as Robert Mugabe, Augustino Neto, Meles Zenawi, Fidel Castro, Erich Honecker, Joseph Stalin, Augusto Pinochet and Mao Zedong.

In the 1990s, financier George Soros took the board of the Open

Society, of which I was a member, to some countries in eastern Europe 'to see for ourselves'. The last bit of socialist conscience I had dissipated after walking the streets of Poland, Hungary, Yugoslavia and Ukraine and seeing empty shops and listening to stories of rampant corruption, media suppression, inferior health-care systems and ineffectual industries, all made worse by the growing class and gender inequality. This was an eye-opener and broke down all the Marxist claptrap I had imbibed as a young social anthropology and sociology student.

The astounding thing is that while middle-class socialist politicians live bourgeois lives, travel the world, enjoy the benefits of globalisation, the internet and global information technology, they speak a language out of synch with the modern democratic society that allows them their lifestyles.

Why can we not speak of a social democratic form of capitalism geared towards socialist ideals as a viable alternative to address poverty and unemployment? Why can the excessive revenue generated by the government not be used to create employment and fulfil some of the socialist goals that most of us share?

No national democratic revolution or the overthrow of 'colonialism of a special type' will provide answers to these problems. They will, I know for sure, make them worse. What political leaders need tons of is common sense.

☛ Power at any cost has backfired on ANC
The Sunday Independent November 27 2005

'THE IMPORTANT Stalinist culture of both Mbeki and Zuma is fundamentally at odds with democratic principles.'

I Didn't Do It For You: How the World used and Abused a Small African Nation, by Michela Wrong, is a sobering account of the conflict between Ethiopia and Eritrea and how, despite their genetic closeness, they are prepared to blow each other out of existence in their quest for sovereignty. It is the old story of yet another African bloc struggling with democracy.

Notwithstanding their complex histories, their failure to democratise has more to do with the vanities and egos of two power-obsessed leaders than with leaving a democratic legacy for future generations. The primitive accumulation of power in the form of military might and, in their case, playing off one superpower against another, has ironically left them weak in their quest for self-determination. And this lies at the heart of the conflict in the continent.

The Mbeki-Zuma soap opera is another manifestation of the same. When Mondli Makhanya (*Sunday Times* November 6 2005) says all analysts had missed 'the level of simmering discontent', his 'all' of course excludes those from other political camps who view this feud through a different lens and who provide more compelling arguments than the hackneyed explanations offered by the leftist orthodoxy.

While he credits the media for identifying the problem as a 'brutal battle for control of the ANC', he claims to have the only insight, namely that this is 'a rebellion against the head of state by the party that runs the state'.

His conclusion – that the solution to the current debacle is for Mbeki to take the ANC and the state with him and 'to humble himself and ask what he has contributed to the climate of dissent' – is to expect an abusive parent to continue to look after the child because there is no better.

Many of us predicted that Mbeki's rule could only lead to the kind of chaos we are witnessing today, because the belief that the solution to the current debacle is to be found within the ANC alone is deeply flawed; the ANC is a master at sowing the seeds of its own destruction. Its modus operandi is fundamentally anti-democratic, moulded in the belief that it alone should control all the levers of power. This obsession is finally blowing up in its face. The National Prosecuting Authority, the Scorpions, the public protector, the intelligence services and even the police have all become servants of the ruling party, and now that the party is divided, they too are divided.

Anthony Butler, a political science professor, concurs with Makhanya and came up with an even more bizarre analysis (*Business Day* November 9 2005). Recognising all the faults of the ruling party, he nevertheless concludes that: 'In these circumstances, the best scenario may well be fifteen or twenty years of ANC dominance – creating a period of stability in which liberal institutions can entrench their authority.

'The government will face a real but unrealistic threat of defeat by a credible opposition. Meanwhile, citizens will use other mechanisms of accountability to limit the abuse of executive power. When the ANC eventually begins to lose its electoral and organisational power, liberal institutions will then be robust enough to cope with the immense internal strains generated by a more fluid political system.'

This is like arguing that US President George Bush should remain in power because only he can quell the unrest and political chaos in Iraq.

Butler's analysis also fails to recognise that it takes about fifteen to twenty years to undo democracy in Africa. When political chaos reigns, state and civil society institutions do not become stronger. Their powers are eroded by partisan politics, especially where the majority party becomes the party of unfettered power and patronage.

Under such circumstances, Parliament readily submits to the executive and lacks the balls to hold government accountable, as we have seen here with the erosion of Scopa (the standing committee on parliamentary accounts), the Scorpions and others. As in Zimbabwe and other African countries, state institutions are easily destroyed by an overweening executive and also hard to resurrect once they are down. The Mbeki-Zuma feud is a clash between the politics of exile and the politics of democracy. Both leaders are products of the machinations of exile and the Stalinist culture they imported into the Union Buildings once Mbeki assumed office, obliterating the democratic ethos Nelson Mandela left behind. What we are witnessing on the streets and within the ANC structures is a conflict between the masses nurtured on a diet of consultation, dialogue and debate, encouraged by the United Democratic Front, and the closed society of ideological battles, conspiracies, intelligence, spies and police infiltration so typical of liberation movements in exile. When the ruling party uses state resources to control and maintain power, it is sure recipe for disaster.

The paranoia of the ANC in exile was understandable, but to perpetuate that modus operandi under a completely different dispensation is to look for trouble. All of us who are familiar with that culture hoped it would never take root here; but it has predictably taken a course all of us feared would happen. The politics of exile is threatening to destroy this country because we, who know better, are allowing it to happen.

Some of us will continue to subscribe to lame-duck analyses like those of Adam Habib, Makhanya, Butler and others who assume the answer lies within the ANC, and that the battle for the hearts and soul of the masses has to do with economics alone. This kind of reductionism becomes a self-fulfilling prophecy, and the more those analysts think our salvation lies within the very party that is destroying us, the more they need a drastic course in the fundamentals of democracy.

The tenure of Tony Blair, the British prime minister, is under threat because his own party is holding him accountable. Equally, Bush's presidency is vulnerable because his own constituency is raising questions about the secrets and lies behind the war that caused international repercussions. While we sanctimoniously batter western democracies and their leaders for their lack of judgement and undemocratic behaviour, they at least have democratic mechanisms and electorates that will vote them out of office at the next election.

Here we have no such hope. Parliament is dead, the media is compromised, MPs are self-serving and the Chapter 9 institutions (established to support constitutional democracy) are a joke.

To suggest, as Makhanya does, that 'unless the power and legitimacy of [Mbeki's] office is restored in the minds of party activists, the real casualties will be constitutionalism, respect for the rule of law, clean governance and sound policy-making' is a myopic perspective.

We are in crisis precisely because of the ANC. The institutions of Parliament that should ensure accountability and entrench democracy are all compromised and there is not one that lives up to constitutional scrutiny.

The constitution is a direct challenge to a Stalinist modus operandi. A party that believes its future is wrapped up with the future of the country, regardless, will try to retain power, even if it ruins the country in the process. Unless analysts honestly engage with the language of democracy, party political competition, the role of opposition, the rule of law and democratic governance, no market or socialist economy will provide the goods and services a poor nation like South Africa needs. Democracies work so much better in open, transparent and uncorrupt societies where human rights and the rule of law are pre-eminent.

For as long as we think our salvation lies within a party that is fundamentally corrupt and undemocratic, I will find solace in the bumper sticker that says: 'God is dead, Marx is dead and I'm not feeling too well myself!'

Western Cape (Stormy Cape)

☛ **On the Cape Flats, Madam sings its own De la Rey**
Business Day February 22 2007

A LOT of polemical dust has been kicked up about Bok van Blerk's controversial song, 'De la Rey'. Some argue that the song is about Afrikaners harking back to a privileged past; others see it as a call to Afrikaners to rise up against a loss of power.

To Max du Preez: 'the De la Rey phenomenon is simply a manifestation of frustration and insecurity, a feeling of being marginalised in the ANC-dominated new SA. It is more about perception than reality. They really feel like "second class" citizens.'

Du Preez argues further that the De la Rey phenomenon is a reaction to the over-assertiveness of black South Africans, who see themselves as the rightful owners of this country, against the white 'settlers', 'intruders' who continue to haunt them with their economic, educational and professional prowess. More than that, the song is about the *bittereinders*, who felt betrayed by their Afrikaner comrades, the *hensoppers*, who joined the British forces under Lord Kitchener, whose sole purpose was to induce Afrikaners 'to hate each other more than they hate the British' and thus achieve the main objective of the British.

This song indirectly is a condemnation of the likes of FW de Klerk, Pik Botha and Marthinus van Schalkwyk, considered sellouts and despised for 'cosying' up to the ruling elite instead of promoting the rights of an Afrikaner minority feeling increasingly socially excluded by black domination.

Right here on the Cape Flats, a similar phenomenon is emerging few people are aware of. Madam, the Movement Against Discrimination of

Indigenous African Minorities (Madam), came into being in 2004, started by four correctional services officers who were victimised and suspended for going public about alleged discrimination against coloured people in the correctional services department. The marginalisation of senior correctional officials Johnny Jansen, Achmat Jacobs, and Benjamin Masala, among others, who allegedly were demoted in favour of African appointees, was the driving force behind this movement of whistle-blowers, who refused to be silenced by an African majority who they felt clobbered them into submission. They viewed their ostracism as an attempt to marginalise minorities, who because of their efficiency were considered a direct threat to African dominance in the prison service, which has reached serious levels of decline and has become a den of iniquity since 1994.

Grouping together predominantly to fight for the restoration of the 'Khoisan Nation' in SA, Madam's president, Johnny Jansen, says his mission is to 'restore the identity of coloured people in SA'.

'"Coloured" was never a born identity, it was imposed on us by apartheid. My political struggle against apartheid was the hope that in the new SA I will become a true South African and that we'll get rid of the term coloured. But to my surprise, this new government still labels and sees us as coloured. I was involved in the liberation struggle, but now I am considered coloured again.'

Madam, claiming to have more than 5 000 members, meets regularly around their mission to compel the ANC 'to get rid of the lie that coloureds were brought to the Cape by Jan Van Riebeek'.

'We want to be respected and recognised as the descendants of the first indigenous people, the Khoisan. This heritage will make us true Africans and, by implication, equal benefactors of the resources of this country, which seem to be pillaged by Africans.'

So serious is Madam about its mission that it has linked up with Prof Rodolfo Stavenhagen, Special Rapporteur to the United Nations on Indigenous People, who after having met representatives of Parliament, government, indigenous groups and their leaders, recommended that the term coloured be excised from SA's lexicon.

What do the enthusiasts of the song have in common with Madam? They are all reacting to their own comrades, by whom they feel betrayed. The call to De la Rey *'om die Boere te kom lei'* is similar to Madam's appeal to members' history to rekindle pride in their origins. Feelings of betrayal are strongest when they are perceived to come from within the group in question. Hence, the struggle between the *bittereinders* and the *hensoppers* continues apace in another guise on the Cape Flats. Unless President Thabo Mbeki takes note of these political disaffections, he might have to deal more seriously with the 'state of the excluded nation' at the next opening of Parliament.

☞ Bring back the old Cape gang, regardless of cost
Business Day September 21 2006

PHANTSI democracy. *Phantsi! Phantsi* democracy, especially in Western Cape!

Phantsi transparency, efficiency, integrity and hard work! *Phantsi* service delivery, economic growth and job creation!

Phantsi mayor Helen Zille, *phantsi*! Bring back former queen-bee mayor Nomaindia Mfeketo and her hive of secret affairs; bring back the master of mismanagement, former city manager Wallace Mgoqi and his Ikhwezi team of affirmees. Bring back bodyguards, fancy cars, advisers, lawyers, directors, managers, consultants who can't do the job. Bring back the whole damned lot so that they can get on with the job of pilfering state resources.

Bring back fraudulent Jewellery City; bring back the Big Bay scandal; bring back the secret mayoral committee; dish out tenders to friends and family behind closed doors. What are friends for, after all? Bring back corruption; bring back incompetence; get rid of skilled technical expertise; down with organograms; down with human resource management; bring back deficits; bring back increased rates. Bring back retrenchments but increase the budget for salaries; decrease the budget for services. Get rid of the fire department; get rid of the hospitals; get rid of the metro police; get rid of everything and everyone that works.

Bring back comrades De Lille and Grindrod. Reward them for weakening opposition with ministries in the African National Congress (ANC) government. Squash the coalition, bring back 'transformation', bring back racial politics; destroy the infrastructure; use section 34 of the Municipal Structure Act and section 16 (11) of the Western Cape Determination of Types of Municipalities Act to get power at any cost; use any act that will cripple the coalition; bring back the executive mayoral system but use it only for the benefit of the ruling party.

Use MEC Richard Dyantyi; use premier Ebrahim Rasool, use minister Sydney Mufamadi, use all the useful idiots willing to do President Thabo Mbeki's dirty work for him! And 2010 shall be a miracle and we shall all live happily ever after.

It is embarrassing to witness senior ANC leaders accompany their convicted comrades to jail with comfortable regularity and not a hint of shame. Surely there must be some party members who cringed at the spectacle in front of Pollsmoor where Tony Yengeni shamelessly invoked the words of Jesus: 'Father, forgive them for they know not what they do.' What he should have said was: 'Father, forgive them for singling me out when 300 MPs implicated in the travel scandal should have been at my side today at this prison.'

The message conveyed to the public is one of contempt. With this kind of behaviour becoming the norm, the rule of law is under threat in a country where crime is now second nature.

The rule of law prevails:
- Where people understand the predominance of regular law over the arbitrariness of the state;
- Where all – including public officials – are equally subject to the law administered by the ordinary courts;
- Where the freedoms of citizens are respected by the law justly and fairly, regardless of class, race, gender, etc.

High-profile ANC support for Yengeni was a flagrant defiance of all these provisions and can be linked to the consistently partial way in which the public protector has exculpated members of the executive embroiled in allegations of corruption or some or other kinds of transgression.

The Public Protector's Report (No1/2006) shamelessly exonerates Deputy President Phumzile Mlambo-Ngcuka for her jaunt to the UAE in December, accompanied by her husband, her children, and others. Total costs for the return trip: aircraft operating costs, R347 847; fuel, R130 470; landing and handling fees, R50 000; accommodation and allowances of crew, R35 736; air ticket for private secretary who travelled in advance, R28 568; subsistence/travel allowance of private secretary, R2 262; catering on the South African Air Force aircraft, R10 000. In other words, the entire vacation cost the taxpayer R604 883.

Our protector justifies his decision on the following grounds:
- That the deputy president needs state protection at all times when working or on leave. Yet she travelled to London on a commercial flight a week before. The reason given: 'The South African National Defence Force was not able to field an aircraft in time to meet the planned schedule.'
- While members of the cabinet may not use their positions to enrich themselves, or improperly benefit any other person, or risk a conflict of interest, or solicit or accept a gift/benefit to buy influence or favour, this trip to the UAE and the benefits enjoyed by the deputy president and her entourage were within the prescribed codes of the Ethics Act and Ministerial Handbook.

But the deputy president seems to have violated all of these provisions, no matter what circuitous logic Lawrence Mushwana uses to justify her trip. Whereas the ethics code requires that all gifts be disclosed and declared, this trip, according to Mushwana, 'did not constitute a gift in terms of the executive ethics code and was not a personal gift but a gift to the office of the presidency'. But she went on holiday!

Speaking of being more equal than others, the public protector has singularly redefined the notion of a 'gift' as defined in the ethics code. This is an extraordinary provision and elevates the deputy far above her station, but it also implies that this country and her position are so unsafe that she needs such extraordinary protection. For God's sake, the deputy president is a public servant, not God.

☛ Moves to undermine Cape coalition bode ill for SA
Business Day April 20 2006

DURING THE RECENT municipal election campaign, President Thabo Mbeki warned elected officials that he would take action against those who denied services to citizens on the grounds of party affiliation.

But this promise was short lived. The election is hardly two months past and, shocked by the outcome – of more than 60% of the votes in Cape Town for the opposition collectively – the African National Congress (ANC) is doing everything to undermine the coalition and its elected mayor, Helen Zille.

Rumours abound that a senior ANC minister has visited one of the smaller parties, offering it all kinds of incentives to break up the coalition. Secret meetings are being held between ANC politicians and officials to strategise the downfall of the Democratic Alliance (DA) partnership.

On three occasions officials who should be neutral have countermanded the decisions of the multiparty government in council. The city asked for control of the VIP protection unit to be returned to the councillor support department from the city police. This was countermanded by city manager Wallace Mgoqi. The city asked for all tender meetings to be opened. This was countermanded by Mgoqi's representative, Ike Nxedlana, who said publicly that he would refuse to open the meeting to the public. The city asked for alternative sites to Greenpoint to be considered for the stadium for the Soccer World Cup. Municipal operations chief Rusj Lehutso said the decision had already been taken by Fifa, national and provincial government, and so there has been a refusal to act on this.

The unusually pugnacious Wallace Mgoqi has come to symbolise how fundamentally undemocratic the ANC is when it comes to real competition at the local level. His refusal to accept the advice of the city's legal counsel that he go on leave until the matter of his contract is resolved, proves this. The city's legal advice, from one senior counsel and a professor of administrative law, is that his contract is invalid.

Mgoqi has flatly refused to go on leave, arriving with burly bodyguards at council meetings to intimidate the new council. He continues to sign documents on behalf of the city and still enters contracts – all of which will be null and void if the city's legal advice turns out to have been right. This could cost the city millions. He persists as if the new administration does not exist.

Obsessively engaged in toppling a legitimately constituted administration, the ANC shows how insecure it is about Zille as mayor. Her track record as an efficient, uncorrupt and hardworking politician is a direct threat to its record of gross mismanagement under mayor Nomaindia Mfeketo who, with Mgoqi, virtually ran the city into the ground. More seriously, the message the ANC sends to public officials is: 'Play our game and you can reward yourselves as you wish.'

On these grounds alone, Mgoqi should be fired. He was not only openly aligned to the ANC as city manager, he was also, judging from the unprocedural awarding of tenders to cronies during his administration, deeply incompetent in his post. Among others: Big Bay 1, in which Jonga Entabeni Consortium received prime land for R36 million less than other offers; Big Bay 2, the sale of 65 residential erven to ANC cronies, one of whom included his wife as a beneficiary; the illegal changing of bylaws governing land sales; and the success of the Cell C tender despite Nashua being the recommended supplier.

In its short stint as the new local government, the coalition has already exposed a number of corrupt tender deals – such as the multimillion-rand Jewellery City project awarded to former South African Local Government Association (Salga) CEO Thabo Mokwena, who, despite being known for mismanaging Salga, continues to benefit from irregular deals at exorbitant rates (*Cape Argus* April 13 2006). Mgoqi also irregularly approved a 99-year lease on the foreshore for this project.

These are just the tip of the iceberg. Since 1999, the ANC has steadily eroded the institutional memory of the city by offering retrenchment packages to its skilled professionals so that today the city is saturated with incompetent staff who sabotage good governance.

The executive directors are in a swirl trying to make sense of how departments are functioning. The payroll reveals duplication of posts, lack of accountability, bizarre reporting structures and a complete disconnect between the top and bottom layers of posts. Signed contracts cannot be found and trying to make sense of what is going on will take the DA and its partners another term.

Having lost the election, the ANC continues to govern through incompetent officials, whose jobs are on the line and who now find it convenient to call it a 'racial purge'. The ANC has demonised the DA to such an extent that it cannot afford for it to succeed. This is what citizens should be worried about.

Should the ANC lose a national election, the consequences will be too ghastly to contemplate. The ANC believes that it is its revolutionary right to rule in perpetuity and will use Stalinist tactics to squash any political competitor out of existence. The recent publication by *The Economist* 'A Survey of South Africa' echoes these warning signals. It is time to take note.

☛ Stalinist cabal parodies ANC's promise in Cape
Business Day July 22 2004

SOMETHING is rotten in the city of Cape Town. Governance is a far cry from what the African National Congress (ANC) promised it would be under the new mayoral system.

The language of transformation used with nauseating frequency during election time is not reflected in the kind of governance under the new order. While key words such as democracy, transformation and transparency mark the current political discourse, in reality a Stalinist cabal rules the city.

Described by a former mayor as an 'impregnable fortress', the mayoral committee operates in total secrecy. Meetings are closed to the public, agendas and minutes are not published. Decisions are reported to the council months after they are taken. No debate or questions are permitted. Opposition parties have no seats in accordance with proportionality, and are in effect silenced.

The analogy with Parliament and the cabinet is often made to justify operating in secret. Yet this comparison is out of place. The committee hardly deals with security issues, unless drains, potholes, sewage, electricity and roadworks qualify as such!

Complaints about the flawed tendering process reveal that in this climate of secrecy the law of the jungle prevails. The city's forensic investigative unit is, at the request of the public protector, investigating two tenders for roadworks in Gugulethu and Tambo Village.

The Big Bay tender award has also been overturned by an appeal committee of the city.

The officials and legal adviser reporting to the tender and procurement committee on the roadworks tenders did a thorough job assessing all applications for compliance. All the tenders with bad references and track records, and lacking resources were duly eliminated. Those getting the highest adjudication points were recommended for awards.

For some reason, ANC councillors favouring the worst firms were able to convince the mayoral committee and council to overturn the recommendations.

The awarding of the Big Bay tender was more alarming. The city received six tenders for this property, but the mayoral committee awarded the tender to the fourth highest tender at R36 million less, without following due process.

The tender and procurement committee didn't even have a proper opportunity to consider all proposals before it, to make a fully informed recommendation. The committee also lacked a quorum when it referred the matter to the mayoral committee.

Partial decisions of this nature are of course always open to litigation. Not only does the city lose when tenders are awarded to the worst bidder, the prospect of the costly litigation negatively affects good governance.

Third-rate firms are hardly able to ameliorate the challenges facing the city of Cape Town. And these challenges are formidable, as shown in the report of the integrated development plan 2003-04. With unemployment at 21% generally, and 30% for blacks, generating economic growth that will lead to jobs will require the wisdom of Solomon in a municipality that is cash strapped. The growth of informal settlements, the decline in the provision of housing and the increase in TB rates, prove that the situation in the city is deteriorating.

The politics of secrecy do not create a climate conducive to public sector delivery. The executive mayoral system, as it operates now, is structurally incapable of lending itself to open, accountable, transparent governance.

As a citizen of the city of Cape Town, I object to the secrecy with which we are being governed, given that we pay the highest per capita rates at R666.55 a year. Capetonians should demand that our executive mayor operate like democratic mayors elsewhere in the world – where their electoral mandates comes from policies and the constituency to whom the mayor accounts and is beholden.

The mayor is silent and invisible, described by some as a 'Queen Bee in her malignant hive'. For someone who comes from an admirable history of struggle and detention, a victim of a repressive regime that operated in secret, I expect the mayor to live up to her commitment to democracy and openness.

The essence of democratic governance is building public trust. This is achieved when the mayor's office is open and accessible to the public and when decisions are communicated honestly. The way it operates now leaves much to be desired.

☛ No gentle use of power from this mayor
Business Day April 28 2005

IN THE debate unleashed by Prof Malegapuru Makgoba, vice-chancellor of the University of KwaZulu-Natal, in which he crassly compared white males to baboons, there were several voices of reason – among them those of Prof Mike Morris, a veteran activist and leftist sociologist, and Prof Rob Morrell, a seasoned intellectual at the University of KwaZulu-Natal.

Another was that of Prof Marcus Ramogale, deputy vice-chancellor of the University of Venda. Writing in the *Mail & Guardian* (April 15 to 21 2005), he said: 'As an African elite, we have been entrusted with power, which we must exercise in a non-threatening manner for the common good. To exercise power in a gentler style is not "subservience". It is an expression of unassuming self-confidence and comfort with one's convictions and humanness. The challenge thrust on us by the responsibilities that come with power is to use it differently from those who once oppressed us.'

While the 'Home for All' campaign is raging in Cape Town, its architects use race and racism, once again, as a mobilising tool to divert attention from the rampant poverty, unemployment and the lack of housing that bedevil Western Cape. The electorate will, once again, be subjected to the political machinations of its elected officials who treat citizens here as nothing but voting fodder.

More annoyingly, they find respectable organisations and individuals who will use surveys, opinion polls and their expertise to give credibility to charges of racism as though this is the issue, and not housing, unemployment and rampant poverty, which should receive priority.

Of concern to me is the mayoral committee, which operates in secret, dishing out tenders, procurement deals and parcels of land to friends and cronies on the basis of race and without following due process.

Someone who will not be using power in a gentler style in the coming months of an election year will be Cape Town mayor Nomaindia Mfeketo and her excessively-paid team of executive directors.

Recently, on the Tim Modise show, she said that transformation was moving more slowly in Cape Town than in other cities. How does she measure this? She conveniently ignores the fact that research as well as police and hospital statistics show that the most virulent race hatred manifesting itself in the Mother City is xenophobia. Local Xhosa-speaking people in informal settlements such as Du Noon have lashed out violently against black refugees fleeing the despotic regimes of Zimbabwean President Robert Mugabe and others.

Do elected officials ever try to find reasons why racism is rearing its ugly head, wherever it might occur? Could it be a reaction or backlash to their own racially inspired policies of exclusion and forms of governance?

The mayor continued that there were public places in Cape Town, particularly restaurants, where you simply did not see black people. This might be true for a number of historical and class reasons, but she ignores the fact that our constitution specifically guarantees freedom of association and that black people are not barred from frequenting restaurants, theatres or cinemas. The racially designed spatial planning of the city under apartheid will take years to undo.

The bigger worry, however, is that this black government has failed even to begin to address this problem. The N2 Gateway Housing project is an ad hoc solution to a problem that has inspired greater racial tension and it eschews all the features of a properly planned long-term solution to the housing crisis in the province.

Further, safe and affordable public transport that links townships to the city might ameliorate the problem.

Mfeketo's statement also ignores what our political history will confirm, and that is that no South African city was more of a thorn in the flesh to the likes of John Vorster and PW Botha than Cape Town. The city's buses, for example, were desegregated decades before those of other cities and a long line of mayors took the struggle to the National Party, including the likes of Frank van der Velde, now a prominent ANC member.

On April 12 2005, Mfeketo attended the opening of the home affairs national immigration branch in Cape Town. In the presence of President Thabo Mbeki, seeking to heighten racial tension, she claimed that immigration officials (read white) use racial profiling to subject people with 'darker skins' to random identity checks. 'I am also pulled to the side every time I come from some international trip.'

As she is clearly confusing the duties of customs officials with immigration officials, I should point out that luggage checks are done by customs officials and that she could only have been pulled aside by immigration officials if she was entering the country with a foreign passport.

This did not prevent sycophantic immigration officials from suggesting that special facilities be set up for the black elite, thereby, in an instant, recreating the exclusive race facilities of our apartheid past.

☞ Public servants can lead us by example
Business Day March 13 2003

THAT Marthinus van Schalkwyk and not Cheryl Carolus is Western Cape premier shows how far we have regressed. The dissonance between what Van Schalkwyk represents and what diverse Cape Town, once the epicentre of the United Democratic Front, is all about, troubles me.

At a party in honour of Oprah Winfrey at Kirstenbosch, Van Schalkwyk, unable to deal with the greatness the African National Congress thrust upon him, strutted about self-consciously, acting out the caricature he has become.

Every announcement or press statement he makes is accompanied by his photograph, lest we forget who the premier is. His megalomaniacal antics in retail stores and aeroplanes are now well recorded. Rumour has it his colleagues rise as he enters the room, and address him as no less than '*Meneer die Leier*'.

In the circumstances, it is very difficult to take the office of the premier seriously, and to separate the office from its present incumbent. 'The premier is a hard sell' is a recent confession made to me by a New National Party MP. The Roodefontein scandal is not helping, with Peter Marais and David Malatsi determined to finger him, claiming they have evidence to back their allegations.

I mention this because so many public officials, in our brief spell of democracy, have sullied their reputations and parties with random acts of self-interest. The result has been a growing lack of respect for politicians and disdain for the state has now become commonplace despite columnist Cyril Madlala's view that we should respect the office no matter who occupies it.

Live television, furthermore, has done much to add to the public's growing cynicism by exposing politicians for what they often are: cantankerous, self-serving, lazy, entitled and childish. Marais, Malatsi, Tony Yengeni and Madikizela-Mandela, to mention a few, have done their fair share to add to these epithets.

The public is angry that Yengeni was paid a salary for two years while suspended when he knew he had lied. We want to know whether or not the auditor-general will demand that he pay us back. Will Madikizela-Mandela be called to account for the serious charges against her?

Do we as citizens not have a right to demand she be called to account? Surely we can turn this climate of cynicism around by making our voices heard.

The constitution clearly requires public officials to be fit and proper persons. It makes provision for appropriate legislation to be tabled to enforce public accountability. May one be one or the other? No. They go together. The injunction is to be fit and proper, the adjunct to being faithful to the Republic of SA and obedient to the constitution.

It means public officials put themselves at the centre of what it means to be democratic, to respect the rule of law and uphold the culture of human rights. It means being honest, with no criminal record, not being insolvent, and respecting values enshrined in the constitution.

It is a call to lead by example and to put the country's interests above their own. Moral integrity is the cornerstone of an honourable public life and the main ingredient for those who wish to take the campaign of moral regeneration seriously. The appellation, honourable member, should be earned!

What the Harksen, Palazolo, Yengeni, Woerfel, Zama forestry, and the Agusta Riccardo sagas highlighted were how bribable politicians are. These serial revelations of corruption have pointed to what, I suspect, might be the tip of the iceberg.

Deals are being struck as we speak between the rich and the powerful and the post-1994 alliances between the former apartheid rich and the black nouveau riche make for fascinating reading.

Closer scrutiny will show how the rich switch allegiances depending on who is in power. Filthy lucre is no respecter of persons and public officials had better realise it. Ronald Reagan was right about one thing when he said: 'Politics is supposed to be the second-oldest profession. I have come to realise it bears a close resemblance to the first.'

'But at least with the oldest profession, one often gets value for money,' says William Saunderson-Meyer!

☛ Politicians score points as tik lays waste to coloured youth
Business Day April 10 2007

I WAS appalled last Sunday at the unholy spat that erupted between Abie Isaacs, a member of the Mitchells Plain Community Policing Forum (CPF), and Imam Fasiegh Adams on SABC's *Interface*, badly chaired as usual by Udi ya-Nakamhela.

Instead of focusing on the scourge of drug abuse, especially tik, in Mitchells Plain and its deadly effects on our youth, Ya-Nakamhela allowed the debate to degenerate into a political bun fight simply because the executive mayor of Cape Town, Helen Zille, has come out in support of the People's Anti-drug and Liquor Action Committee in its fight against drug lords and drug dealers.

Isaacs came across as one of those typical Stalinist hacks, who believe the CPF has a monopoly on dealing with issues that affect the community. He had the audacity to brag that they had been working in the area for the past decade, questioning the bona fides of the Democratic Alliance's (DA's) and other parties' support for this initiative. Now that other agencies are coming in to join hands in the fight against crime, the CPF labels them as supporters of vigilantes in order to discredit them.

While they accuse Zille of politicising the issue, they forget they have behaved like the handmaidens of African National Congress (ANC) politicians for years, so that very little has been achieved in the fight against drugs in Manenberg, Bonteheuwel, Mitchells Plain, and elsewhere. If Western Cape community safety MEC Leonard Ramatlakane knows about the drug houses and who the drug lords are, as he claims, why has he done nothing about them for so long?

Tik has become a political football precisely because the politicians have done so little about it, ignoring the havoc it has wreaked on our children's lives, and now that Zille has joined the fray all hell breaks loose. And can one blame the parents for asking: is it because tik affects mostly coloured youth that the ANC government does not give a damn? The

Medical Research Council reports that most tik users are below the age of twenty, 88% coloured, 72% male and come from most coloured townships.

In 1999, the US government recognised that obesity was becoming a life-threatening problem. The office of the US surgeon-general set up state-based programmes to tackle the disease. The surgeon-general's office acknowledges the seriousness of the problem by publishing the number of deaths per year attributable to obesity – 300 000 – claiming that obese people are more likely to die from heart disease, diabetes, cancer, breathing problems, arthritis, reproductive complications, and limited mobility than people of normal weight. State-based programmes range from school-based 'healthy choices' programmes to rural schools nutrition programmes to community garden and environmental education programmes. These programmes are monitored and evaluated and, more important, are seriously funded by the government.

Something similar needs to happen in SA if the government wants to get serious about eradicating the tik problem. Tik is not just a crime problem. It is a serious social problem, hence substantial resources such as clinics, rehabilitation centres, funding, national programmes and staff need to be invested in responding to it. More important, political parties need to join hands, as with the fight against HIV/AIDS, to find joint remedies, resources and solutions to the problem.

The only way to gain citizens' trust is to be responsive to the problems that assail communities , instead of political point-scoring. The big lesson that the Treatment Action Campaign (TAC) learnt was that trying to solve the HIV/AIDS problem within the ANC was as helpful as keeping incest in the family. Recently, the TAC has joined hands again with civil society, willing political actors and faith communities to counter the cynicism that comes from the government.

That the Mitchells Plain CPF wants to stifle awareness-raising campaigns initiated by community leaders such as Adams, labelling them vigilantes instead of giving them support and demanding resources from the government, shows how much contempt they have for community leaders – regarding them solely as voting fodder. As with HIV/AIDS, tik affects our economically active population, and we neglect the youth at our peril. Many families are affected by drug abuse and many parents are clueless as to how to address the problem, as few institutions exist to assist with the problem. Drug rehabilitation centres are expensive and out of reach of those who need them most.

Communities have become tired of being used as political footballs and the *gatvol* factor is leading to violent uprisings. The TAC has realised through many a court order that it cannot operate and make demands within the party.

Political maturity across political parties, in collaboration with civil society, is required if we collectively want to wipe out drug trafficking and drug abuse in the townships, where unemployment is rife, where recreational facilities are lacking, where job opportunities are few and where education is a low priority.

☛ The rise and rule of the Cape Flats war machine
Cape Times February 18 1998

GANGSTERISM is a threat to the stability of society in many ways – as we have seen in Manenberg and over the past two years since Rashaad Staggie's death. Not only do gangsters kill each other but many innocent people are caught in the crossfire as they continue their war for power and turf. Gang rivalry also destabilises prisons to such an extent that maintaining discipline has become a virtual nightmare for correctional service officers.

The recent eruption of gang warfare in Manenberg demonstrates yet again how a whole community is held to ransom as gangsters, armed with submachine guns go for each other while even the police take cover. Instead of mobilising forces to disarm and arrest those openly committing crime, the police service seems unable to intervene timeously, nor have they been capable of preempting such attacks. In fact, allegations of police complicity in the drug trade are rife, making it difficult for the police to get to the bottom of the activities of gang syndicates.

Within the first twenty days of this year, about twenty people were killed and sixteen wounded in the drug wars and clashes between gangsters and Pagad. As a result, the government seems, for the first time, to have come down quite hard on gang leaders and Pagad, arresting, where necessary, those responsible for fomenting crime. Government action is to be welcomed, but it comes too late, given the death toll.

While gangsterism is as old as the Cape Flats itself, we need to be reminded that the present low intensity warfare between Pagad and the gangs started in May 1996 when the former constituted itself with the primary objective of 'taking out' gangsters and drug dealers in their efforts to combat crime. Accusing the government of being ineffectual in dealing with crime, Pagad gave an ultimatum to the Minister of Justice Mr Dullah Omar demanding, inter alia, that the death penalty be made mandatory for drug dealers; that the assets of gangsters be confiscated; that R10 000 bail be imposed on drug users; that no bail be granted to drug dealers; that sentences for first offenders be more severe; and that controls be stepped up at harbours and airports.

Unhappy with the government's response, Pagad adopted vigilante tactics, rounding up drug lords and threatening gang bosses, resulting in the public lynching of the Hard Livings gang boss, Rashaad Staggie. A reformed group of gangsters formed Core (Community Outreach Forum) in reaction to this horrendous deed. They committed themselves to peaceful ways of preventing crime on the Cape Flats. Core also presented a memorandum to the government inviting them to hold talks about gangsterism as a social-political phenomenon and the contribution Core could make towards the peace process on the Cape Flats. In many sectors, Core was not taken seriously and its members were accused of still being involved in criminal activities.

In the meantime, Pagad stepped up their attacks on Core – petrol-bombing and attacking houses at random, leaving Core no option but to remobilise in retaliatory action. Pagad's hidden agenda as an anti-state organisation soon became more obvious as it started to defy the law and declared war also on the police. Pagad's anti-state activities and fundamentalist Islamic rhetoric angered many clerics, who issued a joint statement to condemn what seemed to all to be terrorist activities. The eventual disintegration of Pagad ironically also led to the disintegration of gangs into rival groups, so that in the attacks and counter-attacks between the main protagonists, it was never clear who was striking when. It became easy to blame a third force.

In a BBC documentary Rashaad Staggie and his twin brother, Rashied, bragged about their lives as gangsters and their lucrative business. And Pagad paraded up and down the streets of Cape Town, armed to the teeth in full disguise; with not a whimper from the police. These guys were clearly throwing down the gauntlet to the government, but their challenges were met with a deafening silence by the national Minister of Safety and Security, Mr Sydney Mufamadi, and the provincial MEC Safety and Security, Mr Gerald Morkel.

At the time, the only noble attempt to deal with the problem came from the Western Cape Anti-Crime Forum, which gathered for a meeting with key state officials, inter alia the Minister of Justice, the attorney-general, the police commissioner, clerics and some crime-prevention NGO's. Even though the President tried to address the problem in later months, the government failed to seize the crucial moments in August 1996, when most leaders were prepared to assist his efforts. The renewed conflict between gangs shows it has become so endemic that Mandela's promise that 'fire will be met with overwhelming fire' urgently needs to be put to the test.

The government must be seen to be serious about stamping out gangsterism. The Minister of Safety and Security seems to be reluctant to enter the fray, leaving the burden unfairly on the Minister of Justice. MEC Morkel is equally invisible. I believe that the state has the capacity to deal with gangsterism in spite of certain inadequacies in its machinery. It should start by invigorating the National Crime Prevention Strategy, a comprehensive plan to combat crime.

In the short term it should disarm gangsters; speed up investigations against those charged; break up crime syndicates; and strengthen intelligence networks within the police and the community to stamp out police corruption. In the long term it requires all relevant government departments to contribute to anti-crime policies and plans in a holistic fashion. Cabinet ministers, directors-general, and civil servants are required to look beyond their departmental needs and budgetary constraints to address creatively the causes for crime and the opportunities for crime. In addition, effective socioeconomic solutions to crime prevention should be made a priority.

Human rights training about the Bill of Rights and the need for a new human rights culture needs to become part-and-parcel of our school curricula and inculcated into the youth from an early age. While statistics around certain types of violent crime seem to have stabilised, police reports confirm that the incidents of rape and sexual violence against women and children have increased. Victim support is therefore urgent, requiring extra budgeting as well as specialised skills. Finally, I believe that the government should hold talks with gang leaders. Many gang leaders have embarked on their ruthless road to anarchy on the grounds that government is prepared to tolerate some forms of gangsterism more than others. The Cape Flats gang leaders will tell you that while they are being targeted as the dangerous criminals who should be eliminated, gangsters such as members of the CCB, Askaris, and Koevoet, created by the apartheid state to kill opponents, seem to have more legitimacy and, therefore, are more eligible for pardon.

Gangsters, too, want a truth and reconciliation process.

☞ Atlantis a telling example of state not hearing poor
Business Day October 18 2002

KEN OWEN's parting shot as he leaves for his sabbatical in France is for South Africans to stop whining. Easily said for someone who can afford holidays, unlike the majority who live in abject poverty. For him there is indeed nothing to whinge about. As a self-appointed representative of the voiceless, I will whinge as much as I like, and would like to recount two recent experiences.

I was invited to attend a talk by the New Zealand Prime Minister, Helen Clark, at the University of Cape Town on September 6 2002. Interestingly her talk drew parallels between our common colonial histories and how rugby defined the tense relationship between New Zealand and SA prior to 1994. Her explanation of the economic resurgence of New Zealand as an important player in the global markets included mistakes made by her predecessors, lessons learnt and strategies used to boost economic growth.

Clark was extremely impressive, honest, forceful yet modest. She displayed all the qualities any country's leader should have. Her incisive mind and jargon-free English impressed the audience and we all left feeling, if only!

Driving back to my office, we were flagged down by traffic cops flashing blue lights, forcing us to make way for the presidential cavalcade coming over De Waal Drive at breakneck speed, endangering the lives of all concerned. Many possible accidents were averted miraculously.

Delusions of greatness can be dangerous and a threat to public safety. Zimbabwe's Robert Mugabe and Namibia's Sam Nujoma are known to indulge in similar displays of reckless grandeur, which in some instances have led to the loss of life. Why should we tolerate such unlawful behaviour from the president whose job it is to protect our rights?

Another incident warrants mention. Last Saturday I attended a community meeting in Atlantis. Several politicians were invited as guests to the launch of a multipurpose community centre in Atlantis. A big crowd gathered in the grounds to witness the hoisting of the flag by a youth brigade and to listen to the speeches. On the podium were two MECs, a deputy minister, an MP and some public servants.

Sadly, the sound system did not work so no one could hear the speeches. The crowd got angry and went up to the podium to alert the master of ceremonies to the problem. The irate marshals pushed away each one who went up to complain. The audience was not amused.

Inspired by the sour smell of cheap alcohol, the inebriated masses let us know in no uncertain terms how they felt.'*Hoekom moet ons hier staan in die hitte wanneer ons nie kan hoor nie?*'

'*Die government praat van partnerships maar hulle kan nie eers a PA system organise nie.*'

'*Julle praat met die land Engels, maar as julle hier kom, dan praat julle Afrikaans. Wie dink julle is ons?*'

In the meantime the political speeches went on regardless. The politicians were not even aware they were not communicating. Access to information and services, one of the key objectives of the new community centre, was flouted within the first minutes of the launch. Another objective, to encourage community participation, was cruelly undermined as complainants were chased away from the podium.

When the outside proceedings were over and the crowd moved into the hall to hear a continuation of the speeches, people outside asked disappointedly:

'*Is die show nou oor?*' '*Waarom was hulle hier?*' '*Ons het skaars die band gehoor.*' '*Dis die enigste entertainment wat ons nog die hele jaar gekry het.*'

Atlantis is worse than it ever was. Intended as a decentralised economic growth point by the apartheid government for coloured people, this project ended up as a colossal failure. The factories there soon relocated when government withdrew incentives, leaving the bulk of the community jobless. The new government has done nothing to include it into its broader economic and development plans.

The obvious poverty and drunkenness juxtaposed with the opulent cars and bodyguards at the launch provoked unrepeatable racial slurs that can only be understood as anger at the insensitivity of elected officials to the burgeoning poverty of a deeply alienated electorate.

Against this background one can only commend the community workers of this multipurpose community centre for trying against all odds to create an oasis in a desert of abandonment and neglect. *In vino veritas!*

Good Governance (Stumbling State)

☛ A crime that many of SA's ministers keep their jobs
Business Day June 14 2007

PRESIDENT Thabo Mbeki will go down in history as someone who fired only one person from his cabinet, not for mismanagement but for being a political competitor.

This when more than half his ministers are incompetent and pose direct threats to the wellbeing of the public. They are allowed to continue, however, regardless of the havoc they wreak on the nation in their respective portfolios.

Ministers from the departments of correctional services, safety and security, home affairs, justice, labour, health, public enterprises, transport, agriculture, constitutional development and communications, to mention a few, should all be given the boot for the gross mismanagement of major aspects of their portfolios.

For one, it is unfathomable why Mbeki has reinstated the sickly and sickening Health Minister Manto Tshabalala-Msimang, despite her spectacular failure. But then, we should not forget that as someone connected to one of the most senior members of the African National Congress (ANC), she may not be dumped. Maybe the president keeps her on so she can benefit from the substantial pension benefits ministers get upon retirement as a reward for her self-denying loyalty to him. Or maybe he did so just to spite the Treatment Action Campaign.

Given the decline of the public sector, Tshabalala-Msimang is not the only one who should be fired. At least half the cabinet should go. The gross mismanagement of the Sector Education and Training Authorities (Setas) is good enough reason for Labour Minister Membathisi

Mdladlana to be fired. The continuing debacle around South African Airways is good enough reason to give Public Enterprises Minister Alec Erwin the boot; eNaTIS is one among many reasons Transport Minister Jeff Radebe should be relieved of his duties. Equally, marching orders should be given to the Nqakula couple. One of them has done very little to reduce the unacceptably high levels of crime in SA. The other has literally run home affairs into the ground.

I can go on and on about our cabinet ministers, whose services should be terminated for good reason, but the one who escapes scrutiny is Agriculture Minister Lulama Xingwana. Her failure to stem the farming crisis is astounding. The *Cape Times* reported recently that 20 000 farmers have left the land because of 'low import tariffs and the dumping of cheap agricultural products from rich countries where farmers are heavily subsidised'. Add to that the more than 2 000 farmers murdered since 1994, and the picture looks grim.

Nothing is done to protect agriculture, leaving a tenuous food security situation. We are ironically losing farmers to Mozambique and other neighbouring African countries, where many have started new lives with the support of their new host countries.

One agricultural union claims the government is the biggest single threat to commercial farmers and has warned Xingwana that any agricultural policy driven by ideology and not for economically sustainable reasons will lead to chronic famines and food shortages.

As with the doctors who leave in droves, so too, farmers are leaving in great numbers, not least because of land expropriations due to land claims and the lack of support from the government. The Land Bank, which should be helping farmers, gave an R800 million loan to Pamodzi Investment Holdings – a nonagricultural investment – whose shareholders include ANC high-ups Kgalema Motlanthe and Manne Dipico, yet it cannot help farmers and subsidise those who have been adversely affected by drought, global competition, a weak export market, and other factors. The Land Bank's constitutional duty is to provide affordable finance for the development of the agricultural sector, not for the development of the bank accounts of ANC cronies.

Can anyone explain who decides that R800 million of the Land Bank's funds go into an investment company in which senior ANC politicians have major shares, bankrupting the bank and leaving it to rely on the state to bail it out? Where is the logic in this? Where are the checks and balances? Can we imagine the amount of support and subsidisation possible to farmers with this amount of money?

The Land Bank has never recovered since the departure of Helena Dolny, who would never have allowed it to deteriorate to the level we have now. Her successors, the former CEO Alan Mukoki, chief financial officer Xolile Ncame and risk manager Godfrey Masilela, earned exorbitant salaries and bonuses while seriously mismanaging the bank. Where are these people? Why does Mbeki allow such major forms of mismanagement when Jacob Zuma is dragged into court for amounts that pale into insignificance by comparison? The mind boggles.

☛ Blind lead the blind through a moral wasteland
Business Day February 8 2007

THE PUBLIC, and criminals in particular, are laughing their heads off at politicians who preach moral regeneration when the politicians themselves are morally degenerate.

As I write this column I hear on a news bulletin that the politicians implicated in the travel scandal will not be disciplined as Parliament lacks the mechanisms to institute disciplinary measures against them. Why, might I ask, could they discipline former chief whip Mbulelo Goniwe for sexual harassment, but not crooked MPs who stole taxpayers' money?

Is it that because the president knows that the very edifice of Parliament and the ruling party would collapse with about 300 MPs being probed at the same time?

Just as the church has no right to preach to others when it lacks moral probity, so politicians are treading on dangerous ground with their appeals for moral renewal. It is clear that the more anarchic this country is becoming, and the more government deviates from its social contract with its citizens, the more the political leaders sound like vacuous televangelists.

The last people we want sermons from are our political leaders, who have been found wanting on every score. Parliament, for example, under the leadership of Baleka Mbete, is a cesspit. Implicated in a driver's licence scandal, she was nevertheless promoted to speaker of Parliament despite evidence of guilt. Withholding the PricewaterhouseCoopers audit report when it was first released, she allegedly made it public only after senior MPs were sanitised from the list, exposing the small fish to the might of the law.

Add to this the criminal behaviour of former chief whip Tony Yengeni, the recently fired Goniwe, the oil scandal, the deputy president's expensive flying habits and the controversy surrounding police commissioner Jackie Selebi, and we have a deadly cocktail of graft.

The criminals know that the legislators have violated the highest lawmaking body in the land and have no right to preach to them.

The result is a country where the rule of law is constantly tested. We might have the finest constitution in the world but we also sit with the unfortunate legacy of a culture in which the law was used to discriminate against people and to violate their human rights. So it is that today people have no respect for the law. We see it on our roads, we see it with domestic violence, we see it in private school thuggery, we see it with internecine gang warfare, we see it with family murders, and we see it in Parliament.

In 1994, we had the opportunity to redirect this unfortunate trajectory, but instead, duplicitous standards of governance and the selective use of the law for those in high places have been directly responsible for the excessive crime that we have today. It is an expression of the rebellion against a state that has become endemically corrupt, greedy, inhumane, acquisitive and uncaring. The growth of the corruption industry among political 'gangsters' sets the context for gangsters who constantly explore ways to buck the system. What we see is low-intensity warfare between criminals who are angry and a government that does not give a toss about its citizens.

A few years ago I received a doctorate from Uppsala University in Sweden. The day it was conferred, we were all invited to a ball in the castle up on the hill. Clothed in our ball gowns, we went for a feast that lasted late into the night. After the ball, on our way home, I walked to the parking lot where our car was parked, accompanied by my host. But she walked past the car. When I protested, she responded quietly: 'In Sweden no one drives after having drunk even a glass of wine.' I was a human rights commissioner at the time and, to my shame, I said: 'Agh, just drive.'

No one will know.' She simply looked at me, astounded, as if to say: 'We just don't do that.'

Everyone left their car in the lot and either walked home or took a taxi. It suddenly struck me that this kind of behaviour is typical of a country where the rule of law has become second nature to people; where people understand the predominance of regular law over the arbitrariness of the state; where all (including public officials) are equally subject to the law administered by the ordinary courts; where personal freedoms of citizens are respected by the law justly and fairly, regardless of class, race or gender.

The rule of law will never become endemic as long as our rulers deny its culture in their own lives. It is easier to talk about morality than it is to talk about the Bill of Rights, because the concept of morality is as fuzzy as the brains of those who endlessly beat the moral regeneration drum. The Bill of Rights, on the other hand, is definable and focuses on the needs of citizens. It requires political will and the resources to implement it.

Government's constant appeal to morality is about putting the onus on civil society for the dysfunction of the state. But this distinction is important because it partly explains why, for example, the law must provide regulatory frameworks for divorce but it cannot tell people not to have affairs; and why, similarly, the state has a duty to protect gay people from discrimination, but has no right to interfere with their sexual preferences.

Those who have no moral compass themselves are disqualified from pointing the way to others – and so we have the blind leading the blind, with devastating consequences.

☛ Mbeki's silence rotten as Land Bank dirt piles up
Business Day March 27 2008

AT A DINNER party recently I was involved in a heated debate with someone who worked for the government, over whether or not President Thabo Mbeki is corrupt. He disagreed vehemently with my assertion that he was. For this man, corruption is defined narrowly, as someone using his position to enrich himself; but the meaning of corruption is much broader.

The *Cambridge Dictionary* defines it as 'dishonestly using your position or power to your own advantage'. The way Mbeki has used state institutions to entrench his power base is corrupt. Corruption also means covering up for those who are corrupt when you have the power to deal with it.

According to media reports last year, Deloitte sent a forensic auditor's report to the cabinet about the endemic corruption within the Land Bank. The cabinet allegedly handed the report to the police to investigate, but then withdrew it.

My response was, 'Why?' The answer was given in last week's *Mail & Guardian* – It seems Land Affairs and Agriculture Minister Lulu Xingwana is being sued by the estranged wife of the acting CEO of the Land Bank, Phil Mohlahlane, in a divorce suit. The divorce papers reveal a web of intrigue between the minister and Mohlahlane that involves all kinds of perks and privileges and, in the meantime, 'bank officials had defrauded the bank of more than R2 billion to fund investments by close friends and business associates'.

That Mbeki does not fire this minister and demand an open investigation surely points to something rotten in the Presidency. Since Helena Dolny was indecently fired in 2000, the Land Bank has had several CEOs, has undergone several restructuring efforts and transformation, but has amounted to nothing but a cesspit of indolence, incompetence and embezzlement of taxpayer's money. This is not affirmative action, it is gross nepotism and cronyism under the guise of employment equity.

The African National Congress government rides roughshod over us, the citizens, taxed to death to support the profligate lifestyles of public officials. Mbeki has allowed this kind of unaccountability to become part of the social fabric of SA. We are governed by political gangsters, with a few exceptions, and the only way Mbeki maintains control is by having dirt on his colleagues.

On June 14 last year, I wrote the following in this column: 'The one who escapes scrutiny is Lulama Xingwana, minister of agriculture. Her failure to stem the ongoing farming crisis that we have in SA is astounding. A recent *Cape Times* article reported that 20 000 farmers have left the land because of "low import tariffs and the dumping of cheap agricultural products in SA from rich countries where farmers are heavily subsidised".

'Add to that the more than 2 000 farmers murdered since 1994, and the picture looks grim. Nothing is done to protect agriculture, leaving a very tenuous food security situation. We are ironically losing farmers to Mozambique and other neighbouring African countries, where many have started new lives very successfully with the support of their new host countries.

'The Land Bank, that should be helping farmers, gave a loan of R800 million (33% of the bank's total R2.4 billion capital base) to Pamodzi Investment Holdings – a nonagricultural investment – whose shareholders include Kgalema Motlanthe, Manne Dipico and others, yet it cannot help farmers and subsidise those who have been adversely affected by drought, global competition, a weak export market, and other factors ...

'Worse, the Land Bank expects government to inject R700 million to keep the bank afloat, which the government has unquestioningly agreed to do.

'The Land Bank has never recovered since the departure of Helena Dolny, who would never have allowed the Bank to deteriorate to the level we have now.'

So, who will prosecute Mohlahlane for the missing R2 billion? And when will Xingwana be fired?

☛ Mbeki resting on laurels that few can discern
Business Day February 17 2005

PRESIDENT Thabo Mbeki's state of the nation speech was disappointing for a number of reasons, not least for mentioning deposed Haitian leader Jean-Bertrand Aristide more than the HIV/AIDS pandemic. The speech did not even mention the word HIV – in a country with one of the highest infection rates.

There was no Festus Mogae urgency to reduce the pandemic as a top government priority; instead a feeble boast that SA has one of the best programmes in the world, when government has not even reached its own target of providing antiretrovirals to 53 000 people.

There was no plan for speeding up the provision of antiretrovirals or concern for the thousands of AIDS orphans, cared for by struggling grandmothers and welfare organisations. Because of this grave oversight, I find the President's speech wanting.

Lauded by many, Mbeki's address lists the achievements and failures of his government, but for the most part the script was unreadable and way over the heads of the people of Manenberg, Harrismith, Diepsloot, Hanover Park, Phomolong and Crossroads, with its tedious list of summits, strategies, programmes and action plans. An audit of these would reveal that not much is happening.

Codes of good practice for broad-based black economic empowerment, the National Skills Development Strategy, integrated development plans, the Small Enterprise Development Agency, community development workers, the Izimbizo, Project Consolidate, Batho Pele, Letsema and Vuk'uzenzele.

Nice sounding, sexy titles often designed before an election to catch the ear of the electorate, but mostly vacuous and cumbersome to administer. This is borne out by the mismanagement of the National Development Agency, most sector education and training authorities, the social-grant programme, some multipurpose centres, and the failure of Batho Pele and Vuk'uzenzele to deliver.

Threatening to wield the whip against lazy civil servants is a bit rich when Mbeki knows that race-based rather than competency-based appointments are responsible for the alarming rates of incapacity within the public sector. Appeals to our hordes of skilled emigrés to return to fill the gap are revealing.

The sooner he admonishes his ministers to adopt policies with a long-term view to address problems bequeathed to us from apartheid, the sooner they will find sustainable solutions to housing, education and health care. Ad hoc, persona-linked remedies will not address the deep-seated problems that have become endemic in poor communities.

And so, to the middle classes at whom Mbeki directed his speech. It was a dangerous soporific, focusing on the good life. With a thriving economy, a strong currency, a wallowing business elite and a fairly stable democracy, our alarm systems are down in the way the previous regime lived through apartheid's golden '70s unaware that Soweto was brewing.

When Barney Mthombothi, editor of the *Financial Mail*, laments his inability to attract anyone from business to comment on the president's weekly online letters, it comes as no surprise. As the main beneficiaries of this golden era, the business classes are reluctant to rock the boat, lest they fall victim of the president's pen and the state's largesse.

And here lies the rub. Mbeki's speech is dangerous precisely for that reason. While he does have laurels to rest on, his government cannot afford to be complacent. He needs to communicate his poverty reduction programme to the poor as clearly as he is able to threaten them. The Diepsloots, Harrismiths, Phomolongs will multiply and soon fulfil a prophecy he once made, that when the poor rise up, they will rise up against all of us, as evidenced by the 'September Revolution' raging in the Free State.

The revolt in Phomolong in the Free State may well come to be a direct threat to the power of the state, and not just a 'genuine protest over slack service delivery' as reported in the *Sunday Times*.

Real power resides in local communities and unless government realises this and takes drastic measures to remedy the 139 'chronically ill' municipalities mentioned in the Local Government Survey, it will soon be able to discern between threats to state power and revolts over slack government delivery.

When the poor, schooled in the slogans of the Freedom Charter, rise up and make demands then the ANC should begin to worry! This is our wake up call. We ignore these subterranean tremors at our peril.

☛ Democratic charade misses the point of dialogue
Business Day February 9 2006

AS A PASTOR's daughter I become nervous when people quote the Bible for their own ends.

So when President Thabo Mbeki quoted from Isaiah to portray an upbeat economy and future electorate, I complained to a friend about the misuse of scriptures, whose apt response was: 'What we need is a Jesus with a whip who will drive out all those MPs who desecrated Parliament with the travel scandal. Jesus not only condemned them for turning the house of prayer into a den of robbers but also took decisive action.'

This is what Parliament needs.

To me Parliament is nothing but a democratic charade – an act or event which is clearly false. A president who commands a lawless cavalcade – that shoves everyone off the road, that blares its sirens all day long, announcing to the unimpressed Capetonians that he is around – would earn more votes if his axing of Jacob Zuma really meant the beginning of clean governance.

What we witness instead with the state of the nation address is the emission of yet more hot air, exacerbating the already soaring temperatures of Cape Town.

All the pomp and circumstance, Health Minister Manto Tshabalala-Msimang's hat notwithstanding, hides an institution rotten to the core. What confidence is inspired when already at the beginning of the session it is announced that Deputy President Phumzile Mlambo-Ngcuka will not be investigated. When Harry Charlton, Parliament's former chief financial officer, is being persecuted for doing his job properly, what will the year hold for those of us who long for a Parliament that exercises oversight instead of rubberstamping the executive?

Inkatha Freedom Party leader Mangosuthu Buthelezi summed up Mbeki's speech to the core: 'I cannot correlate the ructions out there to the president's rosy speech.' African Christian Democratic Party leader Kenneth Meshoe rightly condemned Mbeki for hardly mentioning concrete plans to combat the scourge of HIV/AIDS and to reverse the escalating pandemic.

This reminds me of how far we have departed from the role and function of Parliament. Ralph Heintzman, a distinguished Canadian writer and academic, said one of the single most important features of a parliament is its deep symbolic value as the citadel of dialogue and civilised debate: '(The) daily confrontation of government and "loyal" opposition in the House of Commons symbolises the inner dialogue, the continual sequence of question and answer, which distinguishes the truly civilised mind and is reflected in the social and public life of a civil community.

'Just as a genuinely sound mind does not suppress either of its two fundamental impulses but listens instead to both, and tries unceasingly to achieve a synthesis in which their opposition will be reconciled, so too the good society recognises that opposing tendencies are not each other's enemies but each other's partners instead, and their indispensable complement. They are linked by an educational contract which is at once the condition and the sign of civilisation.'

The idea that inner dialogue and disputation are indispensable to democratic states emerged in Greece in the fifth century BC. It was embodied in the philosophical method of Socrates, whose thought, as transcribed by Plato, almost always took the form of dialogue.

What fuels the belief in the importance of dialogue is the conviction that the truth of any matter, whether philosophical or political, can best be reached through debate between parties that often disagree.

Opposition was crucial because without it there could be no dialogue; and without dialogue, one could not begin to approach the truth. No one person, and no one party, can lay absolute claim to the truth, whatever their credentials. And the person or party that does so is almost certainly going the way of Zimbabwe's Robert Mugabe – to fanaticism, fascism and thuggery.

The institution of parliament should, therefore, be the embodiment of Socratic thought. It should be the definitive institution for debate, dialogue and civilised opposition. It should be the symposium for SA's political, cultural and social quandaries. Parliament should fundamentally be about cross-examination, adversarial but civilised dissent and frank Socratic discourse.

It is about the 'transacting of the people's business in public', to quote Gerald Schmitz, a Canadian parliamentary researcher. It provides a forum in which points of view can be argued and in which, through the constant battles of opposing ideas, we can hope to find the truth.

Not surprisingly, then, history shows us a long line of rulers who have sought to undermine parliament. As Socrates discovered when he was sentenced to death for provoking debate with the democratic Athenian government, something in people forcefully resists self-examination.

Ruling parties hate answering questions about their performance and motives, they hate being demanded to do so and they hate being shown up for doing so poorly, everywhere in the world.

🐖 Evil depth of SA's crimes calls for drastic measures
Business Day May 4 2006

A FEW DAYS before the unspeakably brutal assassination of Brett Goldin and Richard Bloom, I noticed a little news report in the papers that went virtually unnoticed.

A Bloemfontein farming couple, aged more than 80 and 70 years respectively, was assaulted by five armed men. The old man was dumped in a scalding hot bath until the soles of his feet fell off and the guys jumped on the chest of the old woman breaking her ribs, damaging her lungs and her heart.

I read and reread this incredible story simply because my brain could not absorb such evil. Not long after, four corpses were found in a field in Philippi, all of this hot on the heels of the horrible murder of Judge Ngoepe's angelic-looking granddaughter.

These murders unleashed a groundswell of emotion that demonstrated the public's frustration with the levels of crime, which seems not to abate no matter what the statistics say. Talented people are wiped off the face of the earth by young people who should still be at school or in college. Callers to radio stations, text messages, and letters to the editor revealed a vulnerable nation living not so much in fear of crime itself as with the fear of being the target of the unmitigated cruelty that accompanies crime in SA.

Why is crime in SA so evil? Babies, young girls and grandmothers are raped; old people are hacked to death; women live in a state of fear; and government inspires no confidence in the justice system's ability to stem the tide.

Last week I visited a maximum security prison, and all the inmates I dealt with were murderers. Many of the men had already served five to ten years of their life sentences, and all looked incredibly young, which means they committed their crimes when they were teenagers.

We cannot explain these evil crimes in terms of our past even though apartheid did play a role in brutalising people in ways we shall never know. Nor can we blame it all on poverty because many countries with similar and worse poverty do not have the levels of crime we see here. So what is going on here?

Have we provided the context for the levels of crime we are experiencing today? At the time of the truth commission in 1996, several gang leaders approached me as human rights commissioner, complaining that political 'gangsters' were promised the option of immunity but not them. They asked me if I could set up a meeting with Dullah Omar, the then justice minister, where they would request immunity for certain crimes in exchange for information on police who were working with the gang leaders and drug lords. For several reasons this meeting did not take place, among them being that government felt we should not negotiate with criminals. As much as I understood the reasons, I firmly believed it was a moment lost.

Many politicians are perceived by criminals to have become instantly wealthy. The criminals reckon politicians do not have to be educated or work hard to be rich, so why can't we do the same? They are not role models, and so through crime and drug trafficking we gangsters can also live rich. What we see in the townships is the glamorisation of crime, and many have told me that what they earn through real work is pocket money compared with the money they get through crime.

Government has failed to act and set boundaries for criminals, so criminals use their anger and criminality in a pseudopolitical context to continually test the limits of a weak justice system and its boundaries, which are extremely malleable and elastic.

Our sentencing regimes are no deterrent. A crucial part of any argument against the death penalty is the assurance that brutal criminals will be kept locked behind bars. With recidivism rates of 80% and with government's failure at rehabilitation and reintegration, prisons have become hotbeds of gangsterism and crime, where criminals operate between communities and prisons, keeping the networks alive no matter how long they are incarcerated. Prison has no effect. With a rape culture that is endemic parole is often threatening to the public and should be feared. That is why people are calling for the death penalty.

As someone who has opposed the death penalty all my life – through columns and speeches and letters to the editor – I am beginning to rethink my firm conviction on this matter, only insofar as SA is concerned. The only way we will be safe is when those who take life are denied the right to life as the only means to reassure the public that murder will not be tolerated. Further, government has repeatedly pardoned criminals with heinous track records, some of whom committed even more horrendous crimes on their release only to be sent back to prison again.

Gangsters reward contract killings. Goldin and Bloom's killers have cooperated with the police because the act of killing brings with it a reward of moving up in the ranks of the 'Americans' gang. Prison is no deterrent; in fact going back enables the gangsters to continue their activity with more clout and power, as they will have gained the respect of their rivals. Jonny Steinberg has written about this in his columns on these pages, and in his award-winning book, *The Number*.

We will never address crime unless President Thabo Mbeki authoritatively and unequivocally condemns murder every time it happens, and sees to it that the maximum punishment is meted out effectively. His silence over the brutal murders that happened last month was conspicuous. Government is not interventionist enough. In fact, the tolerance of white-collar crime and the growth of the corruption industry among political 'gangsters' sets the context for gangsters who constantly explore ways to buck the system.

Before 1994 we robustly sang, 'We shall overcome'. Today it more appropriately means, '*Ons sal iets oor kom*', if we do not do something drastic soon.

President must get to grips with crime
Business Day August 14 2003

A FEW WEEKS before National Women's Day, eight-year-old Sasha-Lee Crook was snatched from her home. She was found dead, mutilated beyond recognition, on a vacant piece of land near her home. The police did not do the most basic of investigations.

Soon after, the young Ms Drennen, year-old baby Layla and mother-in-law-to-be were brutally raped, shot and dumped along the road while their attackers pillaged everything in their path. These young murder suspects were arrested soon after.

In the same week before Women's Day, ten cash-in-transit heists were reported in the media – and suspicions were confirmed that this criminal activity has become almost commonplace in SA. Not a word of reassurance or condemnation from the president or the national police commissioner. Clearly the national crime prevention strategy has failed, and the commissioner should take responsibility for this. Lives are cheap, and victims of crime have become statistics.

Why do we as citizens accept this? Why do we accept the current state of affairs as a quiet admission that government is incapable of protecting its citizens? Surely we should demand more? Surely an economy cannot flourish if its base is not protected. Word that hundreds of prisoners are to be released adds to the despair, not because they should not be released but because petty criminals often become murderers. In this country offenders kill for R5, for a cellphone or a handbag.

The problem is compounded by the unacceptably high rates of recidivism. While the release of prisoners is a necessary evil to relieve the heavily overcrowded prisons, government needs to face the fact that prison rehabilitation is a low priority and not enough effort and resources are invested to make the release of prisoners unthreatening to the public. And so the cycle continues.

What is to be done?

Lack of governance in this country is palpable. Public-sector delivery is weak, crime is rampant and poverty due to extremely high levels of unemployment plagues this new democracy. The African National Congress (ANC) government should take control and start governing.

The president and deputy president need to fly around the world less and get to grips with the needs of citizens and the seriousness of the situation, and tackle the criminal justice system with all the commitment it deserves. Or else national police commissioner Jackie Selebi should admit the problem is too big for him, and do something drastic.

Government should admit that it focused too long on the wrong priorities such as black economic empowerment, mining and other charters, oil and arms deals, resolving conflicts in other African countries and so on. All these could be laudable if only it concerned itself first with the basics of governance. Training in detective work, forensics, prosecution, conviction and, most of all, visible policing is an absolute necessity if we want to turn the crime epidemic round.

Last week Western Cape newspapers ran a feature on gangsterism in the province in all its gory detail. Why is it that when so much is known so little is done to eradicate this scourge on the Cape Flats? That children are caught in the crossfire of gang rivalry is almost accepted, and little is done about it. Schools in Hanover Park, Manenberg, Lotus River and Mitchells Plain are the battlegrounds of gangs with little hope of protection from the police.

Criminals know crime pays and they can get away with it. They know the criminal justice system is weak, and exploit its loopholes with daunting regularity.

I am writing this column from a terrace cafe late at night in Toronto, feeling absolutely safe as a woman. In a town where crime is minimal, visible policing is the order of the day. On this Women's Day the temptation to emigrate is strong, and I fully understand why there is a huge colony of South Africans here.

As someone who strongly supported the ANC government, I suddenly realise that if I emigrate it will not be because blacks are governing this country. It will be because blacks are not governing.

☛ Hard-won freedom must not remain a paper tiger
Business Day December 13 2002

THERE IS so much disgruntlement about the declining standards in the health sector, the inability of government to deal with crime, the burgeoning poverty crisis and the looming AIDS pandemic that people are asking: what has the struggle been for?

Is there anything other than our macroeconomic policy and our constitution that we can be proud of? Where does all the revenue that is generated go to if it does not reach the 22-million poor? How is it possible for the Growth, Employment and Redistribution (Gear) strategy and the constitution to coexist with such extreme forms of poverty?

In this atmosphere of despair people need to know that there are remedies.

One such, freedom of association, is one of the most empowering clauses in our new constitution. We now have the right of association with any party, any group and any organisation that we were denied under apartheid.

Before, the entire apparatus of the apartheid state was geared towards restricting South Africans in the associations we made in almost every aspect of our lives. It determined whom we married, where we lived, what school we attended, what political organisations we belonged to (or not). People were detained without trial, banned, murdered and tortured for having practised freedom of association.

The old state sacrificed the individual to conformity, and by the State Security Council under PW Botha went to great lengths to cultivate a conformist nation that said '*Ja baas, nee baas, skop my onder my gat baas!*'

Conformity, centralised control and the adulation of politicians were in part what kept the majority of white South Africans loyal and subservient to the apartheid government.

Under African National Congress (ANC) rule, similar trends are developing in another guise.

Consensus building, African nationalism, political correctness and censure of those who refuse to conform are all elements that smack of the past. The lack of internal democracy within the ANC, the centralisation of power in the presidency, the disrespect for opposition, all point to a conformity that should have us in a state of worry.

Fortunately, our current constitution has restored to us that freedom of association that the former government tried to destroy. The constitution will not transform our lives, but does give us the ability to make that choice.

Our vote need no longer be based on the symbolism of what the struggle and its heroes depicted. We can now make choices in favour of good governance. We take responsibility for the success or failure of this democracy. Opposition, a vibrant Parliament, an independent media and respect for human rights are what our democracy needs. Freedom of association means that we are now free, even to destroy ourselves. That is the most frightening aspect of this freedom.

Freedom to destroy has to do with our president's unqualified support for Zimbabwean dictator Robert Mugabe and his ruthless reign of terror. Freedom to destroy has to do with the use of state's resources to cover up government corruption, as witnessed with the arms deal. Freedom to destroy has to do with the neutralisation of Parliament and watchdog bodies such as the public protector, the auditor-general and the public accounts committee that readily submit to the will of the executive.

Freedom to destroy has to do with the failure of government to account for R1 billion when people are dying of poverty; or Eastern Cape's inability to spend 80% of its budget when it is the poorest province in the country. Freedom to destroy is to prioritise R164 million to buy Rooivalk helicopters, a jet of R540 million for the president, millions for conferences to sort out the Congo and the African Union, when citizens live in shacks, and lack water, housing, health care, etc.

Freedom to destroy has to do with the denial of antiretroviral medicines to millions infected with HIV/AIDS, so much so that we top the infection rate internationally. Freedom to destroy has to do with a government unable to reverse the escalation of violent crime, especially against women and children.

It also has to do with low conviction rates for serious crime and the inability of government to protect its citizens.

We do not have to tolerate low standards of democracy and service delivery. Or, is there a fear that no other party is able to do better than the ANC, so we might as well contend with the devil we know?

This is a dangerous precedent. Majoritarianism is not good for democracy anywhere.

Democracy needs opposition for it to function effectively. It needs elected officials who will put the welfare of this country before lust for power.

☛ Trusting Mbeki on Selebi takes a leap of faith beyond most of us
Business Day December 1 2006

CRIME affects all people equally in SA. Women live in constant fear of being raped, assaulted, robbed, and murdered – not to speak of crimes against children.

The country's crime statistics on murder, rape, cash-in-transit heists, and armed robbery, according to a recent *Financial Mail* report, beat the war statistics of Iraq and Afghanistan.

In this climate of national '*gatvolness*', the allegations against the national police commissioner Jackie Selebi are serious. For Selebi to claim that Glenn Agliotti – accused of having masterminded Brett Kebble's murder – is his friend, is completely unacceptable, not to speak of the string of other shocking allegations against him.

The public has a right to demand action against Selebi. And when a group of religious leaders went to the Union Buildings to seek some explanations, it gave us hope, or so I thought. Their request for a commission of inquiry was dismissed out of hand by President Thabo Mbeki. Claiming that the information at his disposal did not warrant any action against the chief of police, the president asked the clerics to trust him.

As far as Mbeki is concerned, the dossier of allegations and the evidence provided in the *Mail & Guardian* against SA's top cop apparently are not enough evidence for him to act.

For a national head of police to be embroiled in allegations of such serious criminal activity at a time when the rule of law is under threat, is the height of political irresponsibility and should be dealt with by a judicial commission of inquiry. Is the term 'prima facie' still a red herring?

For now Selebi is off the hook and, unwisely, the co-chairmen of the Religious Leaders Forum, Ashwin Trikamjee and Bishop Ivan Abrahams, acquiesced to the president's request with fatalistic resignation instead of showing some righteous indignation.

'If we cannot trust the president, whom can we trust?' they asked.

Now we all know that for clerics trust has always been an occupational hazard, but they must not expect us just to do as they do when all the evidence seems stacked against our police chief. More than trusting the president, they should trust their own instincts and those of the public.

They should have challenged Mbeki on his double standards and asked why he summarily sacked his great contender, Jacob Zuma, on a whiff of scandal, when a dossier in Selebi's case has left him unmoved.

Why was he ever willing to appoint the Hefer and Desai commissions, at great cost, to probe issues that had more to do with internal African National Congress (ANC) battles rather than national politics?

In the old SA we in the liberation movement disparagingly called the Dutch Reformed Church the 'National Party at prayer' or the 'Dutch Deformed Church' for consorting with the ruling party. When Allan Boesak declared apartheid a heresy and challenged his own church for condoning apartheid, they felt deeply maligned.

Ten years after the birth of our democracy, our religious leaders sounded very much like the 'ANC at prayer' with their lame commitment to trust the president.

With scant commitment from the president to allay the fears of the public that he will clean out the rot in the South African Police Service, starting with the head, and having squandered our trust – particularly on crime – the president can hardly expect us to trust him.

Our constitutional right to a crime-free country is being undermined constantly by political leaders who play roulette with our right to freedom and personal security. On a grave matter such as the credibility of the national police commissioner, when crime is at an all-time high, Mbeki cannot expect us to trust him.

How much more evidence does Mbeki need before he sacks Selebi? And for how long will the clerics trust Mbeki before we see some good old-fashioned Boesak-style civil disobedience?

On Selebi's track record as police commissioner alone he should be fired. All the stuff about Agliotti, Kebble, the bribe of R50 000 that he allegedly took from Clinton Nassif, and the allegations of a crime ring at Airports Company SA, just make matters worse and presidential action against him all the more justified.

My dilemma with Mbeki's double standards was captured neatly in a text message sent to the *Cape Argus* last week: 'Why should we trust Mbeki on Selebi after his previous appointment of Zuma as head of moral regeneration?'

☞ Unrest, gags and insults call back unhappy past
Business Day August 3 2005

MAY 27 2005 could have been a day in 1976, in apartheid SA. The *Mail & Guardian* was gagged. Judge Vas Soni ruled that the public interest in knowing details of the corrupt relationship between the African National Congress (ANC), PetroSA and Imvume was secondary to protecting the dignity of Imvume and its CEO, Sandi Majali.

In that same week ANC chief whip Mbulelo Goniwe's diatribe against the Democratic Alliance (DA) echoed the anti-Semitic expletives used by the Nationalists against Helen Suzman.

At the same time, township protests broke out all over SA against poor service delivery. Television images were reminiscent of the 1970s and 1980s as police aimed their guns at the poor protesting against the lack of sanitation and housing.

As in the past, the poor were not intimidated by the police. One community leader crisply articulated why his community was protesting. 'With every election housing, water, sanitation are promised – and nothing ever happens,' he complained. 'We are sick and tired of promises!'

Struck by the wave of community anger, government hastily introduced Project Consolidate to remedy the situation in 136 dysfunctional municipalities out of 280. This intervention, while necessary, comes a little too late.

Township dwellers are using the tactics of protest learnt at the feet of their ANC masters to hold them accountable. Blaming a third force sounds too much like the Nats in the late 1980s and underestimates the electorate; accusing the DA of fomenting violence is to credit the opposition with power the ANC doubts it is capable of mobilising. And to blame poor service delivery on a lack of capacity has become a hollow refrain when there are enough competent people around who could do the job.

The poor protest because they see the difference between the lifestyles of their elected leaders and their own miserable lives. They see the smart cars, the Fabiani suits, the diamonds, the mansions, the corruption scandals, the jets, and they know that each German luxury car could buy them five or six houses.

The poor also know that there is a link between their poverty and the endemic corruption within the ANC, as demonstrated by the Schabir Shaik trial. Corruption within the National Party is beginning to look like a tea party next to the ubiquitous arms deal, the Shaik trial, the parliamentary travel scandal, Oilgate, Truman Prince – all happening at the same time. They know there are many more corrupt cases being swept under the carpet. They also know that no matter how corrupt, few get fired despite the president's statements that corruption will not be tolerated.

The electorate has become tired of the forked tongue – the talk left, walk right syndrome. They are cynical about the moral regeneration campaign run by moral degenerates. If the president is serious about cleaning up, he should start with his own ranks. He should purge the cabinet and Parliament of those who enter political office to enrich themselves. Perhaps his reluctance stems from the fear that once he starts, few comrades will be left in his government.

There is a growing fear that SA is becoming like the vampire state described in Robert Guest's *Shackled Continent*: 'Several African leaders have grown skilled at enacting the letter of reform while sabotaging its spirit ... Belt-tightening measures hurt schools and hospitals, but ministers still get their Mercedes limousines, and the military budget is never cut ...

'The African vampire state is hard to reform because most necessary reforms would reduce the power and wealth of the people in charge. And the people in charge do not, on the whole, want to lose their privileges. Even business leaders, who you might expect to favour market reforms, are often so reliant on state patronage that they actively oppose them.'

In this climate of discontent, the ANC would be unwise to invoke the Freedom Charter to show that it cares. To use it as a mobilising document around the election might just backfire horribly. The charter might just serve to mobilise the poor against a corrupt government which they trusted to provide them with basic services, health care and jobs.

There are many in the ANC who are unhappy with the status quo and who are against the growing corruption. But to quote Dietrich Bonhoeffer: 'Not to speak is to speak; not to act is to act.' Where is the moral voice within the ANC? Are we to be subjected day in and day out to the growing corruption and failure to deliver? Are we to be subjected to the idiocy of the likes of Goniwe, who is an embarrassment to his party and his political namesake, Matthew Goniwe?

☞ Death of John Muller, a hero who shamed the ANC
Business Day May 13 2004

IN MATURE democracies, where tax-paying citizens can vote for individual politicians of their choice and hold them to account, such public servants are expected to maintain high standards of probity.

What is anathema in such democracies are officials who either lie in Parliament or mislead the public by being evasive or economical with the truth.

An example of this ethos was the resignation of the British defence minister, David Profumo, after it transpired he lied about his involvement with Christine Keeler. In the US, President Richard Nixon resigned over Watergate, and even under National Party rule, a lie in Parliament over covert government funding for the *Citizen* signalled the end of Connie Mulder's political career.

These are not, though, norms to which the African National Congress (ANC) adheres. Proof of this was provided by a recent story in

Rapport on the death in penury of an honest and honourable man, whose life was irrevocably changed for the worse when he blew the whistle in 1997 on corruption in the Mpumalanga traffic department.

Traffic official John Muller's revelations, with documentary evidence, led to the appointment of the Moldenhauer Commission and the recently elected speaker of Parliament, Baleka Mbete, being implicated in an illegal driving licence scam.

Instead of being rewarded, Muller was branded a troublemaker and, although later cleared of trumped-up disciplinary charges, was effectively driven out of the public service and financially ruined.

Those he implicated, Mbete, Steve Mabona and Stanley Soko, received the support of the ANC, were promoted and have gone on to thrive and prosper. Government has, indeed, introduced legislation such as the Protected Disclosures Act, and created anticorruption units such as the Scorpions. The president has also expressed concern about the sense of entitlement so endemic in the ANC's rank and file.

These are, however, only whispers in the wind, unheard and unheeded in the cacophony of gravy train grunting, in the tumult at the trough. Noble sentiments count for nothing when party-elected officials do not buy into democratic value systems.

The status quo was defined with disarming candour when then Mpumalanga premier Ndaweni Mahlangu said at his first public appearance it was normal and acceptable for politicians to lie and when, during the Sarfu case in 1998, department of sport director-general Mthobi Tyamzashe told the court he saw nothing wrong in lying to protect the president.

The expectation of integrity from politicians and public servants appointed by the ruling party also counts for nought when it closes ranks to protect those shown to lack it. The martyrdom of Stompie Seipei, the cover-up of Jessie Duarte's indiscretions, and support given to Allan Boesak are just a few examples. Norman Mashabane, ambassador to Indonesia, is acquitted of 21 counts of sexual harassment while the victim gets posted off to Seoul.

The ANC has learned that a resigned and long-suffering public, drowning in a never-ending sea of sleaze, has a short attention span; today's scandal will swiftly be forgotten as it is invariably overtaken by tomorrow's.

It accordingly prevaricates, knowing each breach of trust will quickly fade from public memory. Thus when, in June 1997, Penuell Maduna knowingly made false and defamatory accusations in Parliament that the auditor-general, Henri Kluever, had covered up strategic fuel fund losses, he was in breach of the constitution and rules of Parliament.

The subsequent appointment of a public protector's tribunal cost the taxpayer R20 million, yet he received no significant sanction. The fact that Nkosazana Dlamini-Zuma was less than candid about European Union funding for *Sarafina 2* was similarly ignored.

Those in the ANC brave and principled enough to oppose such practices are immediately and harshly dealt with. Luckily for Andrew Feinstein, he had the resources John Muller lacked and survives in exile abroad.

Poverty stricken, Muller lost his car, almost forfeited his home, and eventually died as he could afford neither the necessary medication nor the heart operation that would have extended his life.

Not for him the yellow silk suits, the Mercedes 4x4s. He was naive enough to believe the 1994 promises of governance from 'the moral high ground' and died a virtual pauper, broken on the wheel of the ANC's duplicity.

☛ Babies perish even as ministers lead charmed life
Business Day June 23 2005

THE DEATH of infants under any circumstances is tragic.

The headlines capturing the brutal murder of six-month-old Jordan-Leigh Norton evoked deep feelings of sadness and affected South Africans profoundly.

The joy of conception, the expectation as one carries around a foetus for nine months, culminating in a painful but miraculous birth, have been wiped out in one fell swoop by murderers motivated only by revenge and filthy lucre. The innocent victim of an apparent love triangle, Jordan-Leigh's death reminds us of the depravity of human nature.

While this death competed for media headlines with the drama around former deputy president Jacob Zuma, another tragedy hit our country, barely noticed, caused by gross neglect.

On June 8, fourteen babies in KwaZulu-Natal succumbed to a bacterial infection and died, within hours of each other, with barely a squeak from the media. Yes, the incident was reported but in a rather low-key way.

These babies were the victims allegedly of unhygienic conditions prevalent at the Phoenix Mahatma Gandhi Memorial Hospital, which is severely understaffed and under-resourced. It serves about 1.5 million people and handles about 1 200 deliveries a month.

What makes these deaths more disturbing is that they were wholly preventable. The filth in which the *Klebsiella* bacteria thrives caused it to sweep through the neonatal intensive-care ward, killing babies fresh from their mothers' wombs.

Klebsiella is a hospital-acquired infection that strikes the urinary tract, surgical wounds, and blood. The infections occur because of invasive treatments with such things as catheters and breathing tubes. Through these devices bacteria enter a person's body, but, with extra care, infections may be prevented.

But the immune systems of babies are often too underdeveloped to fight the bacteria, hence the deaths. In the absence of a resident microbiologist who would normally monitor such conditions, it comes as no surprise that so many babies succumbed to the bug.

Eclipsed by the Zuma melodrama, these avoidable deaths passed almost unnoticed. The subsequent call by the health minister for an investigation is not good enough. In any civilised country, the minister would have had to resign over such a fiasco — and this is a fiasco of epic proportions.

Regrettably, in SA, ministers are rarely fired, no matter what they do.

Zuma's dismissal is a rare event in the history of our democracy, hence the incredulous reaction from the public. President Thabo Mbeki fires people only when it serves his purposes.

He knows how to invoke the full spectrum of the law when he wants to get rid of somebody who is a threat. And, make no mistake, Zuma was a threat to the African National Congress (ANC) and to the country.

When the electorate clamours for similar action against other errant ministers or officials, the demands go unheeded, depending on who the minister or official is. The law is not applied without fear or favour. There have been many instances when senior ANC officials should have been fired for their ineptitude or corruption but who were instead promoted after their misdemeanours became public.

A cursory internet survey of cabinet ministers who were fired around the world makes interesting reading. In April 2003, Beijing mayor Meng Xuenong and China's health minister were fired after the disclosure of a tenfold increase in Sars virus cases in the capital. They were charged with mishandling the outbreak of the deadly illness.

President Bingu wa Mutharika of Malawi fired his education and human resources minister for, among other things, spending 2 165 000 kwacha (about R10 800) of public funds on his wedding. Since Mutharika took office in May last year, a number of former cabinet ministers and senior politicians have been arrested on allegations of fraud, corruption and tax evasion.

Eleven days after his inauguration, South Korean President Kim Youngsam fired three ministers to root out corruption. Those ousted were the welfare minister, who was found to have amassed a fortune through questionable real estate deals, the health minister and the construction minister, whose misdeeds have yet to be exposed.

Hungarian Prime Minister Ferenc Gyurcsány replaced his finance minister, Tibor Draskovics, who had held the position for fifteen months, during which time the current account deficit soared to almost 10% of gross domestic product (GDP), and the budget deficit reached 5.3% of GDP.

German Chancellor Gerhard Schröder dismissed his defence minister, Rudolf Scharping, after it was reported in the magazine *Stern* that he had been paid DM140 000 by a public relations consultant with links to the arms industry two days before a general election. German cabinet members are not allowed to earn anything other than their salaries.

Many of these ministers were fired for what the ANC might consider to be minor offences. Our health minister still reigns supreme, regardless of the HIV/AIDS pandemic. If ever anyone needed to be fired it is she.

Batho Pele has become an empty slogan because in her portfolio she has violated the very values and principles governing public administration enshrined in the constitution.

☞ HIV sufferers still left out in the cold

Business Day February 26 2003

TWO weeks ago someone who works in the same building as I approached me to ask for some help for a sister who has chronic TB and whom she suspects is HIV positive. Because of my connections with HIV/AIDS organisations and activists in the country, I started phoning around.

After the seventh call I was referred to a clinic in Cape Town that seemed willing to help. The interrogation, however, was what unnerved middle-class me with all my connections, not to speak of the colleague, a cleaner, who asked for my help. She witnessed the grilling.

Why does she not go to the clinic in her area? Who is the sister who is making the inquiries? How reliable is she? What is her connection to you? When last did she see a doctor? Can she afford treatment?

After I had painstakingly tried to sketch the conditions under which this poor woman lived, I was asked to spell out my credentials. I was told that she would receive help only if I wrote a letter, stating who I was, who the sister was, and reassure them that the sister would volunteer to be tested. We were asked to guarantee that she would stick to the medication should they decide to help.

After all this my colleague gave up because she least expected that from my office she would be subjected to the kind of treatment that African people have become so used to in township clinics, which are supposed to prioritise primary health care above all else.

So being part of the Treatment Action Campaign (TAC) march of 30 000 people on February 14 2003 was my opposition to a government that does not give a damn about the people who voted it into power. It was my opposition to African National Congress members who sang the president's praises after his state of the nation speech that has left the nation in a state of despair.

The problem with Thabo Mbeki's address was that he spoke on everything in general but nothing in particular, except Iraq, of course. And that is what enraged the public and journalists.

The particular item that the TAC wanted to hear was that treatment would be made available and accessible, now, *sekunjalo*, to those whose lives and livelihoods are being threatened by the killer disease that is decimating South Africans quick and fast.

Meanwhile, my colleague's sister has capitulated under the strain of not finding aid or an antiretroviral medicine that will relieve her of her illness. Knowingly, she has succumbed to the prospect of imminent death. That, Mr President, is what you have reduced my compatriots to.

Feelings of déjà vu, as we marched down roads regularly trudged before 1994 to protest against the apartheid regime, enveloped us. We were toyi-toying along the same roads against our democratically elected government. Its incomprehensible reluctance to obey the Constitutional Court order, despite the president's brief commitment to do so, is what infuriated the protesters.

Repeated ad nauseam through loudspeakers: 'This march is not anti-government, but an appeal to government to implement the Constitutional Court order', was a last bid to bring government on board as a partner in the fight against AIDS. Alas, it fell on deaf ears. And that is just what was wrong with the march.

For me it was a march against a recalcitrant stubborn government that has come to betray the people who put it into power. It is about a government that has become a law unto itself because of its majority power, and secure in the knowledge that its alliance partners will give it legitimacy no matter what it does.

By saying we are not against government but against its failure to provide treatment, we give legitimacy to a government that is committing genocide against its own people.

Where you have a crime against humanity of such proportions, surely perpetrators like Tshabalala-Msimang and Manana should be hauled before the International Human Rights Tribunal. As our publicly elected servants they have, in the midst of an epidemic, failed to provide emergency medical care. On this score, even an Inkatha Freedom Party or Democratic Alliance government would be better.

☛ When presidents go paranoid, NGOs beware
Business Day October 13 2005

AS A director of a nongovernmental organisation, I do not take kindly to President Thabo Mbeki's provocative comments about NGOs. It was with disquiet that I read his statement at the launch of the peer review in Midrand at which he questioned the independence of African civil society organisations.

He accused certain civil society organisations – such as those funded by the Americans, the Swedes, the Danes, the Japanese – of having hidden agendas and therefore not being truly African civil society organisations.

'Do they reflect us, the ordinary people they should be representing, or do they represent other interests?' This question was one of those classic Mbeki-isms intended to sow discord between government and civil society. When he says 'African society is beginning to question', one cannot help but ask, what is African society? Who is he referring to? African society can mean anything or nothing, depending on how the term is used.

Commendably, civil society members responded with righteous anger. On John Perlman's radio show, SAfm's *AM Live*, one caller reminded Mbeki that government had probably received more funds from donors such as the European Union, USAid, DfID, Sida, Japan, and Danaid, than any NGO we know. And what, asked the caller, was government's agenda in taking funds from these agencies?

Is this not a case of the pot calling the kettle black? Mbeki has the audacity to accuse the NGOs of hidden agendas when he himself harbours a secret, refusing to disclose who donates funds to his party.

Another caller reminded the president of the vast withdrawal of funds from NGOs after 1994, leading to the considerable weakening of civil society in order to strengthen government's capacity to provide services and consolidate democracy. Government poached hundreds of professionals from NGOs to boost the skills of the public service, adding insult to injury.

When presidents become paranoid, their first line of attack is usually the media, then Parliament, then the judiciary and then NGOs. Those NGOs, relied upon to assist the liberation struggle, ironically are often the first targeted after liberation precisely because governments know they are prepared to risk life and limb to safeguard democracy.

NGOs have an important role to play with opposition parties in holding government accountable. The Treatment Action Campaign, the rape crisis centres, the Landless People's Movement, the Anti-Privatisation Movement, the Centre for Violence and Reconciliation, the Centre for

Democratic Enterprise and the Black Sash are but a few that have done incredible work not only in holding government accountable for services, but in giving voice to the poor and marginalised.

This does not mean we are above reproach. Some NGOs do have agendas, but these are as obvious as the sky is blue.

My own organisation, Impumelelo, has recognised a vast number of NGOs all over SA doing wonderful work, in partnership with government, to improve the quality of life of the poor. Impumelelo receives quite a number of project applications from government, but if it were not for civil society initiatives employing a huge labour force and an army of volunteers, SA would be worse off than it is now.

The hundreds of volunteers involved in home-based care, palliative care, voluntary testing, counselling and treatment of the HIV-infected millions are doing more than half of government's work. There are those that assist government in the fight against crime. Rape crisis centres, domestic violence and abuse centres such as Mosaic and the Saartjie Baartman Centre, the Institute for Security Studies, Business Against Crime, to mention but a few, are indispensable to crime prevention in SA.

As for hidden agendas, most NGOs are compelled by the very nature of their operation to be transparent, or they simply would not get funds. With the scandalous misappropriation of funds in the 1980s, donors have imposed even more stringent requirements before they will consider giving money to NGOs.

NGOs have to be registered at the master's office, with a constitution and a governing board in place, and have their finances audited by reputable auditors.

Mbeki is either out of touch or is picking a fight. He should know by now that international funders worth their salt publicise their criteria for funding openly – in the media or in their organisational brochures readily obtainable from their offices or on the internet. If the president suspects any of hidden agendas, as intelligence chief he can find out what they are on about.

☛ Ministers rate 'I' for incompetence on my card
Business Day July 21 2005

EVERY YEAR the *Mail & Guardian* rates the performance of ministers on a scorecard. Very seldom do I understand the grounds on which they are rated.

Crime, disease due to HIV/AIDS, tuberculosis, malaria and road accidents have reached such unacceptable levels that I cannot fathom why the relevant ministers are in office.

Ministers have a duty under the constitution to respond to the needs of the people and provide services accountably. Health and transport have failed dismally in reducing deaths by prevention.

The health department is a disaster. Hospitals are understaffed; medicines are in short supply; linen disappears; and hospitals, generally, are in a state of decline. HIV/AIDS and tuberculosis are steadily increasing. Nurses and doctors are fleeing SA and the accusation that the west is poaching our health professionals rings hollow. There are no incentives to stay, given the lack of resources and respect for the profession and the failure to make the health of the poor a priority.

How Health Minister Manto Tshabalala-Msimang obtained a C for general health and an F for HIV/AIDS, God alone knows. Maybe the F stands for f...ing bad. With more than 22 babies dead from *Klebsiella* bacteria, and 40 more that died two years ago, not to speak of the spreading pandemics, the African National Congress should explain why she is still in office. These neonatal deaths are unforgivable and anywhere in the world, except here of course, the media would call on the minister to resign for failing to take responsibility.

The worse the situation becomes the more Tshabalala-Msimang interferes in the running of the health sector, promising now to take over the work of the Medicines Control Council, not to speak of the black economic empowerment intervention in private health care.

The mind boggles.

The traffic department, equally, has reached its sell-by date. On Friday morning I witnessed the most unspeakable carnage on the N2 in which 88 people were injured. Thirty-five vehicles – minibus taxis, cars, a truck, and two buses – were involved.

'Morning fog sows motorway mayhem,' screamed the *Cape Argus* headline, followed by another idiotic one two days ago: 'Deluge sets off string of crashes.' It is not the weather that causes accidents; it is negligent drivers who do not slow down. On that same day, 23 lives were lost in a horror bus accident in Eastern Cape.

These accidents were all avoidable were it not for the usual taxi mania and traffic offences that law-abiding citizens endure. Reckless taxi drivers break every rule of the road while traffic cops sit idly by on the side of the road. I often wonder why their misdemeanours are overlooked when others are fined so easily.

The worst is having a taxi collide with you. The drivers never take responsibility, no matter what the court rules. In my instance, the court ruled in my favour, gave the taxi driver a suspended sentence and ordered him to pay my costs. He never obliged. He was in contempt of court, but the law was ineffectual in tracking him down.

No wonder SA's road safety is the fourth worst in the world, with collisions costing about R16 billion a year. The campaign has seen more people Arrive Dead than Arrive Alive, and has done little to reduce the carnage. The statistics are alarming. A person is killed every 48 minutes; an accident occurs every four seconds; there is one death for every 570 vehicles; six out of ten accidents involve alcohol; one out of every 45 road users will end up in a trauma unit at some point.

South Africans' dance with death is described fully in a report entitled the 'Road Traffic and Fatal Crash Statistics 2003-04', issued by the Road Traffic Management Corporation last month. I have never seen such a thorough report dealing extensively with road traffic indicators, age of the vehicle population, the number of fatal crashes, their cost, and the like. I cannot understand why the transport minister cannot deal with the carnage on our roads, given that he sits on all the information required to sort out the problem. All it takes is political will. The number of fatal traffic crashes increased from 7 260 in 1998 to 10 530 last year. There was an increase in deaths from 9 068 in 1998 to 12 727 last year.

Probably more people die in SA through AIDS, accidents and murders than in any war now raging. But we turn a blind eye because life is cheap, and the poorer the life, the cheaper it is.

In SA, Robert Guest's poignant question rings true every day: 'How can we teach people safe sex when they will not even wear seat belts?' It is only in Africa where these two issues are inextricably linked.

☞ Inquiries aplenty, but none into ANC abuses
Business Day August 4 2005

REMEMBER the time Helena Dolny was unceremoniously booted out of the Land Bank simply for doing her work rigorously?

The reason behind this purge is now obvious. Corrupt deals such as the R800 million loan by the bank for a non-agricultural endeavour to Pamodzi Investments – in which two senior African National Congress (ANC) members, Secretary-General Kgalema Motlanthe and presidential adviser Manne Dipico, have shares – would never have been allowed under Dolny.

This loan was not intended for agricultural purposes but to facilitate Pamodzi's buyout of Foodcorp, one of Africa's biggest food companies. It represented more than 40% of the Land Bank's reserves and would have seriously compromised its already inadequate servicing of its core business – the desperate need of farmers and community farming groups for money to buy equipment and supplies. Minister Thoko Didiza claims this transaction is a normal Land Bank deal and will not investigate.

In Tony Leon's weekly online letter (July 29 2005) he reminds us that, unless we distinguish between party, business and the state, this incestuous pillaging of the state coffers will continue.

The Oilgate 'scandal reveals how the ANC has conflated and confused its party interests with the state interests and the private business interests of its leaders.

'The breakdown of the boundaries between these three spheres means corruption is slowly becoming institutionalised ... Until we have strict safeguards in place that prevent public officials from making private fortunes through the transactions of state-run companies and state financial institutions, and which also prevent high-level government officials from moving straight into top jobs in the private sector, institutionalised corruption will remain a feature of public life in SA,' Leon wrote.

The raiding of state coffers continues apace and President Thabo Mbeki's commitment to clean governance remains to be seen. His selective application of justice gives no confidence that he is serious about eradicating the scourge. To get rid of Jacob Zuma he invoked the full might of the law. The former director of the National Prosecuting Authority is called a spy and a commission overseen by Judge Joos Hefer sits for weeks trying to get to the bottom of this. An expensive commission chaired by Judge Siraj Desai investigated Jurgen Harksen and his relationship with Gerald Morkel, then mayor of Cape Town, simply so that the ANC could take over the city and find evidence to beat the Democratic Alliance in Western Cape.

The ANC has been good at setting up commissions to investigate matters that boost its own, rather than the public's, interests.

Where favoured ANC officials are alleged to be corrupt, the rule of law does not apply with equal rigour. The oil scandal implicating Deputy President Phumzile Mlambo-Ngcuka simply gets referred to the public protector, in the full knowledge that Lawrence Mushwana will never rule against her. The man should go!

The protracted parliamentary travel scandal is allowed to flounder and now the scurrilous Land Bank deal, questioned by the bank's own auditors, is swept under the carpet.

Appropriating government resources has become the raison d'être of the ANC, referred to mockingly by columnist Robert Kirby as the Association of Nepotists and Cronies. The R100 million scandal in the Bloemfontein municipality adds to the feeding frenzy that seems to gain momentum the closer we come to the end of Mbeki's tenure. The litany of irregular tender procedures in Cape Town makes a mockery of Mbeki's so-called zero tolerance of corruption.

Increasingly, institutions such as the Industrial Development Corporation and the Land Bank are used with impunity to enrich politicians and government cronies. This lack of accountability is made worse by Mbeki's reckless gift of R6 billion to dictator Robert Mugabe.

Using the most bizarre rationale, what I call African logic, Mbeki and Finance Minister Trevor Manuel's quiet diplomacy gives way to the megaphone in support of a political low-life who has systematically destroyed Zimbabwe. The illegal seizure of land, the erosion of checks and balances such as Parliament, the judiciary, the media, the opposition and the rule of law, and now Operation Murambatsvina, have qualified one of the world's worst despots for a R6 billion reward.

'Are we asked to allow people to die of hunger on our borders. Clearly we have a responsibility. It's a responsibility we take very seriously,' says Manuel.

Does he think we are stupid? Responsibility to whom, might I ask? No wonder the masses are *gatvol* and rising up all over SA.

☛ Government for the people rings hollow
Business Day June 5 2003

THE SCANDAL relating to the arms deal will not go away. Every time government tries to squash the investigation and cover its tracks, the more it rears its ugly head.

As an exercise, reading the successive headlines in the *Mail & Guardian* for the month of May 2003 alone shows that corruption is far more widespread than we think. We read in the media of its occurrence with growing frequency. Prominent political figures, ministers, senior public servants and even the president are being implicated in all kinds of deals.

First, it was Winnie Madikizela-Mandela's conviction on 43 counts of fraud and 25 counts of theft that started the ball rolling for the month. This was followed by the headline, 'Transnet rocked by R1 million bribe'. The next edition read, 'Shadow falls on Lekota', exposing the defence minister for failing to disclose his business interests in various ventures such as BZL Petroleum and Landzicht Winery.

Next in line – 'Things fall apart: Incompetence in Mpumalanga' leads to an even bolder headline inside the newspaper, 'New financial scandal in Mpumalanga', referring to the gross financial mismanagement of a province characterised by Stalinist leadership.

'Mega oil scandal rocks SA' ends the month with an even more disheartening revelation of oil deals between Nigeria and SA, the proceeds of which ended up in the Cayman Islands, instead of SA.

These serial acts of corruption point to a paralysis in the state, and a failure by Parliament and the Chapter 9 Institutions to hold government accountable to the public. While all the checks and balances are in place, these institutions have failed to oblige government to control itself. The checks and balances themselves have become suspect.

Political appointments to these institutions have compromised the integrity of these agencies and the very constitutional values upon which they have been based. The result is a deeply suspicious public that no longer trusts them. I don't.

Found wanting, the offices of the auditor-general and the public protector cannot be relied upon to do the job, not to mention the national public prosecuting authority.

Set up to strengthen constitutional democracy, the Chapter 9 Institutions and other relevant state organs are obliged to be independent of government, and subject only to the constitution and the law.

Government has no right to interfere with them and they are obliged to be 'impartial and (to) exercise their powers and perform their functions without fear, favour or prejudice'.

These provisions demand we strike a balance at all times between effective government on the one hand, and accountable government on the other hand. Parliament's duty is to oblige government to control itself, but when we have a two-thirds majority in Parliament and a speaker that belongs to the ruling party, our confidence wanes.

The weakening of the standing public accounts committee, and the marginalisation of all the MPs who insisted on being independent of party influences, have further fuelled suspicion that suppression of the truth is more important than accounting to the public how its finances have been prioritised.

It is said, every nation has the government it deserves. South Africans, black South Africans, in particular, don't deserve the government we currently have. Having been denied democracy and basic human rights for almost a century, what we now deserve is a government that will distribute resources more equitably and uphold the promises that ushered it into power, justice, transparency, and accountability.

Instead, to quote the late US journalist and critic Henry Mencken, our 'government is (increasingly) becoming a broker in pillage, and every election is a sort of advance auction in stolen goods'.

The spoils are distributed to the inner circle and black economic empowerment is nothing but a euphemism for looting state coffers and entrenching loyalists in the structures.

After decades of resistance to oppression, South Africans now deserve a government that puts its citizens first.

Society pays the price for neglecting prison reform
Business Day August 30 2002

THE CONTROVERSIAL presidential pardon of Dumisane Ncamazana and the Jali commission hearings have highlighted an issue that is often ignored by the criminal justice system. That is the problem of recidivism.

Dumisane has a track record for murder like no other. Before 1994 he was found guilty of going on a shooting spree, and of having later escaped from jail. The Truth Commission with the support of the police and correctional services rightly denied him amnesty on some grounds. His status as a political prisoner is at best dubious, as a killer, not. On those grounds alone, he should not have been pardoned.

The justice minister cannot say that there is no way of predicting that he or any other prisoner with a serious criminal record would do it again. The high rate of recidivism among SA offenders is common knowledge and borne out by statistics. Many South Africans are victims of recidivists. More than 50% of convicted offenders return to jail after a previous sentence.

As human rights commissioner I had to monitor a search in 1997 for hand grenades. One of the gang leaders at the time planned a revenge killing in Pollsmoor Prison, and had smuggled weapons into jail for this purpose. The prison authorities went on the offensive and all of us were alerted to the sophistication with which these crimes are planned in prison.

The hearings at the Jali commission reveal that SA prisons are dens of iniquity. It is for this reason that the Human Rights Commission prioritised an investigation into the prisons, as one of its first projects. Even though this report did not see the light of day for months thereafter, it did finally come up with findings and recommendations that went unheeded.

I am prepared to bet that the Jali commission findings will concur with the reports of the rights commission. These recommendations were, however, simply ignored, and now the chickens have come home to roost – with a vengeance.

As commissioner responsible for Northern and Western Cape I investigated about fifteen prisons in 1997 and wrote reports on each of them, which I submitted to the rights commission as part of the overall investigation into prisons.

My office also conducted investigations into two mass assaults of prisoners at the maximum security prisons of Pollsmoor and Helderstroom. Our reports prompted an official inquiry into the events at Pollsmoor in particular, conducted by advocates Motata and Kotsi in 1997.

Their findings concurred with observations I had made in my reports. They found that prisons were overcrowded and understaffed; that drug trafficking was the order of the day; that gangsterism was rife in prison, with networks extending into the townships; that staff smuggled drugs to inmates; that warders were routinely bribed; that some warders were drunk on the job; that warders flouted security measures; that inhumane conditions stifled creative management practices; that rehabilitation was either insufficient or nonexistent; and that prisoners were locked away from 2.30pm onwards without evening meals.

In my reports I raised additional concerns: that the rape of initiates and juveniles was a common practice; that money circulated freely in the prisons; that gangs such as the Hard Livings, the American Boys, the Sexy Boys, 26s, 28s, the Royal Airforce have operated in tandem with outside gangs from time immemorial; and that many prisoners lived under inhumane and unacceptable conditions in overcrowded cells.

An old refrain from prisoners was that their inhumane treatment in prison warranted them taking revenge on society when they left prison. Under these circumstances, the high rates of recidivism are perfectly understandable. Crime in prison is a way of life and very often a struggle for survival.

Had Motata's list of recommendations been taken seriously by the prison authorities, it would have obviated a need for the Jali commission today.

The challenge for government is to break this cycle of violence and to seek ways to transform prisons into places that prepare offenders for reintegration into society. Presidential pardons are not the answer and should be used with discretion.

The old adage, that the state of a country's prisons is a reflection of its democracy, is rapidly becoming a reality in SA.

I hope Correctional Services Minister Ben Skosana will rise to the challenge and act on the Jali commission's recommendations, and all the preceding recommendations, and transform our prisons for the common good.

They may kiss babies, but beware

The Sowetan April 28 1999

POLITICIANS are extremely friendly and articulate, especially at election time – qualities that dissipate soon after the election. This nauseating upsurge of friendliness, inspired more by the possibility of easy procurement of salary than by any commitment to serve the electorate, should be treated with the suspicion it deserves.

We should be wary of politicians who suddenly kiss babies and the elderly but whose welfare policies are against this sector of society; politicians who shake hands with all and sundry but refuse to meet with those who request meetings; politicians who stride smiling into shopping malls but who are inaccessible at crucial times; politicians who visit squatter camps and the rural areas but who are never seen again until the next election; and politicians who woo women voters but who are intrinsically sexist. Politicians should be subjected to close scrutiny before we decide to vote for them. Elections should be taken seriously because it's the most crucial opportunity given to the electorate to hold politicians accountable. It is the clarion call for the electorate to exercise their democratic right to assess government performance and to make choices.

On balance, many politicians are found wanting so the electorate should look at the different parties' manifestoes to see how they hope to address human rights concerns. The AIDS epidemic, sexual violence against women and children, crime, job creation, unemployment, health care and housing are key indicators of measurement. Ask politicians to give concrete proposals how and in what time period they will address these concerns and judge them accordingly.

Here are some pointers:

South Africa is the rape capital of the world. The statistics indicate a steady increase in gender-based violence despite the existence of very progressive laws, a Gender Commission, a Human Rights Commission, an Office on the Status of Women and 25 percent women parliamentarians. According to the 'Human Rights Watch Report' police receive about 32 107 rape reports annually but for every rape reported it is estimated that twenty to 39 more are unreported. Women should therefore insist upon better services to transform the police and police stations, the courts and medical care.

Ask the politicians what they will do to bring down the incident of rape over the next two years; ask them how they would ensure that rapists remain behind bars; ask what treatment (both medical and psychological) will be available to survivors and ask how they will hold the commissions accountable in establishing a human rights culture. Most notably this would require commissioners to leave their plush offices and engage in boots-on activism. Politicians need to monitor police stations, district-surgeon clinics and hospitals, agitate for more sexual offences courts and propose a more holistic approach to crime-prevention. If they don't, then they don't deserve your vote!

Not one party has a holistic approach to the AIDS epidemic. This is scandalous in view of the millions of South Africans already infected and with as many as 1 500 new infections occurring daily. A third of pregnant women who are HIV positive will give birth to HIV-infected children. One third of these will die in their first year. With 29 deaths per 1 000 births, we need to ask why government has not done more to prevent and control the disease. AZT treatment is not made available to pregnant mothers despite reliable medical opinion that it prevents mother-to-child transmission. The epidemic has enormous implications for our nation's future health as well as for the economics of the country. Unless parties spell out their plan of action to deal with the AIDS epidemic, do not vote for them.

Unemployment has increased dramatically in the last five years despite government's job creation proposals. The Growth Employment and Redistribution (Gear) policy predicted an increase in formal employment – from 1.3 percent in 1998 to 4.3 percent in 2000 – but in reality there has been a steady decline in formal sector employment. The latest census reveals that the total number of people employed in the formal economy fell by 5.2 million between June 1996 and June 1997. It is important to ask the politicians what their party's policies on job creation are.

As for crime, one gets a sense that some politicians gloat over the high levels of crime. It seems to be the only area in which they are in agreement with the electorate over quick-fix-solutions, namely amputation, vigilantism, and the death penalty. The call by some parties for a referendum on the death penalty is gross political opportunism, inspired by votes rather than by a genuine concern to improve the criminal justice system.

The clamour for the death penalty is making for some strange political bedfellows. These parties, despite their divergent political positions, are inspired by populist sentiments for retribution rather than justice. Calls for the death penalty give the mistaken impression that there is a seriousness about addressing crime which diverts attention from the more complex measures needed to address crime.

Given police ineptitude, the low (20%) conviction rate and the regularity of prison escapes, the public should seek more urgent, appropriate and proactive measures from politicians to deal with crime. How does one apply the death sentence to 80% of offenders who are not caught? Candidates for the gallows are alarmingly high given that 20 000 people on average are murdered annually. Even if we manage to convict 50% of those guilty of capital offences, there is no way the state would execute 10 000 of its citizens annually. It may as well open a human abattoir.

Clearly the emphasis should be elsewhere. Many murderers and rapists are going scot-free because investigators do not prepare evidence properly, because prosecutors are overworked and courts understaffed, and because prisons are overcrowded with thousands of awaiting-trial prisoners. Ask political parties for concrete solutions and insist upon visible evidence that crime is being reduced, controlled, prevented and combated. Insist on speedy convictions, refusal of bail to rapists, hijackers and murderers, proper investigations and empathetic services to victims. If these issues cannot be addressed constructively, dump the party.

Don't vote for those who make promises but who have a track record of non-delivery. Don't vote for parties who call for the death penalty; they will invariably support differential treatment for different races and classes of offenders. Don't vote for those who are against corruption but who do not suspend those close to them who are corrupt. Don't vote for those who feel entitled to big salaries but never volunteer to take a cut in salary or live simply so that others can simply live. Vote for a clean, accountable and transparent government which will give priority to the needs of black women, children and the poor.

Media (Media Meekness)

☛ Dumbed-down SABC still its ANC master's voice
Business Day April 19 2007

THIS PAST WEEKEND, SAfm's news bulletins unashamedly promoted the African National Congress (ANC), giving it excessive airtime compared with other political parties.

The first news item, for example, reported at length on President Thabo Mbeki's Gauteng *imbizo* and his well-meaning but ineffectual promises to the residents of Soweto. This was hardly news, but then it was followed by the deputy president's inane comments on something or other, at which point I switched off the radio.

I got to my office on Monday and the first e-mail was from a journalist expressing her outrage at Jeremy Maggs' interview with Snuki Zikalala on *Media SAfm*, the latter proudly extolling his plans to set up a special news bureau for Africa to counter what he considers the un-African myths of the BBC, CNN and Al-Jazeera.

This interview was preceded by an even worse one, between Movement for Democratic Change leader Morgan Tsvangirai and Tsepiso Makwetla, who obviously reserves her venom for people she perceives to be ANC antagonists. Under her direction, *The Editors* has reached rock bottom, with her agenda as transparent as her lack of expertise.

It occurred to me that the Sisulu commission of inquiry into the allegations of blacklisting achieved very little, if anything at all.

Even after a series of public outcries against the SABC's open political bias, CEO Dali Mpofu's chip-on-the-shoulder comments in response to the commission's report inspire no confidence whatsoever: "This battle is not about one or other commentator or a "blacklist" or Zikalala. It is about wresting control of the SABC, of the hearts and minds and ultimately, of the country, from us barbarians . . . It is over for good. The savage natives are in charge and democratically so.'

Indeed. The evidence that the barbarians are in charge, desperate to control the minds of the masses, is writ large on the SABC's screens and radios. The endless talk shows with their mediocre content are increasingly relying on an ignorant public for their *raison d'être*.

When the state contributes to the national dumbing down of the public and uses its media to keep the public ignorant, it shouldn't be surprised when the public riots in reaction to poor service delivery; it shouldn't be surprised when we fail to transform male behaviour in curbing HIV/AIDS; nor should it be surprised when the ANC rank and file votes against Mbeki, as happened at the previous national general council meeting.

The SABC is just another cog in the national dumbing-down machine.

The looming presidential succession battle will make matters worse and the prospect of being force-fed propaganda until the next election is simply too ghastly to contemplate.

Since June 15 last year, when I wrote at length about the high attrition rate of good journalists at the SABC and its biased and selective reporting; and Anton Harber's subsequent column on October 11 2006, in which he hoped that the commission's recommendations would see some heads roll, nothing has improved.

Viewers and listeners continue to be subjected to semiliterate, young and inexperienced presenters and commentators who do not even understand the text that they read.

Last Friday, for example, *Morning Live* on SABC 2 yielded another idiotic cameo. Reporting on the Paul Wolfowitz 'scandal' at the World Bank, the presenter concluded that this was why transformation of the World Bank was urgent, as though the one issue had anything to do with the other.

If one measures transformation by nepotism, then our government is seriously untransformed.

I quote a most unlikely source, Marthinus van Schalkwyk, former premier of Western Cape, when he made a submission to the SABC in 2003 on its draft editorial policy:

'The SABC, as our public broadcaster, has the potential to be the single most important instrument of positive change, nation-building, education and development. Equally, it has unmatched potential to discriminate, misinform, indoctrinate, and polarise our people. The thin dividing line between these two pictures is the quality, substance, and implementation of the SABC's editorial policies.'

I quote him because as a former National Party stalwart involved in undercover politics he knows what it is for the public broadcaster to be abused by the ruling party because his former party has been there and done that.

☞ Now the media thinks it can silence 'whingers'
Business Day July 13 2006

THREE recent editorials stick in my craw. 'Avoid political point-scoring on crime' screams the headline in the *Financial Mail* (July 7 2006).

'The debate about crime ... has, in some quarters, gained unusefully hysterical proportions with the fearful and pessimistic haplessly combining their efforts ... The police can be forgiven for wondering sometimes whose side the scaremongers are on' (*Weekend Argus* July 8 2006).

Similarly, the editorial in *The Sunday Independent* (July 9 2006) is almost apologetic that one of our literary notables, André Brink, has written about his family's close shave with crime. Lest we all sink into despair, it is quick to point out we should not forget 'what a wonderful country we are' with our booming economy, having just recently emerged from the brink of civil war.

Having a burgeoning economy and a great constitution mean nothing when we are forced to be prisoners in our own homes, locked up behind security gates and alarms while big, burly male politicians walk about with bodyguards, telling us not to whinge.

Now the president too has warned 2010 sceptics that he, according to the *Cape Times* (July 10 2006): 'would confront those who consider it their "permanent job" to paint a negative image of the country.' No, Mr President – we are not painting a negative image; your colleagues in the cabinet are giving even 'negative image' a bad name! Few in your cabinet can do their jobs, and if you want our support then fire some of them and appoint others who can.

Why does the media think it is its duty to muzzle us and opposition politicians, as though only it has a right to criticise? When so many of us are affected deeply by crime, losing loved ones and breadwinners, no one, not even the president or the minister, has the right to tell us to shut up. When travelling along the N2 freeway becomes life threatening, we have a right to moan or march them out of office until our right to freedom and security of the person is met.

Being a woman in this country is life threatening, despite the president's lip service to gender equality. Women and girl children constantly have to look over their shoulders. What troubles me most is how we acquiesce to being bullied by incompetent politicians using the state's resources to enrich and entitle themselves when they have nothing to offer and cannot deliver even the most basic of services.

If we can claim to host the 2010 World Cup, then we can do something drastic to reduce the horrendous levels of crime. If Eskom can deliver energy-saving bulbs and gas stoves to the nation, then government can deliver antiretroviral medicines to the millions who need them. SA is adept at showing off its prowess to the world when it comes to international events. But when it comes to looking after its own citizens, it fails miserably.

We are a gullible nation. We allow politicians to treat us like dirt, and that is why they have no respect for us, the citizenry. In Cape Town, Western Cape Community Safety MEC Leonard Ramatlakane promised 24-hour patrols on the N2 to prevent more of the fatal stone-throwing we have had over the past month. But to date there is no visible policing and the province is blaming the city for not coming to the party.

In the same vein, more than 40 babies have died from *Klebsiella* in KwaZulu-Natal over the past three years, Xhosa initiates are dying of botched circumcisions, yet Health Minister Manto Tshabalala-Msimang adorns the pages of the *Financial Mail* as one our most influential women in the country. Influential *se voet*!

She is an embarrassment and deserves the Spanish Inquisition or, to quote commentator William Saunderson-Meyer, do we need to wait for ministers to die before they get fired? Why do we, the public, not start a civil disobedience campaign against the likes of ministers Charles Nqakula and Tshabalala-Msimang?

A journalist friend of mine suggested that we block the N2 until the police do something about the stonings that threaten Capetonians. On Monday, Ramatlakane's spokesman, Makhaya Mani, admitted they were not capable of preventing stonings on the N2, and complained that our expectations were too high – yet we want to host 2010.

The problem is: our expectations are not high enough, if the media is anything to go by.

To revert to my opening quotes – there are many editors and journalists, mostly white, who find it difficult to criticise incompetent ANC ministers unconditionally. When they do, they have to cast aspersions on the opposition or white people who, according to them, invariably criticise 'to score points', or who are 'unusefully hysterical', or who 'with the fearful and pessimistic haplessly combine' forces to trash government for their own ends. Increasingly, it is becoming dangerous to be right when government is wrong, as Voltaire warned a long time ago, yet the media keeps putting brakes on our right to be right instead of encouraging us to be bold about our civic rights.

The local media needs basic lessons in democracy, one of which is its duty to hold government accountable. This central function it holds in tandem with the opposition. A former Canadian prime minister, John Diefenbaker, reminds us that the role of opposition in democracies is manifold: 'Opposition must ask questions, extract information and cross-examine the executive. The opposition must expose flaws in government policy and seek to influence policy in the interests of the general public or of its particular constituency. The opposition provides voters with choices by offering alternative policies, promoting different ideas and visions, and proposing different political leaders. The opposition must monitor and promote the effectiveness of checks and balances on government power and, by so doing, defend the rights of minority groups against power abuse by the majority. The opposition must constantly seek to increase its support so as to be prepared to become the alternative government' (*Opposing Voices*, pages 120-129).

The taxpaying public has a right to moan when government fails to deliver or abuses taxpayers' money. We have a right to demonstrate and picket peacefully and to present petitions until government can no longer stand us. We even have a right to expect the media to assist in this regard!

☛ Journalists also close ranks

Business Day September 25 2003

JOURNALISTS do not differ in any way from politicians when it comes to silent diplomacy about those who, in their own ranks, transgress accepted ethical codes.

This is not new. One of the Pahads was quoted in a Sunday paper recently as saying journalists, like lawyers and doctors, close ranks to cover up malpractice by their peers.

Nowhere was this more obvious than Allister Sparks' commentary in his book, *Beyond the Miracle*. To illustrate his point that blacks are increasingly abusing the practice of accusing whites of racism to divert justified criticism, he cites the Helena Dolny case.

'In its most striking instance, this weapon was used to destroy the career of ... Helena Dolny ... an agricultural economist whom Mandela appointed to head the Land Bank and transform it into an institution that would help re-establish a black agricultural class ...

'Dolny was tackling her job with a passionate commitment when out of the blue in May 1999 the chairman-designate of the bank, one Bonile Jack, wrote a letter to president-in-waiting Thabo Mbeki, with a copy deliberately slipped to *The Star* newspaper, accusing her of "racism, nepotism and mismanagement". A judge later found the allegations to be "defamatory and baseless", but after six gruelling months of public traducement (in) which it became clear this was part of an orchestrated campaign to squeeze her out of her job, Dolny resigned in despair.

'Three years later *The Star* published a front-page apology to Dolny in which it acknowledged the statements it published about her were not true. But the damage was done – to herself and the country.' *The Star*, in the apology cited (published on the eve of Dolny's pending libel suit) was as culpable of a cover-up because it failed to mention the name of the person who had misused his media influence to viciously prosecute a palpably false case against Dolny.

As a result of this apology Dolny did not proceed with the case.

Business Day, while it had the courage, at the time, to question and criticise the falsehoods being communicated in a clear campaign to unjustifiably besmirch Dolny, also refrained from outing the person who, along with Bonile Jack, was jointly responsible for executing what it quite justifiably described as an 'anti-Dolny vendetta'.

The *Mail & Guardian*, while raising the same concerns, was also party to the cover-up. The journalist referred to was Prince Hamnca and the senior who guided him was Mathatha Tsedu, who now holds the most influential post in SA's newspapers – as *Sunday Times* editor.

Ethical journalism's most fundamental rule is *audi alterem partem* (tell both sides) and, as Dolny reveals in her book, *Banking on Change* (Viking, 2001) the deliberate negation of this rule defined the parameters of her subsequent vilification: '*The Star* cast their reportage of events in the most unfavourable light possible, and moreover chose to limit their coverage when there were facts to be reported that were in my favour. The positive parts of the Katz report were largely ignored; Judge Coetzee's verdict at the High Court got but a few lines on page two, compared to comprehensive coverage in other dailies such as *The Citizen* and *Business Day*.'

In the most recent issue of the *Sunday Times*, Tsedu cites his journalistic ideals as the reason why he did not run a story – provided for the paper by its reporter, Ranjeni Munusamy – on the fact the national director of public prosecutions, Bulelani Ngcuka, was being investigated as a possible apartheid-era spy. He said a newspaper had to ask whether publication was in the public interest. What a pity he did not aspire to the same lofty ideals when he chose to run with the false information given to him by Jack.

Could the difference be Dolny was a white woman with no great influence in the African National Congress whereas Ngcuka is just the opposite? In her book, Dolny asks much the same question.

The recent failure of local newspaper journalists – with the honourable exception of Robert Kirby and David Bullard – to condemn the repeated plagiarism of Darrel Bristow-Bovey, simply reinforces my point.

☛ 'Consensus politics' just a way to silence dissenters?
Business Day May 27 2004

IMMEDIATELY after President Thabo Mbeki's optimistic state of the nation address, the cameras of the South African Broadcasting Corporation (SABC) switched to opposition leaders for comments.

Presenters Kim Cloete, Clayson Monyele and Vuto Mvoko presented a carefully choreographed line-up, giving ample time to each party leader to express his or her views, except for the leader of the official Democratic Alliance (DA) opposition.

Tony Leon was positioned neatly next to Kgalema Motlanthe, the African National Congress (ANC) secretary-general, giving the impression that Leon was elevated to his rightful place.

However, the agenda behind this juxtaposition with Motlanthe soon became clear: Mvoko was going to manage Leon's comments to his liking. Surely, Motlanthe did not need to be there to reinforce what Mbeki had just said for an hour? It was important to hear Leon's views without the intervention of three SABC announcers, junior soccer players, and so on. Was this intended to restrict Leon's time and minimise what he had to say?

Why do the media fear someone they repeatedly dismiss as a political lightweight? Leon must surely be a force to be reckoned with – how else do we explain the SABC's partial treatment of him? Why don't they allow the public to hear Leon's views uninterrupted?

Need I remind the SABC that the ANC gained a two-third majority vote with its help. The state broadcaster can now relax and be more even-handed with Leon. Or was Mvoko's final question to Leon: 'And what about consensus politics?' a euphemism for, 'Will you shut up in future?'

Disappointingly, Patricia de Lille, leader of the Independent Democrats, sings the same tired song. From someone whose claim to fame is to stir shit, this refrain is hardly convincing. Support for constructive, as opposed to destructive, criticism seems to be her new slogan, implying the DA is a proponent of the latter.

De Lille should know by now that one person's destructive criticism is music to another's ears. And who, for that matter, determines what is destructive or constructive? While a general consensus might mean all parties agree, it should be remembered that agreement is not necessarily the same as the truth.

Consensus politics has its place, and has had its place in our history. The constitution is the result of consensus battered out at the Convention for Democracy in SA. With the basics in place, SA should allow and manage its pluralism in all its diversity, in line with constitutional values.

It is the task of Parliament, of the opposition, of the media, of business and civil society to hold government accountable, especially with its firmly entrenched majority. Since the ANC has the support of the entire media and controls most state institutions, consensus politics is hardly the only way to go.

Can we imagine a state where we all agree with Health Minister Manto Tshabalala-Msimang's handling of the HIV/AIDS pandemic? Where we all support the president on his views that HIV does not cause AIDS?

Where we all agree that R60 billion should be spent on arms? Where we all agree Jean-Bertrand Aristide should live on our taxes? Where we all agree we should provide Zimbabwe with electricity regardless of how President Robert Mugabe spends money? Where we all agree with Black Economic Enrichment?

History is replete with political leaders and parties who silenced dissent and ruthlessly crushed opposition under the guise of consensus politics. Hilda Bernstein realised late in life that Stalinism was wrong. In her book, *A Life of One's Own*, she admits with great difficulty that where Soviet leader Josef Stalin's followers failed, was to notice tendencies early on in his rule that would later lead to their demise. 'Stalin's strengths lay in his rigid management of the party machine that controlled appointments to key posts ... he gathered round himself a body of faithful henchmen whose political fortunes were linked with his and who owed him unquestionable personal allegiance.'

His vanity demanded 'absolute obedience and recognition of infallibility. He would permit no covert criticism, and no expression of dissent was allowed to appear in the party press or journals,' she wrote.

I would sooner live in a robust, vibrant democracy than in a polity based on consensus where the ruling party reigns and remains supreme. Those who fear criticism should be feared.

☛ Smug white journalists strangers to democracy
Business Day January 26 2006

THE SABC no longer apologises for its blatant promotion of the African National Congress (ANC) almost every night on its various news bulletins, flashing the ANC's logo and flag more than any news item on its agenda.

The recent complaint of unfair treatment by the Democratic Alliance (DA) elicited the following response from SABC group CE Dali Mpofu: 'Equitable coverage does not mean we give every party the same amount of minutes and seconds,' claiming it was absurd to give the same treatment to all 98 registered parties (*Sunday Times* January 22 2006).

The notion that the majority party should be given coverage in proportion to its votes is the kind of nonsense that inspires tyranny and perpetuates the idea that those in power should be given more power to keep them in power. There should be a rule that no journalist or editor should practise journalism unless they treat all political parties evenhandedly, especially during elections.

On December 27 2005, driving back to Cape Town from my holiday, I was shocked to hear a debate being fuelled on whether or not we should do away with the notion of 'official opposition'. The debate is scheduled for the parliamentary rules committee soon, and one would think that at least a spokesman from the affected party would have been invited to participate in the debate. But the sole spokesman was Corné Mulder, fuelling the Anglo-Boer war as only the Freedom Front knows how to do, happily inciting divide-and-rule politics.

Despite repeated calls from listeners that this is yet another measure to dilute opposition, Mulder repeated the claim that Tony Leon has no right to speak on behalf of the opposition – as though he has ever done so. As far as I know Leon has never spoken on behalf of other opposition parties but the DA. To do that would be absurd – the variety and range are such that one cannot speak on behalf of all of them.

The media has a duty to promote democracy. But its partisanship undermines rather than consolidates the democracy we still enjoy. A piece in the *Sunday Times* (January 15 2006), condemning Deputy President Phumzile Mlambo-Ngcuka for her pricey holiday at taxpayers' expense, is a prime example of the partisanship I have come to despise in the media. While everybody uses the information they get from the DA for their own ends and to sell newspapers, they despise that very party for doing its job properly.

'Repeatedly, the opposition party brings to light matters of importance, only to drown them in an overkill of blame and self-congratulation.

Douglas Gibson ... chief whip and terrier, appeared on national television this week. His smugness, coupled with his characteristically irrelevant and malevolent chirp that Bulelani Ngcuka is wealthy enough to foot the Abu Dhabi trip, inspires a solution' (*The Sunday Independent* January 15 2006).

There is nothing more irritating than smug white journalists who call the opposition smug, yet they alone claim the right to criticise. What journalists in SA need is a basic course in Politics 101. One journalist on SAfm last Sunday commented that it was a pity Mlambo-Ngcuka had made this faux pas given her standing with the business community, hoping this incident 'does not take away from what she has done'. He seems to forget she became deputy president with the scandals of the diamond tiara and the Imvume-PetroSA oil saga hanging around her neck. Her holiday in the United Arab Emirates is just more of the same. Her appointment turns out to be a poisoned chalice.

To say the president's office should clarify the rules regarding perks is to avoid the nub of what is at stake here. The ANC has been very adept at adopting rules to accommodate its undemocratic inclinations and it will easily make rules that allow it access to state resources at will, as exemplified by Jacob Zuma's excessive use of state air travel for his private use when he was in office.

What the media needs to call for unequivocally is the resignation of public officials who enrich themselves at taxpayers' expense and who misappropriate funds for their own purposes no matter how small. And Murphy Morobe's unforgivable gaffe, that R700 000 is 'a drop in the ocean', demonstrates exactly what the ANC is all about – R700 000, R1 million or R5 million are no longer big amounts. When ruling parties like the ANC become used to enjoying the state's largesse, and stealing large amounts of money, R1 million no longer seems much. Lest we forget, between Frederick Chiluba, Daniel Arap Moi, Mobuto Sese Seko, Robert Mugabe and Sani Abacha, Africa could have written off its own debt a long time ago, instead of depending on the west they so despise.

☛ *'Ja baas'* media shirks uncomfortable questions
Business Day September 16 2004

IN THE 'Thick End of the Wedge' (*Business Day* September 13 2004), Peter Bruce takes on President Thabo Mbeki for lashing out unfairly against Anglo American CE Tony Trahar. Why the sensitivity, he asks, or is this yet another attempt to silence critics? Such courage among editors is rare, even though Bruce merely did what editors are supposed to do: ask the uncomfortable questions comfortably.

Editors wield power, and they know it, hence the need to be responsible. Many of them are master manipulators of the pen and of the truth. Mondli Makhanya's column in the *Sunday Times* (September 5 2004), 'Whites must come on board', is a case in point.

He writes about the racism of Hestrie Cloete's family and claims that this growing negativity among whites, symptomatic of them having lost power, is the responsibility of Tony Leon and is his alone, as leader of the opposition. Like Moses, Leon's calling is to lead 'the likes of Hestrie Cloete's family out of the laager and into the transformed SA'.

And since the Democratic Alliance leadership has 'served only to echo the fears and anxieties of those in the white community who feel uncomfortable about the change going on around them', they, more than any other party, owe it to the nation.

According to Makhanya, to criticise Marthinus van Schalkwyk's opportunism is nothing less than destructive politics above which Leon is instructed to rise. Such crass, racist generalisations are best left to John Perlman's callers, not the editor of a leading paper.

If ever any column defies logic, it is this one by Makhanya. It is also deeply racist. To dismiss white people's disquiet over affirmative action, black economic empowerment and corruption as racist responses to a previously comfortable lifestyle, as though blacks are not equally perturbed by these things, is simplistic to say the least. Equally, to place the burden on Leon to help build a unified nation – nation building being part of 'the South African project' – as though it is his job alone, is simply ludicrous.

This quest for 'nationhood' is often a euphemism for national consensus, and national conformity. This is the kind of behaviour PW Botha, under the state security council, created in a volk that said *'ja baas, nee baas'* for almost 50 years! Is this what Makhanya wants?

Will Makhanya tell me what the difference is between black people cheering for Robert Mugabe and white people calling blacks kaffirs?

While eloquent analysis is often found to explain black support for black dictators, white racists are never afforded the same privilege.

If the fourth estate remains as lily-livered and as equivocal as demonstrated by Makhanya's column, we are all doomed to politically docile and ineffectual opposition, as everywhere in Africa. The constant need to racialise and discredit opposition in this irresponsible way has more to do with the hang-ups and vested interests of editors and journalists who do more to assist the ruling party in entrenching their hegemony, than to cultivate a healthy climate of debate.

The way they package news and use language to undermine people they do not like (yes, it is often personal) has become extremely transparent. In *The Sunday Independent* of September 5 2004, for example, Leon wrote a most interesting commentary of the floor-crossing saga that should have made headlines, given the pertinence of the topic at the time. It contained astounding facts, which were conveniently underplayed by the media. For example, he pointed out that:

- The *Washington Post*-Kaiser Foundation survey found that two-thirds of South Africans disapproved of floor-crossing;
- The African National Congress (ANC) retained the salaries of the New National Party (NNP) councillors who crossed to it, their salaries being at least twice what an ordinary councillor would earn;
- The ANC was able to hold the threat of losing these salaries and perks of office above the heads of NNP office-holders. Some of these posts were actually created by the ANC after the first round of floor-crossing – to reward NNP councillors who had left the DA.

Leon's punch line, that this 'amounted to a legal form of bribery at the taxpayers' expense', turning 'councillors from public servants into political mercenaries', got lost, stuck as it was in some insignificant corner of the paper.

And so it is in this vein that the media contribute to the creation of consensus politics.

☛ Embedded scribes grovel to new elite
Business Day July 17 2003

WHO THE HELL are these Yankees denying us the right in our own country to report on their president's visit, complain John Battersby and S'thembiso Msomi in last week's Sunday papers, not in those words, of course.

'I realised that it was possible to be a stranger in your own country,' moans the deeply affronted Battersby in *The Sunday Independent*, clearly peeved at how the US press corps controlled journalists' admission to this media event.

Rightly, he condemns what he suspects to be a complete manipulation by the US media of President George Bush's trip to Africa and concludes with an uncharacteristically rare insight.

'I began to understand why the gulf between US perceptions of themselves and the rest of the world, on the one hand, and the perceptions of the rest of the world of the US, is such a gaping chasm. There is almost no point of reference between the two world views. This week I discovered what a crucial role the White House press machine plays in maintaining US hegemony.'

'My first whiff that my journalistic freedoms were about to be curtailed' are words that resonate with my experiences of the media in SA. Unaware that he and his cronies at Independent Newspapers and the SABC are fast being considered the very embedded journalists that he is warning us about, he pontificates at length about US arrogance.

The SA media have been so conspicuously partial to the ruling party that their role in entrenching the hegemony of government is taken for granted. My freedom to objective reporting has been so severely curtailed by sycophantic journalists that I have developed the same queasy feelings I had when the National Party controlled the airwaves.

When Bush endorsed President Thabo Mbeki's silent diplomacy on Zimbabwe, calling him a 'point man' and 'honest broker', our reporters hailed this uncritically as a major victory for Mbeki instead of condemning them both for disappointing the people of Zimbabwe.

As I write this column I am watching *Dateline* on BBC after midnight. Bush, the UK's Tony Blair, and Mbeki are subjected to the merciless scalpel of the highest calibre of international editors who question their doublespeak.

There was no beating about the bush, as vital questions were raised about 'doctored evidence' justifying the invasion of Iraq, the gaffes by Blair's press secretary Alastair Campbell, and Mbeki's acquiescence to the tyranny of Zimbabwean President Robert Mugabe.

This is the robust journalism we are being denied in SA. Those grovelling interviews with Mbeki in the past few years that make one cringe, come to mind. The recent interview by Phil Molefe with Mugabe, those hollow drumbeats of the numerous African summits by Miranda Strydom, and those diatribes by Ranjeni Munusamy, are exactly what I am referring to, not to mention that famed *imbongi* Snuki Zikalala. If these have not contributed to entrenching the hegemony of the ruling elite, then I don't know.

The axing of CNN and scheduling of BBC late at night are intended furthermore to deny us international opinion on global matters, unless one has DStv.

With regards to the SABC, it is very difficult to respect a board when it is so openly partial to the ruling party. How can I trust the SABC when a senior member denounces objectivity as a key element in journalistic endeavour? How can I believe SABC policy on editorial independence when upward referral is entrenched in its policy? The broadcaster is not to be trusted. It is not what is being said, but how what is said is packaged.

Tawane Kupe (*Sunday Times*, July 13 2003), in pointing to the furore raging between Campbell and the BBC, alerts us to the dangers when a public broadcaster compromises its editorial independence in favour of the ruling party. Campbell's storming of Channel 4 news to give his side of the story would be unthinkable in SA. Can one imagine Joel Netshitenzhe storming an SABC3 news bulletin in like manner, muses Kupe, forgetting that government's self-elected generals are already doing their national duty for volk and *vaderland*.

Afrikaans press carries torch of brave journalism
Business Day October 14 2004

BUSINESS DAY'S David Gleason has fought a somewhat lonely battle against the manifest iniquities of black economic empowerment. Along the way he has had to endure Saki Macozoma's outrageous and libellous slur that he was 'against democracy', and the tepid sneers of columnists who routinely and predictably accuse those with whom they differ of racism.

But I was delighted, on returning from a brief trip abroad, to find that reasoned debate on this issue had found some resonance within the trade unions and the African National Congress (ANC) as articulated recently, first by Finance Minister Trevor Manuel and then by secretary-general Kgalema Motlanthe.

Gleason's honourable discharge of his professional obligations brought to mind a speech made by Naspers chairman Ton Vosloo to the Cape Town Press Club recently. He said that, unlike the Independent Group, for example, the Afrikaans press was not beholden to overseas owners and was thus less constrained.

Some have criticised his speech as self-serving. It affirmed my own belief, however, that the torch of courageous, crusading journalism carried by many from Thomas Pringle to Percy Qoboza, Donald Woods, Max du Preez and Martin Welz, among others, has been dropped, with a few honourable exceptions, by the English press and picked up by Afrikaans newspapers.

This is ironic, as there was a time when the Afrikaans press saw itself as indivisible from the National Party in what it and PW Botha saw as its joint struggle against the 'total onslaught'.

In comparison, the English press, once so strident in its morally justifiable fight against apartheid, seems – now with that enemy defeated – to have muted its voice and lost what should be its focus.

An example: *Die Burger* recently (September 29 2004) carried a front-page lead, an editorial, a column by its political reporter, and a cartoon on a story that, by any standards, was newsworthy. It concerned two black student pilots at the Air Force Langebaanweg training school, 90 minutes from Cape Town.

Fighter pilots carry enormous responsibilities, flying multimillion-rand aircraft that, as numerous tragedies in the past few decades have shown, can in a split second sow havoc among civilians. The selection process is accordingly and justifiably stringent and rigorous, and the norm in military flying schools around the world is that if students fail even a single exam, they are immediately disqualified.

At Langebaanweg, however, the two black aspirant pilots were, despite repeated failures, allowed to continue flying, and the examiners who had failed them were, predictably, accused of racism.

The result, fortunately not tragically, was that one of them wrote off his multimillion-rand Pilatus PC-5 on landing and the other badly damaged his, also while landing. This is affirmative action gone mad, but of the other two newspapers in Cape Town, both belonging to Tony O'Reilly's Independent Group, the *Cape Argus* carried a few paragraphs buried in the middle of the paper and the *Cape Times* ignored it.

When affirmative action is seen as incompatible with merit, skills and qualification, with the criterion of race or gender central, the outcome is often disastrous. Imagine a developing country like ours littered with underqualified doctors, engineers, mechanics, pilots and judges?

These papers, when the possibility exists of showing either blacks as the victims of white racism or the opposition in a bad light, throw all their resources at such stories, lead with them and bay for blood. But, by and large, they ignore the opposite. Two recent examples: the repeated front-page coverage afforded a schoolyard altercation where a black schoolgirl was the victim of racial epithets from a white classmate, and the Democratic Alliance involvement in the Harksen debacle, where no illegality or crime was ever proved. In the first instance dignity, but not lives and multimillion-rand aircraft, was at stake and, in the second, they have not followed up *Noseweek*'s expose of the involvement of leading members of the ANC in the Hout Bay corruption scandal where prima facie, documented evidence of, at the very least, forgery, clearly exists.

The Afrikaans press, in contrast, saw fit to cut its umbilical cord to the National Party several years ago, and much of the best investigative journalism, and the debate that is taking SA forward, is occurring within its ranks.

☞ Déjà vu on SA Bootlicking Corporation TV
Business Day March 3 2005

'ON THURSDAY November 2 1978, amid protestations from minister Owen Horwood and new prime minister PW Botha, Justice Mostert convened a press conference to divulge details of the (Info) "scandal". The next day the press called this the most shocking and disturbing news of the century.' – Les de Villiers, *Secret Information* (Tafelberg Publishers, 1980).

'Botha's response was swift and, as later events were to show, typical. Within hours of Mostert's evidence being released, the government, through the South African Press Association, advised all newspapers that publication of the revelations would be in contravention of the Commissions Act.

'All media ignored the advice and published – with the natural exception of the government-controlled South African Broadcasting Corporation.' – Brian Pottinger, *The Imperial Presidency – PW Botha, the First 10 Years* (Southern Book Publishers, 1988).

I anchor this column with these quotations for two reasons. Firstly, because I hate paying television licence fees and in return being force-fed blatant African National Congress (ANC) propaganda dressed up as news.

Secondly, because of what many would see as history repeating itself in the light of the recent call by the Freedom of Expression Institute for a judicial commission of inquiry into the SABC.

The institute made the call after two analytical surveys found that, in contrast to the news programmes of rival e.tv, SABC news coverage was grossly biased in favour of the ANC. Other political parties just do not exist as far as the SABC is concerned.

What concerns me is that while the institute has highlighted what *The Citizen* recently described as 'taxpayer-funded propaganda in favour of the ANC', nobody seems to be analysing the news that the SABC is deliberately suppressing.

As one example of many, I would refer to the documents recently obtained by Richard Young who, in support of his contention that the arms deal is hugely corrupt, has fought a long, arduous and expensive court battle against government to acquire documents that it is clearly determined to keep secret.

On January 7 2005 the most recent batch of documents released to him in terms of a court order were the subject of front-page leads in *Business Day* and the *Mail & Guardian*.

If these articles are factually correct – and they have not been challenged – then the documents Young obtained compromise not only the office of the auditor-general, but the presidency as well.

Considering the implications of these revelations, it would have been unthinkable in any first-world democracy for the story not to have been the lead on the evening's television news bulletins. Accordingly, e.tv led with the story.

What Independent Newspaper group columnist William Saunderson-Meyer calls the 'South African Bootlicking Corporation' ignored the story in its SABC 3 news bulletin at 7 pm.

I see no difference in principle between the National Party-controlled state broadcaster's suppression of news in 1978 and the identical violation of news ethics by the ANC-controlled state broadcaster this year.

The SABC's constant promotion of the ANC on its evening television news bulletins and its constant suppression of any news seen as inimical to its political masters is both illegal and illicit.

It is illegal in terms of chapter three, section 10 (d) of the Broadcasting Act of 1999, which obligates the SABC to 'provide significant news and public affairs programming which meets the highest standards of journalism, as well as fair and unbiased coverage, impartiality, balance and independence from government, commercial and other interests'.

It is illicit in terms of the SABC's own code of news ethics, which compels it to report in a neutral and objective way. The SABC's media code was further defined and refined recently in an extensive and expensive country-wide and much-trumpeted public participation exercise.

The SABC's failure to broadcast the revelations in the documents obtained by Young in its SABC3 news bulletin on January 7 2005 shows that, unlike e.tv, its coverage is characterised by both fear and favour. And if those who sought to make a contribution through the public participation exercise now see it as a deeply cynical scam, would anyone be able to blame them?

☛ So sue, but Zikalala's partiality is beyond doubt
Business Day May 27 2005

PETER BRUCE's publication of Snuki Zikalala's lawyer's letter (March 17 2005) is contemptuous, and rightly so, of a self-proclaimed commissar who wants to sue *Business Day*'s publisher, BDFM, and Bruce, for allegedly defamatory remarks made by one of its reporters, Jacob Dlamini, about him. Whatever the truth, or lack of it, there were many occasions when Snuki himself confessed to being partial to the ruling party.

The evidence is there for all to see with South African Broadcasting Corporation (SABC) propaganda writ large on our screen day after day. At least half of the news programmes are devoted to the ruling African National Congress (ANC).

If it is not Thabo Mbeki and his forays into Africa with commentator Miranda Strydom close at hand, it is some insignificant minister or apparatchik spelling out some equally insignificant drivel about how great the governing party is.

In an article, 'Making patriotism a virtue' (*Business Day* July 31 2002), Zikalala articulated the basis, rationale and motivation that drives his journalism and news management ethos: 'The white liberal media will defend and shower with praise any black journalist who passionately hates government. This is called freedom of expression.'

To counter this he called for a 'press corps that can work with government'. Just such a press corps, he wrote, existed at the SABC. 'Our newsrooms are full of young and talented cadres who still need to be nurtured.'

An example of Zikalala-type 'nurturing' of 'cadres' occurred on January 31 2005. Having given extensive coverage the previous night to the opening of an international conference on leprosy, the SABC decided not to send a news team the next day. Big mistake – because Manto Tshabalala-Msimang was giving a speech. Mindful of the demand by the ANC at its 2003 national congress for a 'more responsive' SABC, she called Zikalala and irately demanded coverage. And Zikalala, mindful of SABC board member Thami Mazwai's concomitant and supporting justification to Parliament later that year that the SABC should not be driven by western liberal views of media freedom objectivity, hastily and happily complied.

Zikalala acknowledged the inevitable consequence of the goals he articulated in the *Business Day* article. These goals he is putting into practice, as the Tshabalala-Msimang incident proves. Ironically, at a recent World Press Freedom Day seminar in Stellenbosch, he confirmed the obvious; that the SABC, in contravention of its statutory and ethical obligations, is not politically neutral.

Earlier, while watching probably the most obscenely obsequious interview ever broadcast in the SABC's sordid history – Zikalala interviewing Robert Mugabe after the Zimbabwe elections – many of my friends complained how reminiscent this spectacle was of apartheid days.

At the Stellenbosch seminar, in Zikalala's confirmation of the SABC's board-supported, pro-ANC bias, there was honesty but no honour. It was, however, a compelling acknowledgement that the Cliff Saunders era had seamlessly morphed into an era of similar sycophancy mirrored by Zikalala and Paul Setsetse. The latter, in a radio interview with Dene Smuts, defended and justified the corporation's endless coverage of Mbeki in its bulletins, in stark contrast to e.tv's attempts to publish its news 'without fear or favour, zero percent propaganda'. Setsetse claimed the SABC needed to counteract criticism of Mbeki by our independent, privately funded newspapers!

We thus have a state-funded and controlled broadcaster, stuffed with sycophantic party apparatchiks whose sinecures come courtesy of government's cadre redeployment policy. Providing a thoroughly justified imprimatur was Saunders, who, in a letter to the *Sunday Times* last year, praised Zikalala's party political propaganda, indicating that he could not have done better himself! The SABC, significantly, did not deny the gravamen of this panegyrical peer review.

On a daily basis the SABC defiles both the letter and the spirit of the Broadcasting Act and its own ethical charter – because it can. It does this by overtly promoting the ANC through the volume and placement of stories favourable to it and by covertly suppressing stories inimical to its interests. And Zikalala, who once described journalism as a 'noble profession', is thus quite safe in acknowledging the SABC's manifest lack of neutrality/integrity even if, in so doing, he confirms Lord Acton's famous dictum: 'Power corrupts. Absolute power corrupts absolutely.'

We can but hope that if Mandla Langa is chosen as Peter Matlare's successor he will not, like Matlare, turn out to be a man of straw. In the meantime the status quo remains. That reality was, without denial from the corporation, cogently defined last year by *Sunday Times* columnist Phylicia Oppelt: 'SABC TV news sucks.'

Hackneyed digs at Zille expose our gutless media
Business Day May 3 2007

THE MINUTE that Helen Zille announced her candidacy for the Democratic Alliance (DA) leadership, the *Cape Argus* changed tack in how it portrays her – from darling executive mayor to troublesome opposition leader-to-be.

The over-the-top headline, 'De Lille lays into Zille', is completely out of kilter with the substance of the story published on April 23 2007.

Mike Wills' cynical column a few days later continues in much the same vein: 'Her mayorship has been given a remarkably easy ride on this one. The local media have, more or less, tolerated her breathtaking ambition because she gives the impression of having the energy to do six jobs before breakfast, but can you imagine the criticism an ANC (African National Congress) mayor would have received if she had claimed that running Cape Town was a part-time job!'

Criticism from who, Mike? Have you forgotten that under mayor Nomaindia Mfeketo the city was so badly managed that it was run into the ground?

Have you forgotten about the scandals around Big Bay and Jewellery City, and the irregular awarding of tenders to Cell C and BTH? Have you forgotten about Ikhwezi's incompetence? Did you forget that in the past financial year the ANC reduced the staff by 1 000 yet the staff bill went up R250 million? Have you not noticed that since the coalition government came into power, 1 780 staff have been appointed, R550 million having been set aside to appoint 600 more personnel in the near future? You seem to have so much faith in Zille that you expect her to clean up in a year what Mfeketo took five years to destroy.

Another groundless profile of Zille, this one by Kevin Bloom, is featured in *Maverick* (vol 2, issue 6). The article exposes the writer's agenda far more than it does anything about its subject, whose political and ethical credentials are beyond reproach. The only negatives that Bloom can find against her are her 'stoop' and some references to the ostensibly 'opulent' furniture in Zille's office, which, incidentally, she inherited from her ANC predecessor.

And then, of course, there is the old bogey that Zille is confrontational, an appellation often attributed to her current leader, Tony Leon, as though this is some 'liberal white thing'.

Further, as if to give credence to his fatuous representation of her, Bloom quotes an anonymous 'insider', 'a former DA man': 'Helen is very confrontational. She understands black culture to a large extent, she shows the right amount of respect when she's not in front of the cameras. But she stands up in public and she's confrontational. It could be one of her downfalls.'

This is such laughable rubbish and confirms my worst suspicions about that magazine and the media in general. They are fundamentally ignorant of the vibrant role opposition has to play in keeping government on its toes, and they harp on and on like a stuck record about matters of style. In an essay on the role of opposition, I have argued elsewhere that Parliament 'should be the definitive institution for debate, dialogue and civilised opposition. It should be the symposium for SA's political, cultural and social quandaries ... Parliament should be about cross-examination; adversarial but civilised dissent.'

It is about 'transacting the people's business in public', to quote a Canadian parliamentary researcher. Referring to the opposition as aggressive and confrontational is so hackneyed that it no longer has any meaning except to a media that still cringes at the thought of criticising a black government. By smearing opposition, they seek the right to criticise the ruling party because they lack the guts to do so unconditionally.

That Zille is prepared to tackle both the mayoralty and party leadership is unthinkable for most because the majority of politicians cannot do even one job properly. She was reluctant to do both, but when her party prevailed upon her to take on the leadership, she sought advice on how best to do so efficiently. I do not necessarily agree that she should do both jobs but I admire her chutzpah for proposing to do so. My only problem with Zille is that she is far too dutiful – an embarrassment to a breed of politicians who go into politics, according to *Financial Mail* editor Barney Mthombothi, to access 'easy money, in keeping with our national pastime of demanding lucrative awards for little or no sweat'.

The media that try to weaken Zille do so at their own, and our, peril.

Instead of strengthening democracy by respecting her leadership as she tries to clean up the city, bring back good governance and restore the institutional memory that has been lost through rampant affirmative action policies, they cast aspersions on her, because they cannot be seen to be promoting a white woman opposition leader, regardless of her credentials.

ANC desperately covering up Hout Bay sleaze
Business Day November 11 2004

I HAD just finished reading a chapter titled 'Public Deception in Cape Town: Story of an Insider Witness', in *Whistleblowing Around the World: Law, Culture and Practice*, by Richard Calland and Guy Dehn, when the October 2004 issue of *Noseweek* arrived.

This chapter was written by Victoria Johnson, an articulate and brave young lawyer, formerly in the employ of the Cape Town municipality.

In early 2001 she worked in the office of then Democratic Alliance mayor Peter Marais, a National Party member in that ill-fated coalition. Marais had wanted to leave an immutable legacy by renaming two of the city's oldest streets, Adderley and Wale Streets, Nelson Mandela and FW De Klerk Avenues respectively.

He accordingly initiated a farcical and corrupt 'public participation' process. Although opposition to the project was huge and unanimous, Marais and his team decided to counter this with forged letters and petitions of support.

In her chapter in the book, Johnson describes how Marais' spokesman, Johan Smit, delivered these letters to her. 'That afternoon Mr Smit came into my office and handed me a batch of almost 500 "letters" and petitions supporting the mayor's proposal.

'His statement when handing them to me was, "This is how to win elections." As soon as he left my office I looked at the documents and was speechless. A cursory glance made me sure they were forgeries.'

What made that obvious to her was that the handwriting on these 'individual' letters of support and 'petitions' clearly belonged to only a handful of people.

Fast forward to late this year. *Noseweek* shows, in the October 2004 issue, that exactly the same modus operandi was used to bolster a controversial application by African National Congress (ANC) stalwart Shantaal Meter for a multimillion-rand development – with noncompliant building plans – in Hout Bay.

Noseweek alleges that Meter instructed two Hout Bay ANC members to get supporting petitions signed, an impossible task. They transcribed information from the voters roll and, following the Marais formula, signed these fake 'petitions' themselves.

Not surprisingly – and hardly for the first time in our 10 years of democracy – a desperate, retrospective cover-up is being implemented. When *Noseweek* attempted to get details of the Meter application it was told curtly to try a costly and, more significantly, time-consuming, application under the Access to Information Act.

There are, however, two significant differences between the Marais scam and the Hout Bay sleaze. First, the DA immediately acted on Johnson's whistle-blowing report. It called a news conference, and then appointed a commission of inquiry under former judge Willem Heath. In Hout Bay, governing from the 'moral high ground', the ANC shuns such measures.

Second, while the pro-ANC media in Cape Town – namely the state broadcaster and the Independent Group newspapers – relished giving saturation coverage to the Marais and Harksen scandals because they were embarrassing to the DA, they have ignored the Hout Bay scandal, for obvious reasons.

Fortunately, as M-Net's *Carte Blanche* team showed a fortnight ago, a few media organisations still take the fourth estate's watchdog obligations seriously. We could all see, on our television screens, that the handwriting on the Hout Bay 'petitions' was identical for page after page – something *Noseweek* confirmed by hiring a handwriting expert.

Noseweek also quoted Hout Bay resident Veronica Reed, who claims she never signed the petition containing her name and 'signature' and, accordingly, attempted to lay a charge of fraud at the Hout Bay police station. These worthies, obviously acting on instruction, declined to prosecute. Reed confirmed all this in the *Carte Blanche* programme. As taxpayers what should we do when the police openly seem to collude with the powers that be?

Cartoonist Zapiro has seized on the irony of Deputy President Jacob

Zuma being the patron of SA's 'moral regeneration' campaign but, worryingly, Western Cape premier Ebrahim Rasool has also taken of late to parroting the moral-regeneration mantra.

Implicated in all of this, alleges *Noseweek*, is our long-term Public Works Minister Stella Sigcau, whose governance record is not particularly kosher.

We need action, not hot air, and Rasool could start by following Tony Leon's example in the Marais scandal. Get government to release the information sought by *Noseweek*, call a press conference and then appoint a commission of inquiry.

The ANC did this with Harksen – why not Hout Bay?

Foreign Affairs (Foreign Fumbles)

☛ Tainted foreign policy at the root of SA's woes
Business Day June 5 2008

THE OUTBURST of hatred towards foreigners is not a new phenomenon. It is the product of a vision that still sees the world in Cold War terms. It is a vision that has been cultivated by the African National Congress (ANC) since the beginning of the Mbeki era for ideological reasons, encapsulated by SA's stance on human rights issues at the United Nations Security Council.

SA has consistently supported the world's losers – such as Robert Mugabe, Omar Ahmad al-Bashir, Bashar Al Assad, Mahmoud Ahmadinejad and Ismail Haniyeh – against leaders who support international human rights.

This meddling in the affairs of others, for retributive reasons, has come back to bite them. The millions of Zimbabweans seeking refuge here are the outcome of Thabo Mbeki's support for liberation dictator Mugabe. In this he was not alone. He was supported by cronies who refused to tell the emperor he was naked.

They used Parliament, the Southern African Development Community and other agencies to aid and abet Mbeki's mission. Ronnie Kasrils, for example, instead of ensuring that his ministry was carefully attuned to the early seismic vibrations of the restless poor, focused relentlessly on the Middle East. His obsession with Israel averted his attention from the dangers within.

The present deluge of xenophobia has similarly taken the ruling elite by surprise. While Rome was burning, MPs were united in their calls for an increase in salary, claiming that they were unable to live on more than half a million rand a year. This unity is rarely seen in Parliament, except when it has to do with self-interest. If only they were as united in their demand for the dismissal of those rotten MPs involved in the Travelgate scandal, we might be able to deal with the rule of law.

The murder of more than 62 foreigners and a foreigner set alight and emblazoned across the world's screens, have exposed SA for what it is – a hypocrite concerned about the splint in the eyes of others, when the beam blinds it to its own sins.

Those who knowingly supported Mbeki when they knew he was wrong, are now suddenly writing letters as 'concerned citizens', decrying the state of the nation, when all they were concerned about for a very long time were the next black economic empowerment deal, the next tender, and next lucrative post. Remember the capitulation of FirstRand and the clergy on the question of crime? Equally, those who knew a two-thirds majority would be dangerous for democracy now pretend that they were not a part of it; worse, some still believe that the ANC is the only answer to democracy, and will continue to vote them into office.

Rudely awakened from their acquisitive stupor, they now seek ways to connect to the very people whom they have forgotten about and who now despise them.

When our people went on a rampage against foreigners, some leaders had the cheek to lament that these acts of terror against fellow citizens were destroying the legacy of our heroes.

Who are the heroes that they are referring to? Our so-called heroes have destroyed their own legacy, driven not so much by their love for democracy, as their control of the economy and all the levers of power.

This definition of hero is narcissistic. It expects eternal adulation for 'liberating the masses' – as though 'the masses' did not contribute to their own liberation.

Fortunately, admiration for these self-acclaimed heroes is waning, as powerfully signified by the Polokwane revolution. The racial conflagration at present is a brutal extension of it.

In his recent column, John Kane-Berman described, in lurid detail, SA as a failed state in every sense of the word. Most departments are dysfunctional and the entire ANC has to take the blame for this miserable state of affairs and not blame it on a 'third force'. This is exactly what the apartheid government did when they were at their very worst.

Has it ever occurred to the ANC that it might be its own third force?

☛ Oscars for Mugabe and SA's 'internal Zimbabwe'
Business Day April 5 2007

WHILE the movie, *The Last King of Scotland*, was being shown around the country, our own cricket-loving survivor of the British empire, Zimbabwe's President Robert Mugabe, received a standing ovation and a few Oscars from the Southern African Development Community (SADC).

Just last week, Mugabe demonstrated his hold over the club by using the full might of his repressive state to persecute his opposition, knowing full well that not one African leader would dare oppose him. He knows the quest for solidarity with brothers in arms overrides the quest for renewal. He knows his fellow liberation leaders will not let him down, even if he instructs his goons to clobber Morgan Tsvangirai, leader of the opposition Movement for Democratic Change (MDC), to death. He knows that support for the MDC as an alternative government is anathema to African despots keen to preserve liberation movements as ruling parties.

Mugabe, clearly, more than anyone in the SADC and the Commonwealth, has a profound understanding of the mind of the African political leader, an issue that has baffled psychologists, social anthropologists and literary scholars alike since the demise of colonialism. He knows that African leaders, except a rare few, are unwilling to shake off the bonds of their own oppression and will use their psycho-political 'woundedness' to extract loyalty from their followers long after liberation.

The inability to resolve the deep loss of dignity and woundedness wrought by colonisation, and in our case apartheid, leads to a destructive 'acting out' when African political leaders assume positions of power. The seeds of this oppression are so deeply embedded in the victims' psyche that unless they have the courage to resolve it, it leads to all kinds of antisocial behaviour, especially in the political arena, where clinging to power long after the sell-by date has become a permanent feature of the politics of the continent.

John Kane-Berman's recent column in this newspaper was a pertinent reminder that Mugabe's career as a human rights violator started the day he came into office. The pattern of abuse is clear and, lest we forget, the Fifth Brigade's pogrom against the Matabele happened early in Mugabe's reign. So, SA's fear of Mugabe is a recognition that 'Mugabe' is on the rise here too. In condemning Mugabe, President Thabo Mbeki and the African National Congress (ANC) know they would be criticising their own propensity to do the same, especially with a populist contender such as Jacob Zuma waiting in the wings. The failure to deal with Mugabe is our failure to deal with our own internal Zimbabwe.

This dilemma is summed up no better than in a recent interview with the *Financial Times*, in which Mbeki acknowledged the intertwining histories of SA and Zimbabwe: 'So we have this history in common ... When things go wrong in Zimbabwe, we feel that. I am not talking of refugees coming here ... I am talking of marching in step.'

Deep down, our political leaders know that our instruments of democracy are not sound enough to deal with a negotiated settlement that promised delivery of services as a quid pro quo for ANC rule. Under circumstances where it is easy to create a facade of wellbeing through black economic empowerment, affirmative action and employment equity – with very little trickling down to the masses – the situation is potentially explosive for those who want to remain in power, with the poor and unemployed growing more and more restless by the day.

It is easy to amend the constitution to extend the term of office of the president – as happened in Uganda and other African countries, especially where opposition and mechanisms of accountability were weak. SA's constitution cannot necessarily deal with a ruling party that has an overwhelming hold on executive power, where struggle credentials override merit and Parliament is secondary to the might of Luthuli House. It is quite possible to have all the instruments of democracy in place while in fact citizens remain excluded from real power and an equitable share of the state's resources.

African leaders who invoke nationalist rhetoric about identity, race, renaissance, cultural pride, traditions, the renaming of streets, airports and towns as mobilising tools to keep the masses on board, pretend they do this in the interests of their followers and divert them from issues that matter.

In this context, talk of decolonising the mind is counterproductive and reminds one of the late Zimbabwean writer Dambudzo Marechera's potent statement: 'I don't hate being black, I'm just tired of saying it's beautiful.' The negation of previous influences, good or bad, does not recognise the impact the past has had in forming our psyche. Appeals to the African renaissance and essentialism that extol the virtues of black pride in our nationalist identities are fatal if we are unable to resolve our own internal Zimbabwes.

The presidential rhetoric in favour of Zimbabwe and the condemnation of sanctions is the beginning of a betrayal of our inner SA – a psychosocial condition for which there is a remedy: the promotion of a truly open society.

☞ Support for Mugabe brings SA no benefit
Business Day May 22 2003

THERE is nothing more sickening than to see Zimbabwean President Robert Mugabe popping up all over the place, enjoying the largesse of our country and the adulation of our political leaders when he should be standing next to Slobodan Milosevic before the International Court of Justice. Staying at the luxurious Westcliff Hotel, while millions in Zimbabwe starve, was obscene. His attendance at the funeral of Walter Sisulu, a man whose very essence he defies, was a disgrace.

What is more worrying is how President Thabo Mbeki and the foreign affairs office are scurrying about trying to give legitimacy to a dictator who should be consigned to the dustbin of history.

In his weekly letter (ANC Today, May 9-15 2003), Mbeki incredulously claims that 'contrary to what some now claim, the economic crisis currently affecting Zimbabwe did not originate from the actions of a reckless political leadership or corruption' and blames Zimbabwe's ills on abstract historical forces and economic inevitability, not on Mugabe's rotten leadership.

No, according to Mbeki, Zimbabwe's economic decline has to do with a racist negotiated settlement with London, that 'quarantined the matter of land redistribution because of agreements reached' and that 'sought to counter-balance the principle of black liberation with the protection of white property, inserting into the settlement the racist notions of black majority rule and white minority rights'.

This is racist reductionism at its very best and Mbeki attributes no agency to black people for their own liberation from oppression. According to this logic, post-colonial societies and their liberation leaders will remain forever the victims of colonisation. Liberation from colonisation, yes, but never liberation towards a democracy that is sustainable.

Pulled by the rapids of history to destinations not of our choosing, we may as well give up as there is no control over this 'internal logic of various processes in society (that) compels all of us to be carried along by events to destinations we may not have sought'.

By delinking Mugabe's reckless economic agenda from his growing dictatorial tendencies, Mbeki is able to rationalise Zimbabwe's decline. This is as deliberate as it is flawed. Mbeki knows that an economic agenda that is devoid of an equally ambitious agenda for democracy and human rights is bound to end up in a sociopolitical and economic morass, as Zimbabwe is today, but on this score he prefers to remain in denial.

The Zimbabwean disaster is entirely man-made, despite Mbeki's explanations to the contrary. The war veterans, the draconian media laws, the harassment of independent judges, illegal land seizures, the theft of state assets were all politically and racially inspired by a president demanding to stay in power for life. Patronising in its tone, Mbeki's letter is a veiled warning to those who dare to ask questions, who, according to him 'pose as high priests at the inquisition, hungry for the blood of the accused, as though to condemn, demonise and punish'.

This dangerous political standpoint becomes even more threatening when world leaders like the UK's Prime Minister Tony Blair and his lapdog, Jack Straw, cosy up to Mbeki for their own selfish political agendas.

Reeling from severe criticism from within his own cabinet for sidelining the United Nations and support for the unilateral invasion of Iraq, Blair is losing his moral authority over foreign policy concerns such as sovereignty and human rights. Disillusionment with his role internationally is made worse by his promise to soften his stance on Mugabe, ease the anti-Mugabe 'media frenzy' and loosen restrictions on the Commonwealth ban.

With the inauguration of Nigerian President Olusegun Obasanjo looming, Mbeki is being wooed to pave a reconciliatory path to African Commonwealth members, to ease what would otherwise be an awkward celebration with Mugabe supporters.

Why do world leaders from western countries, in particular, tolerate dictators simply because they are black? Colonial guilt and its corollary racial oppression have become so entrenched that both sides are unable to snap out of what have become continental pathologies.

Why should we make do with lower standards of democracy?

When world leaders retreat from holding Mugabe accountable for their own selfish reasons, they implicitly support the tendency of African leaders to rule ad infinitum and with impunity.

From liberation heroes to rotten paranoid thugs
Business Day March 18 2004

WITH only few exceptions, most liberation heroes become rotten political leaders. The metamorphosis from freedom fighter to dictator, in most cases, seems to be effortless.

History is replete with such examples from Latin America, Africa, eastern Europe, and Asia, with names all too familiar – Fidel Castro, Josef Stalin, Milton Obote, Robert Mugabe, Sam Nujoma, Eduardo dos Santos, Daniel Arap Moi, Jean-Bertrand Aristide, Pol Pot and so on.

Those who lead the oppressed to freedom are hailed heroes regardless of their own personal flaws. This is understandable given that a liberation leader usually has to be disciplined, selfless, an excellent mobiliser on all fronts, and a political visionary.

Often with the entire state machinery arraigned against them, they frequently have no option but to resort to undemocratic tactics to achieve their goals. Spied upon, infiltrated and undermined, liberation leaders cannot help but be paranoid and conspiratorial.

A consequence of this has been suppression of internal dissent, the expulsion of dissidents, secrecy and conspiratorial behaviour. This explains the frequent lacunae in liberation histories, aspects best left unsaid lest exposing them detract from what liberation is all about.

In a recent column in *The Sunday Independent*, Michael Holman raised this issue rather pointedly. Deftly weaving the personal with the political, Holman acknowledges that despite all the blame that can justifiably be put at the door of British colonial rule, Mugabe was always a thug.

Like a premature 'obituary' of Robert Mugabe who has just turned 80, he condemns the man for his tyrannical rule, and reminds us Zimbabwe's decline cannot be ascribed to the excesses of British colonial rule alone.

There is a direct link between what Mugabe always was and what he became.

His insatiable lust for power led to his steady erosion of civil liberties and violations of human rights. It came from a desire to entrench his rule for life. How else does one explain remaining in office for more than twenty years?

Lest we accuse Holman of some crude determinism, he does not let Mugabe off the hook.

Throughout Mugabe's history, he calculated his way to the top and how to stay there. The massacre of the Ndebele, the seizure of white farms, the creation of the Green Bombers, the cooption of the war veterans and harassment of the judiciary were orchestrated to ensure his political longevity.

Having failed his constitutional mandate, he seeks a 'refuge in history', as is the wont of most liberation leaders, and blames his government's failure on the west, on whites, on colonial rule, on everything except himself.

Lest we forget, dictators do not become dictators by themselves. They have help along the way, and often those who help do not fully recognise the role they play until it is too late. The cronies abandon intellectual pursuits in favour of the corridors of power, which are more lucrative.

Like most leaders of his ilk, Mugabe used key institutions of state to centralise and entrench his power, in the process becoming like his former oppressors, if not worse. Key sectors of the executive, the legislature, the judiciary, big business, trade unions, the media were all coopted to keep him in office.

In the process, parliament was the first to go and with it the ruthless suppression of opposition. The judiciary was next stripped of its independence, followed by the bludgeoning through of laws that silenced the media ruthlessly.

Political sycophants, the military, and the police knew it was in their best interests to back him. They were rewarded with white-owned farms, land, exorbitant salaries, all kinds of perks and probably Congo diamonds, too.

The moral of my story is this. Leading people to liberation from the evils of oppression does not necessarily make the liberator a good person. Liberation 'leaders' have baggage, and the act of liberation often hides the processes by which people become leaders or are thrust into such roles.

As the systems they have liberated people from have been so bad, the assumption often is nobody can be worse. And so they escape scrutiny. No one dares look too closely at who the liberators are. The silence, and the tolerance of Mugabe's massacre of the Ndebele shows precisely that.

Surely it is reductionist to blame it all on our past. When some Commonwealth members retreat into their racial laagers, refusing to condemn a former liberation leader-turned-dictator, what does that say about us, and our propensity to be the same?

☞ Down a familiar path into the heart of darkness
Business Day December 9 2004

ANYONE interested in understanding why most post-colonial African countries struggle with institutionalising and consolidating democracy, should read Mahmood Mamdani's *When Victims Become Killers*, Robert Guest's *The Shackled Continent* and Michela Wrong's *In the Footsteps of Mr Kurtz*.

These books sum up what happens when ruling parties stay in power forever. The leitmotif in all of them is that a career in politics is the quickest road to wealth, a tendency endorsed by Smuts Ngonyama's recent utterances. To want to be wealthy is not necessarily wrong, but the tendency for politicians to become numb to the poverty and suffering around us seems to be part of the package.

In the past 50 years politicians in southern Africa have in their utterances shown an astonishingly callous indifference to the plight of the poor, the ill and dying and towards their political opponents. And this heartlessness starts with seemingly innocent comments.

In the UDI era of the 1960s Rhodesian leader Ian Smith incarcerated a white critic of his regime, Judith Todd. When Todd went on a hunger strike she was drugged and force-fed. When questioned on this, Smith said he was 'unaware' of the hunger strike, and told an interviewer that: 'If Miss Todd does not wish to eat the food given her, that doesn't worry me a good deal.'

A decade later, National Party justice minister Jimmy Kruger, deliberately misinformed by security police that the charismatic Steve Biko had died as a result of a hunger strike, told the Transvaal congress of the National Party in Pretoria that: 'I am not pleased, nor am I sorry. It leaves me cold.'

The insouciant cruelty of Kruger's remark incensed even the usually supportive Afrikaans press, and the English liberal press justifiably flayed him.

What, then, is one to make of the silence of our newspapers on a remark that left me dumbfounded and convinced that it had been printed in error?

I refer to an interview in the *Sunday Times* (September 19 2004) with Mojanku Gumbi, legal adviser to President Thabo Mbeki. In the article, 'Burning the midnight oil', she is quoted as saying: 'On AIDS and Zimbabwe I have never lain awake at night on either issue.'

Shocked, I bought the following week's issue convinced I was going to read her angry rebuttal and a humble apology by the newspaper for misquoting her.

There was neither. Having just commemorated World AIDS Day and been shocked by government's lame roll-out of antiretroviral medicines across the country, I find Gumbi's remarks reverberate around me as I witness people suffering, despairing and dying, without hope of ever receiving medical care or help.

Gumbi's remarks resonated with the monstrous statements of Smith and Kruger, even though I know Gumbi is not like them. Perhaps my surprise was based on naivety.

After all, the only two issues raised by Archbishop Desmond Tutu in his Nelson Mandela address to which Mbeki declined to respond were HIV/AIDS and Zimbabwe.

Furthermore, we know that the African National Congress (ANC) has repeatedly stymied attempts in Commonwealth and United Nations forums not only to apply sanctions against Robert Mugabe's brutal and corrupt regime, but even to criticise it.

It is also a matter of record that Foreign Minister Nkosazana Dlamini-Zuma has said Zanu (PF) is a 'progressive' regime, which she considers beyond criticism. She also supported plans by Mugabe to have all journalists registered, something that would have nullified what little press freedom remains in Zimbabwe.

On the AIDS question, may we assume that Gumbi's declared indifference to the plight of AIDS sufferers and those orphaned by the disease is clearly and similarly manifest in the ANC's squandering of immense amounts of taxpayers' money to defend court cases launched by the Treatment Action Campaign and other civic-minded organisations?

Do politicians like Gumbi find the widespread starvation in Zimbabwe and the increasing number of AIDS orphans the next best thing to Mogadon for ensuring untroubled sleep? Does the contemplation of the estimated 20 000 Ndebele victims of Mugabe's Korean-trained Fifth Brigade's Gukurahundi campaign in the early 1980s – and all the subsequent abuses – provide a soporific that is superior to the traditional hot toddy?

Do the women in government find the fact that Mugabe, through his state-supported Green Bomber youth movement, has made rape a ubiquitous political tool, in the tradition of Slobodan Milošević's murderous troops in Bosnia, a matter that does not concern them?

Gumbi's words may well come back to haunt her.

All it will take is one angry and charismatic HIV-positive person – a Steve Biko with AIDS – to prove the folly of Jacob Zuma's crass assumption that the ANC will rule, 'until Jesus comes'.

☛ Funny how well Cape Flats manners work in US

Business Day November 20 2003

TO SECURITY personnel in US airports, terrorists have a certain look. How else do I explain the constant frisking, searching and interrogation I experienced for the three days I tried to get home?

I have never had my bags scrutinised as much as on a recent trip to the US and Mexico. It did not matter I was a guest of the Ash Institute at Harvard and of Mexican President Vincente Fox to present our top public sector projects at the World Forum for Reinventing Government.

Flying into Boston was bad enough in terms of security. But coming back from Mexico to Boston was virtually a nightmare. At Washington my bags were opened and searched as never before. Then instead of being sent on for check-in, they stopped me at the next security station for more testing – anthrax, maybe. Why else rip apart my sanitary towels?

While this went on, I did a spot survey to check who was being pulled to one side by the 'Gestapo'. In my queue it was all people of colour: an elderly Indian woman in a sari, a tall West Indian with dreadlocks, two olive-skinned people, who could have been from anywhere, and me.

When I eventually left Harvard for SA on November 8, the second nightmare began. To cut a long story short, my 3.35 pm Delta Flight to New York was cancelled so I missed my 5.55 pm SAA flight for Johannesburg.

By now I was desperate, as I had been away for three weeks and needed to get home for several reasons. After much kicking and screaming, I was eventually sent to another terminal to take a flight to La Guardia at 6.35 pm.

Security here was worse than ever. Somehow, South African passports trigger Pavlovian reactions reminiscent of what the pass did to apartheid police.

I arrived in New York late at night, and Delta 'compensated' me with two faulty phone cards and vouchers for the Ramada. This is one of New York's most disgusting hotels, used by the type of trash one sees on Jerry Springer's shows. They smoked dope on my floor and made a racket. No one dared complain if they wanted to leave alive.

The next day I went to JFK early, determined to secure my seat. When I got there Delta informed me they were not authorised to put me in first class although there was no other seat for me, and that I should fly to Paris, stay overnight and leave for SA from there on Monday.

When people started boarding the SAA flight at 4.50 pm I still did not have a seat. By now, Delta had unleashed my worst Cape Flats manners, and since Americans are not used to that kind of rebellion they suddenly found a business class seat for me.

By now, all my anti-US feelings had reached a peak, further fuelled by my reading of Michael Moore's book – *Dude, Where is my Country?* For those who want to refine their anti-Bush sentiments, it is compulsory reading.

It is one of the most scathing indictments of the Bush administration to date. A call for regime change in the US, it boldly raises all the uncomfortable questions Americans ought to confront if they want to survive this century.

Questions about Guantanamo Bay, the US Patriotic Act (the act enabling erosion of civil liberties), Bush's links with the bin Laden family, the Saudis, defective foreign policies, corruption scandals linked to Enron and all its affiliates, and much more.

He warns Americans that unless they work collectively to replace Bush, Cheney, Rumsfeld and Wolfowitz, the US will slide into a kind of autocratic abyss hard to reverse in a few years' time, with Saddam Hussein being one of the crassest symbols of US foreign policy gone wrong.

If this is the measure of US paranoia, I fear it will be with reluctance that I return to that country while Bush is president, a sentiment uttered by most black South Africans who boarded the plane with me.

☛ Nepad's peer review system needs to be given real teeth
Business Day September 20 2002

NAMIBIAN President Sam Nujoma and Zimbabwean President Robert Mugabe typify the worst excesses of African patriarchy.

Unable to relinquish power and retire gracefully, their behaviour has become analogous to what drives male chauvinists to commit family murders. 'If we cannot own and control you, then we shall take you down with us' is often what finally pushes a man to wipe out his entire family.

Similarly, the destruction of Zimbabwe typifies the impotence of a leader who has lost it. Nujoma's threats to drive out whites highlight his failure after twelve years in office to build an inclusive democracy. Appeals to race and sovereignty have become desperate bids by ageing African dictators to cling to power.

What other possible explanations exist for the destruction of an economy, as in Zimbabwe? If past colonisation justifies driving people from their homes and countries and denying people the right to produce food and earn a living, then African leaders should admit upfront negotiated settlements are not the answer to colonisation. Then we will know what we are dealing with.

I have listened intently to the views of callers to the *Tim Modise Show* on this issue. When they ask why the African Union (AU) is not dealing with Zimbabwe, Tim's reply – like many journalists and politicians – is that the African peer-review mechanism can deal with this dilemma.

The other typical reply is we have no right to interfere in sovereign states' affairs.

I went to take a look at the provisions of this review mechanism, billed as the new panacea for all Africa's ills, of the New Partnership for Africa's Development (Nepad). On the surface it seems all right, but on closer scrutiny it becomes clear it is highly flawed.

It rightly lets African states police each other's adherence to universal standards of democracy and good governance, but wrongly lets African states do so only voluntarily. As a 'mutually agreed instrument for self-monitoring by the participating member governments' its power to influence is minimal.

This is contrary to the traditional understanding of the notion of a 'peer review'. Peers should be universal, not restricted to and confined by continent.

The review mechanism will achieve nothing if African states can become members if and when they please. This is already exemplified by the way the AU has let Mugabe and other corrupt leaders get away with murder.

Peers should consist of true democrats, experts of good governance, whose task would be to admit or reject those who fail to subscribe to Nepad's 'democracy and political governance initiative'. The panel, according to Nepad, will consist of 'persons of high moral stature and demonstrated commitment to the ideals of Pan Africanism'.

Now we all know such leaders are few and far between in Africa, but those who do qualify should automatically constitute the peers of the review mechanism forthwith and proceed to put pressure on states to measure up to their standards. And as for 'the ideals of Pan Africanism', there lies the rub. What are the ideals? Who determines them? Why not the ideals of the Universal Declaration of Human Rights?

Thirdly, as far as I am concerned, admission to the peer group of democrats should hinge on adherence to these tried and tested universally accepted standards, regardless of regional and cultural peculiarities: respect for the rule of law; respect for the rights of the individual citizen; respect for free political association; equality of opportunity; free and fair elections; media independence and an independent judiciary; the separation of powers; democratic election of leaders for fixed terms of office; sound, transparent fiscal, budgetary and monetary policies.

It should be the peer group of democrats that admits or rejects those not complying with the good governance standards, not the other way round. If it is voluntary, what happens when rogue states join? Do they not dilute the ideals of democracy as we have already seen with the AU? The support for the nomination of Libya's Muammar al-Gaddafi to the United Nations Chair of Human Rights is a case in point. Adherence to the Universal Declaration of Human Rights is an old-fashioned remedy that works.

☛ Glossing over truth on Aristide does SA no favours
Business Day June 10 2004

PRESIDENT Thabo Mbeki has an uncanny knack of dabbling with what is taboo, and then trying to give it respectability to suit his often inexplicable agendas.

To be sure, if a constituency that Mbeki does not like condemns someone, that person automatically becomes sanctified in his eyes. Zimbabwean President Robert Mugabe and the new Minster of Environment and Tourism, Marthinus van Schalkwyk, are two good examples of this.

Very much in the same mould, is his welcome to our shores of a much-despised dictator, former Haitian leader Jean-Bertrand Aristide. It is hardly in our best interests to make SA a safe haven for this despot.

But why does Mbeki do so? Why does he risk international disdain for foreign 'policies' that make no sense?

Kader Asmal's argument (*The Sunday Independent* May 23 2004) along with many other mindless editorials, that Aristide should get refugee status as someone driven out of his country, holds no water. Presenting Aristide as a victim of foreign unilateral interventions, and a symbol of resistance thereof, is a load of hogwash in the guise of rational argument.

Here is the truth about Aristide according to the Haitian Democracy Project and my own friends from Haiti:

Although Aristide was elected democratically as president in November 2000, the opposition boycotted the election for several reasons. Only 10% of eligible voters turned out to vote, in reaction to the growing authoritarianism and corruption of his government. The *chimères* – who operate much like Mugabe's war veterans — ruthlessly crushed Haitian dissent, with the support of Aristide's government.

These marauding gangs, assisted by national police, and armed with pistols, clubs, whips, rocks and bottles went into Haiti State University, attacked the rector with iron bars, breaking his legs and wounding 30 students before setting the university on fire.

Under Aristide's rule, Haiti became isolated from the world community through suspension of grants, loans and aid. Transparency International says Haiti is considered one of the most corrupt countries, surpassed only by Bangladesh and Nigeria.

People such as 'the priests and laypersons of the liberation theology wing of the Haitian church, the network of grassroots organisations, peasant co-operatives and labour unions, and every single Haitian intellectual or artist of note' who all formerly supported Aristide's rise to the presidency, now denounce him vehemently.

It is alleged that Aristide's inner circle had drug connections with the Haitian national police, turning Haiti into a drug state comparable with Colombia.

It was against this background that Mbeki, one of only a few world leaders, decided to join Haiti in its 200th year celebrations. Ahead of him went the *Drakensberg* — a South African naval ship, equipped with two helicopters, armoured vehicles, and 133 military personnel — to the besieged city of Gonaïves where Haiti's independence was declared 200 years ago.

During police raids in the city, more than 36 people were brutally murdered, and 85 wounded.

Knowing what we endured to gain our freedom — fighting racist police and Casspirs — Haitians could not believe Mbeki planned a visit to support their despised autocratic ruler, who respected neither human rights nor the rule of law.

Why would Mbeki, asked my friend, tarnish SA's years of struggle for democracy by participating in festivities contested and vehemently opposed by Haitians themselves? Why did our helicopters, as reported by the local news, station themselves in Gonaïves and unload South African soldiers who immediately took up combat positions?

When Mbeki knows he is wrong he finds ways to legitimise the wrong – not least the R10 million spent on the visit to Haiti and the millions that will be spent on Aristide's stay here.

Knowing he will get the support from his cabinet and the majority in the National Assembly, no matter what, he invokes the language of racial oppression to justify his moves. He knows there is enough international guilt about colonialism and racial oppression to let him off the hook. He also knows there are enough spindoctors in the media and crackpot political analysts prepared to attribute noble motives to his bizarre actions. Not so the 100 foreign ambassadors who refused to submit to Mbeki's command to welcome Aristide.

And so the lies about Aristide will continue. Mrs Mbeki may accompany him to church amid great fanfare to make this unholy debacle more palatable, but let me remind readers Aristide left behind an almost irreparable mess, while he will enjoy the fat of our land at our expense.

Gérard Latortue, the current Haitian leader, inherited a devastated country described by my friend as follows: 'Mr Aristide and his goons have plundered the country, burned and looted vast quantities of private businesses ... Haiti has been characterised as a post-conflict country although it has never experienced a civil war or went to war with anybody.'

☛ An unfortunate historical amnesia
Mail & Guardian January 31 to February 7 2003

IN THE strongest terms I take issue with the categorisation of Australia as the equivalent of 'the old South Africa', a suggestion made by Richard Calland last week in his article 'Of sheep and the new Thatcherites'.

The mists of time seem to have enveloped the pages of history where Australia stood steadfast against the old South Africa through the '70s, '80s and '90s. Throughout, there was bipartisan political support in Australia for sporting and economic boycotts against the apartheid regime, complemented by the activism in international forums like the Commonwealth. Australians watched with joy the transfer of power to the new leadership in 1994, and the moves to redress the economic and social injustices of apartheid.

I was part of a government delegation led by minister Geraldine Fraser-

Moleketi to Australia, at the invitation of the Australian government in 1995, to celebrate with us our new democracy. Such hospitality I have yet to experience anywhere in the world as Australians shared expertise and resources with us to help us on our way to developing democratic practices in this country. I am increasingly, therefore, uncomfortable with the shoot-from-the-hip approach to international analysis that Calland and parts of the African National Congress (ANC) and the media adopt when analysing Australia.

It is sad that while the solidarity of dictators during the dark years of apartheid is now rewarded with strong and unwavering ties, the solidarity of progressive developed countries like Australia is forgotten. The frequent public sledging of Australia by the government and media alike in South Africa demonstrates an unfortunate historical amnesia. While accepting of Australia's support in the fight against apartheid, parts of the ANC are now quick to interpret similarly inspired Australian efforts in Zimbabwe as a 'white conspiracy'. So too do they forget the support Australia lent to Zimbabwe's independence struggle. Is it not possible for a developed country to argue in favour of human rights and democracy in Africa?

Calland paints Australia as a 'racially homogenous' society, overburdened with regulation and safe to the point of boredom. While I was amused by his earlier description of Australian sporting efficiency as befitting the tag 'Switzerland of the South', how he arrived at his picture of racial homogeneity is beyond me. Only by staying within the 'cosseted comfort' of Mosman (Sydney's Sandton equivalent) could he have arrived at this conclusion. Australia is one of the success stories of multiculturalism and stands beside the United States and Canada as a 'magnificent tapestry of multi-ethnicity'.

In 2001 almost 25% of the nineteen-million Australians were born overseas. While granted the first ranked of the source countries is the United Kingdom followed by New Zealand, third in line is Italy, then Vietnam, China, Greece, Germany, the Philippines, India, The Netherlands, South Africa, Malaysia, Lebanon and Hong Kong, in that order.

The trend continues with more than 30% of Australia's immigrations this year from Asian countries. The premier of Victoria is of Lebanese origin, the mayor of Melbourne is of Chinese origin, and within his city are more than 140 different ethnic groups.

Australians speak more than 200 languages, 45 of which are indigenous and 460 000 people identify as Aboriginal or Torres Strait Islander. This is far from the picture of homogeneity Calland claims to have seen.

South Africans hate it when generalisations are made about this diverse country. Why should Australia have to put up with such ignorant generalisations?

To his credit, Calland does pick up on the interesting political debate in Australia over indigenous justice. In all healthy societies there are debates like this that keep past injustices in the public domain. But I find it puzzling that Calland equates a growing public debate on this issue with a society teetering toward 'moral indifference'. Surely it indicates the opposite, a society that is dealing with its issues through reasoned debate.

One must be very careful though when attempting to compare the views of the government with the views of the people. To criticise the Australian government, as Calland does, for its decision not to say 'sorry' (instead it 'expressed regret') is one thing, but to presume that that is representative of the view of all Australians is foolish. One needs only to think back to the moving pictures of hundreds of thousands of Australians walking across the Sydney Harbour Bridge in their personal display of reconciliation to see that such generalisations are unfair.

It may sit uncomfortably, but if we look beyond our fiendishly competitive sporting relationship, Australians have a great deal of affection for South Africa. Many are quite taken aback at the venom directed at Australia when they visit here. The fact that someone who writes as well as Calland should pander to the palpably incorrect stereotypes of Australia that circulate unchallenged in this country, is disappointing. As an anthropologist I cannot let Calland off the hook!

Love Her or Loathe Her: Readers' Sentiments

Kadalie kudos

Rhoda Kadalie's regular column in *Business Day* makes my subscription worth its price in gold.

I read it before I even glance at the front page. Her column,'What we black women ought to tell this president' (*Business Day* October 28 2004), makes one wonder why our politicians struggle so much so to say so little in such an opaque manner.

Kadalie's crystal-clear, no-nonsense voice of reason and precise, fearless way with words is a breath of fresh air in a country smothered in befuddled mumbling and tired, confusing jargon like Ronnie Mamoepa's embarrassingly lame apologies for Zimbawean President Robert Mugabe's regime.

Can we have Kadalie for president please?
 Elsa Kruger
 Melrose, October 29 2004

No new ideas

Mark Townsend,'No more regrets for being white' (*Business Day* September 30 2004), and Rhoda Kadalie,'ANC creates a new diaspora with race-based laws' (*Business Day* September 30 2004), are people who want to hold on to advantages they know they gained unfairly.

Kadalie's intellectual hypocrisy is shocking. I doubt she realises that coloureds, whites and Indians continue to earn more than their black counterparts at the same level.

Townsend is one of those white people who think only whites are victims of crime.

He doesn't know that a third of young women in a black township live with rape's psychological scars – and probably didn't even get effective counselling. He hasn't lived in a neighbourhood where answering your cellphone outside your house is considered high-risk behaviour.

The biggest gripe I have with people like Townsend and Kadalie is that they don't offer any ideas on how to level the playing fields, which compounds my suspicion they just can't bear being subordinate to blacks.

Msizi Nkosi
Johannesburg, November 7 2004

Gutless media

Thank you, Rhoda Kadalie, for expressing the opinions of all of us who believe in free speech and accountable government in your column, 'Embedded scribes grovel to the new elite' (*Business Day* July 17 2003).

The vast majority of our news media expresses a sycophantic and acquiescent view of affairs to suit the ruling party. The unquestioning and subservient attitude is an embarrassment to the profession of journalism and a danger to democratic freedoms.

I have never squirmed in my seat as much as when I watched the obsequious 'interview' of President Thabo Mbeki by John Perlman and Tim Modise on SABC television. It could not have been more effectively stage-managed in a totalitarian state.

I say that as someone who was a reporter in London during the heady days of the legendary and formidable press barons, when 'publish and be damned' was the order of the day. In criticising the US, our local apologists seem to forget that the US government comes under the greatest scrutiny and criticism from US media.

Oh that we had more media with the same guts, professionalism and independence – in fact, if Independent Newspapers could live up to its name.

John Wardall
Cape Town, July 22 2003

Pap and wors

The message in human rights activist Rhoda Kadalie's column, 'And SA's new black elite said: Let them eat pap' (*Business Day* August 19 2004), should be applauded and echoed.

The BEE-Shuttle that has helped move our entities, such as ARM, Mvelaphanda, Safika and Shanduka etc to mega-BEE status, must now stop and redirect to actively provide real empowerment to the ones who need to be 'empowered' – our poor. Surely BEE well directed, is the ideal strategy for starting to converge and address our two-economies dilemma.

The black elite can now probably afford the Gulfstream, the catamaran and the caviar.

It is imperative that the spirit of BEE (and the legislative framework that drives it) must significantly embrace our masses (the mineworkers and unionised staff, the ones on our streets selling *Homeless Talk*, the youth who can't afford to pay to get educated at our tertiary institutions, the ones sleeping in tin shacks), where they are the primary beneficiaries rather than elements to be marginally included just to secure a deal.

Surely the time is appropriate to redefine 'broad-based BEE', not as a 'preferred option' in future business transactions, but as a compulsory component (enforced by our individual human conscience and the collective national priority, where the major beneficiaries are the ones who need to be empowered), especially when government or vendor finance is the basis of the transaction.

Lest we forget Spok's famous saying: 'The needs of the many outweigh the needs of the few!' – Pap and wors, please.

Boet van der Peeple
Alex, August 23 2004

Kadalie pushes her own agenda

Rhoda Kadalie's column, 'More to ANC's grassroots revolt than Zuma case' (*Business Day* July 7 2005), throws considerable light on the conservative attitude to the Jacob Zuma affair.

Kadalie claims that protests against poor service delivery and unemployment are, secretly, protests against African National Congress (ANC) elitism and black economic empowerment. She apparently knows 'what the people want', unlike leaders, unionists and politicians, who persist in talking about other things to the applause of the people.

Kadalie adds that these protests are equivalent to the antiapartheid struggle. Since the protests are not against an elite, her argument falls at the first hurdle, but it is still worth examining.

There is a shameful divide between rich and poor in SA, which probably relates to the protests. However, the elite is not the rich as a group, but only the black rich associated with the ANC. Thus, Kadalie is trying to steal the meaning of the protests for purposes either political or racist, while cloaking herself in an undeserved antiapartheid banner.

Then Kadalie plunges into the sewer by stating that Zuma is the victim of a political conspiracy. How does she know this? Self-evidently she has no facts, since she would hardly have hidden them over the past two years. Political wish-fulfilment fantasies are not sound political analysis.

There has been an investigation of the arms deal, and Zuma has been implicated. Naturally, right wingers such as Kadalie wish the process to go on until President Thabo Mbeki is somehow implicated, and the lack of evidence merely proves to them that there is a vast conspiracy.

Kadalie is too dishonest to condemn Judge Hilary Squires, although she merrily includes the National Prosecuting Authority in her fantasy. If there was massive corruption in the cabinet, Zuma would have known of it, and he has nothing to gain by remaining silent if his political career is destroyed.

The decision to prosecute Zuma means that there was no corruption. Kadalie is talking nonsense.
Mathew Blatchford
University of Fort Hare, July 11 2005

Mbeki still in denial on AIDS

All praise to Rhoda Kadalie for 'telling it like it is' in 'What we black women ought to tell this president' (*Business Day* October 28 2004).

What a contrast to President Thabo Mbeki's hysterical stereotyping, in his 'ANC Today' letter (October 22 2004), of white South Africans as racists who consider blacks lustful animals, barbaric savages and potential rapists. With which white citizens does Mbeki consort, one wonders? Certainly racism exists in SA, and not only from some whites, as the exuberant ovation that greeted President Robert Mugabe at the president's inauguration revealed only too clearly.

Mbeki's outburst and his totally irrelevant reply to the questions about rape partially accounting for the spread of AIDS, put to him in Parliament by Democratic Alliance MP Ryan Coetzee, simply emphasise his continued denial of the existence of a virus that causes AIDS. It also highlights government's failure to vigorously combat this pandemic, which will cause the death of the estimated five million South Africans already infected.

I have no doubt that rape is indeed an important contributory factor to the spread of AIDS, particularly the rape of babies and young females. This is partially due to the widespread belief in the myth that if a man with AIDS sleeps with a virgin, he will be cured.

Some years ago when Foreign Affairs Minister Nkosazana Dlamini-Zuma was minister of health, I wrote to her suggesting that a radio campaign be conducted dispelling this myth. I backed up my suggestion saying the control prosecutor at the Protea Courts in Soweto had 400 cases on his books of the rape of girls between the ages of two and fourteen. My letter was not even acknowledged.

Kadalie's column is also in sharp contrast to the feeble explanation by Health Minister Manto Tshabalala-Msimang for government's inability to honour its pre-election promise to have 53 000 HIV/AIDS patients on treatment by March this year, saying that 'she could not force people to use antiretroviral drugs'.

According to government's figures, 11 200 South Africans are receiving antiretroviral drugs. Does she have any idea of the queues of untreated people at the painfully few facilities there are. She, like the president, is in denial about the existence of a virus that causes AIDS.

Helen Suzman
Sandton, November 3 2004

Race still a factor

Congratulations to Rhoda Kadalie in her article, 'ANC win reflects an electorate of low expectations' (*Business Day* March 9 2006), for giving four reasons why the election was not fair: the ANC gets the biggest chunk of the election budget; the ANC conflates party and state and uses state resources to boost its election campaign; the poor take what they can get from a party that commands state resources such as promises of food parcels and places on housing lists; and the ANC hold over much of the media.

There are other reasons for the ANC victory. The demarcation board adjusted ward boundaries to suit the ruling party and deprive the opposition of wards it held. The increase in the size of wards from 16 000 to 18 000 resulted in longer polling station queues. Lack of Independent Electoral Commission personnel, resources and properly trained officials to split up voters rolls into three or four sections discouraged voters from standing in long queues.

Race is still a major factor in almost blind loyalty to a party that did not have a good record of delivery. However, there are signs that more people are considering issues other than race. They sent a message to the ANC, especially in Cape Town, that they are unhappy with local government.

David Quail MPL
Gauteng, March 13 2006

ANC bashing

Rhoda Kadalie's analysis, 'ANC win reflects an electorate of low expectations' (*Business Day* March 9 2006), refers. Benjamin Franklin once asserted that the definition of insanity is 'doing the same thing over and over and expecting different results'. For as long as I have been a reader, I have never come across such vitriol against the same party on almost every subject.

It is interesting to note how Kadalie insists on the distinction between the ruling party and government when there is some apparent form of hegemonic benefit to the party. Such distinction becomes immediately blurred in her eyes when the perceived failures of government get attributed to the party in all its forms.

As for Democratic Alliance posters that were allegedly removed from street poles, this is a cat-and-mouse element of any electioneering that plays itself out not only in De Waal, but in Orania and Boksburg as well!

I am not surprised that Kadalie would stoop so low as to believe that poor people are so cheap that they will exchange their legitimate right to vote with food parcels! The reality is that these people may be poor, but they know who their leaders are and what they have done and will do for them.

Kadalie should be reminded that a 'better life' as opposed to a 'best life' is the mandate on which the African National Congress (ANC) won the elections. We expect the ANC government to continue to provide basic services like water, sanitation, shelter, quality education and jobs to all South Africans. If these are low expectations, then heaven help us all!

The allegations about media bias in favour of the ANC are even more outrageous. Kadalie's column in one of the most prominent and influential newspapers in the country is an ANC-bashing forum.

And every week we have to endure pseudo-academic explanations by a columnist of the same feather, Xolela Mangcu, as to why the ANC should not be trusted. Mangcu has also warned us of 'an impending danger' with the victory of the ANC in these elections! Like before, South Africans will ignore the scare theories and do what is right.

Mava B Scott
Pretoria, March 16 2006

Credit where due

In attacking Rhoda Kadalie while asking 'what exactly is it that she is personally doing to improve the plight of women?' it is clear that Patrick Mkwanazi, 'Talk is cheap' (*Business Day* August 14 2006), does not have the faintest clue as to the work the multi-award-winning Kadalie has done. Nor that she continues to work throughout SA to alleviate suffering and to contribute positively to SA's socioeconomic development.

His ignorance is further displayed by his sarcastically questioning why Kadalie has not made herself available for the Gender Commission – the inference being that if she cared so much about the lives of women, as is exemplified in her columns, she would do so. Clearly Mkwanazi is not aware that Kadalie has, in past years, been repeatedly nominated for a position on the commission.

However, on each occasion the majority of MPs involved in the parliamentary selection process chose not to support her candidature. She can hardly be blamed for being rejected by the African National Congress alliance – who are the final arbiters.

Perhaps Mkwanazi should start campaigning to find out why she is being actively excluded instead of criticising her for something which is totally beyond her control?

Mkwanazi evidently does not know, or chooses to ignore, the groundbreaking work Kadalie has achieved. This includes establishing the Gender Equity Unit at the University of Western Cape; her outstanding contribution as a human rights commissioner, exposing human rights violations in our criminal justice system; and now, as executive director of the Impumelelo Innovations Award Trust, raising many millions of rands to reward best practice in the public sector.

Kadalie has single-handedly created the most definitive database available in the country of more than 1 000 best-practice partnerships between government and civil society.

She supervises case studies on the HIV/AIDS pandemic and on various government departments – including public works, housing, water affairs and the environment and the criminal justice system in general.

On top of all this, she continues a variety of community work.
Suzanne Vos
Rosebank, Cape Town, August 17 2006

Over the top

Rhoda Kadalie questions the South African Broadcasting Corporation's editorial independence in 'Back to the past as SABC bows to its new masters' (*Business Day* October 23 2003).

Our draft policies make provision for a practice established by other credible public broadcasters, such as the BBC, ABC and CBC – that CEs assume full responsibility for all broadcasting operations. Anyone is at liberty to support or differ with it. Our consultation process with more than 1 000 South Africans, including political parties, told us what they liked and disliked about our draft editorial policies.

Kadalie alleges the new SABC is no different from the old apartheid state broadcaster. This is over the top. Ordinary citizens acknowledge and appreciate the efforts we are making to build the SABC as SA's true national public broadcaster.

Reference was made to Peter Matlare's presence at the ANC's national conference. Again Kadalie demonstrated her ignorance.

The ANC extended invitations to a number of executives, business leaders and opinion makers to its conference. There were also a number of editors present, and yet she never suggested that it was inappropriate for them to be there.

Paul Setsetse
GM: Corporate Communications SABC, October 31 2003

Columnist bias

It would be a good idea to get *Business Day*'s columnists to sign an agreement with the newspaper not to intentionally use their columns to promote their political parties.

Not only does Rhoda Kadalie use every opportunity she gets to canvass for the Democratic Alliance, but in 'Smug white journalists strangers to democracy' (*Business Day* January 26 2006), she is also waging war against the media's objective criticism of the party. Her column is nauseating.

Sicelo Bangani
Rondebosch, January 30 2006

Cracking the Whip:
Rhoda's Letters to Newspapers

Why Single out Shaik Family?

With reference to your column 'The thick end of the wedge: An editor's notebook' (*Business Day* November 26 2001) – in which way is the Shaik family good for SA? Their connections to the arms industry and Mo Shaik's promotion to ambassadorial post, I suspect, is a reward for precisely these connections.

Stop pulling the wool over the eyes of the public, Mr Editor, simply because you are moved by the plight of the Shaiks. There are too many struggle families in this country that are corrupt to the core and it is not your job to give them respectability.

Yesterday, the TV show *People of the South* did exactly that by trying to sanitise Allan Boesak by flaunting his role in the struggle.

There are many people who had greatness thrust upon them by apartheid. Many of us were in the struggle for the love of democracy. Others were in it because of their overwhelming love of themselves.

Business Day November 27 2001

Blatant Racism

I have never been so surprised as when I saw the advertisement in yesterday's *Die Burger* under the headline '*Wie is die Coconuts?*'

It was truly ironic to witness the once-proud ANC claiming that so-called 'brown' people are selling out the Nats to the DP. What hypocrisy, what political opportunism, and what is worse, what a display of blatant racism! Do they really think that the millions of educated 'brown' people of our province, some of whom may have voted for the DA, are going to forgive the ANC for calling them 'coconuts'?

And this from a party that brags of non-racialism? Do they not realise that their tactic is as transparent as it is despicable?

I feel ashamed to still be a member of a party whose political buffoonery has descended to the level of our (hopefully) erstwhile mayor.

May I just say to Ebrahim Rasool: Shame on you. You have just lost any respect from at least one 'brown' person in this city. *Pasop!* The coconuts are about to start flying around with a vengeance! There is nothing to be said for a leader who can stoop so low as to resort to racial *opstokery* in his apparently insatiable lust for the trappings of office that the people of the province deprived him of in the last democratic election.

And if the front page report in yesterday's *Die Burger* is correct that you say that you are doing this in the 'interest of the poor people of Cape Town', then you really must have a low opinion of the intelligence of us 'brown' people. We are not so dumb, Mr Rasool, as your stereotyped view of the coloured population would suggest. The last thing on your mind is what the poor of Cape Town are suffering.

One can predict with absolute certainty: you will never be allowed to forget that you have labelled hundreds of thousands of Capetonians as coconuts. You will go down in history as Coconut Rasool. That at least would appear to be an accurate description of what the inside of your skull looks like. Yes, Comrade, you are an idiot to allow a disgusting piece of racism to appear under the name of a provincial party you are alleged to lead.

Cape Times October 2001

Media Destroyers

I am appalled at your suggestion in, 'The Thick End of the Wedge' (*Business Day* March 6 2006), that Patricia de Lille should be leader of the Democratic Alliance (DA) simply on racial grounds. It is like saying Peter Bruce should not be editor because he is white.

We have a new constitutional democracy where anyone is allowed to be leader. Many smaller parties have black leaders, but they did not do as well as the DA with its white leader.

Frankly, given the mismanagement of this economy à la Eskom and the recent fuel crisis, I am beginning to prefer my oppressors to be white.

If black economic empowerment and affirmative action mean black incompetence to the extent that we have seen it in Cape Town, then I would want anybody with skills, integrity and hard work to govern me, regardless of their colour.

Helen Zille has a track record for delivery second to none. Ask people in Western Cape's education department when she was minister; go to Guguletu and Khayelitsha with her. De Lille's political track record is more hot air than actual delivery. Her office is so badly run that I would sooner vote African National Congress (ANC) in Western Cape than for her.

The only gripe people have about Tony Leon is that he is arrogant and combative – as though that has got anything to do with anything. Ninety-five percent of the ANC is combative and arrogant. People never talk about DA policies or what Tony does, but comment on his personality, which is more a figment of the media and its white guilt than anything Tony is.

I believed the media rubbish until I made an appointment to meet him. He is well read, throws a good party and is nice and irreverent.

The media is fast becoming complicit in destroying democracy and the right of opposition to exist by racialising it all the time.

Business Day March 8 2006

Time to stand up

It is a sad day for democracy in SA when an elected mayor has to ask permission of the ruling party to visit a meeting in the township. The African National Congress (ANC) in the Western Cape is hell-bent on destroying the Democratic Alliance (DA) coalition in Cape Town, simply because they have lost an election on the grounds of their gross mismanagement of the city. Instead of condemning their supporters for their undemocratic behaviour, James Ngculu and Max Ozinsky encourage the thuggery by blaming Zille for not informing the ANC ward councillor that she would be attending the meeting.

It would be unthinkable to ask President Mbeki or Premier Rasool to seek permission to visit Independent Democrat or DA constituencies, so why should Zille? And where are the voices of organisations like the Institute for Democracy in SA or the Human Rights Commission in condemning this political intolerance which increasingly has come to characterise responses to legitimate political competition at the local level? It is time the people of Cape Town and all those who voted for the opposition stand up and be counted.

Business Day April 26 2006

Bunch of clowns

Given the drastic decline in productivity due to recurrent power failures, one would think that the government would do its damndest to reverse the downward trend in economic growth.

But no, our president allowed the roads to be closed into the Cape Town city centre on the day of the opening of Parliament, causing gridlock all over the place on the Friday, and denying people their right to work.

Similarly, Western Cape Premier Ebrahim Rasool is closing the roads from Adderley to Long and from Wale to Green streets.

Just who do these politicians think they are at a time when they are found wanting on every score? They not only suffer from great delusions of grandeur, they also thrust greatness upon themselves.

And as for all those politicians who dress up like clowns – just know, there is nothing to celebrate, except hope for a renaissance of Parliament that will start with a total overhaul of those self-serving MPs who occupy a space they neither deserve nor are fit to occupy.

Business Day February 15 2008

Glossary

Aluta continua *The struggle continues*
AU *African Union*

Baantjies vir boeties *Jobs for pals*
Batho Pele *People First*
BEE *Black Economic Empowerment*
Bittereinder *Diehard*
Bosberaad *Village meeting, lekgotla*

Chimères *Haitian partisan political street activists*
Codesa *Convention for a Democratic South Africa*
Cosatu *Congress of South African Trade Unions*

Die government praat van partnerships, maar hulle kan nie eers a PA system organise nie *The government talks of partnerships but they can't even organise a PA system*
Dis die enigste entertainment wat ons nog die hele jaar gekry het. *This is the only entertainment we have had the whole year*
Dit is van laat jou Broeksak, Broeksak, Broeksak *That is what happens when you drop your pants*

eNaTIS *National Traffic Information System*

Gatvol *Fed up*
Hamba kahle *Goodbye*
Hensopper *Quitter*
Hoekom moet ons hier staan in die hitte wanneer ons nie kan hoor nie? *Why must we stand here in the heat when we cannot hear anything?*

IBA *Independent Broadcasting Authority*
IDC *Industrial Development Corporation*
Imbongi *Praise singer*
In vino veritas *There is truth in wine*

Ja baas, nee baas, skop my onder die gat, baas! *Yes sir, no sir, kick me up the backside, sir!*
Julle praat met die land Engels, maar as julle hier kom, dan praat julle Afrikaans. Wie

dink julle is ons? *You speak English to the rest of the country, but when you come here you speak in Afrikaans. Who do you think we are?*

Kyk hoe lyk haar principles nou! *Look at her principles now!*
Kortbroek *Short pants (derogatory)*

Mampara *Fool*
Manne, julle kan darem sing, al het julle nie eers stemreg nie *Men, you sure have a voice, even though you don't have the vote*
MDC *Movement for Democratic Change*
Mbira *Musical instrument*
Meneer die Leier *Mister Leader*

NCOP *National Council of Provinces*
Nepad *New Partnership for Africa's Development*

Om die Boere te kom lei *To lead the Boers*
Ons het skaars die band gehoor *We could hardly hear the band*
Opstokery *Incitement*

Pagad *People against Gangsterism and Drugs*
Pasop *Be careful*
Phantsi *Down with*

Sabra *South African Bureau of Racial Affairs*
SADC *Southern African Development Community*
Salga *South African Local Government Association*
Sarfu *South African Rugby Football Union*
Sars *Severe Acute Respiratory Syndrome*
Schtum *Silent*
Scopa *Standing Committee on Parliamentary Accounts*
Scorpions *Directorate of Special Operations*
Se voet! *My foot!*

TB *Tuberculosis*
Tik *Drug (crystal methamphetamine)*

UCB *United Cricket Board*
UWC *The University of the Western Cape*
UWCO *United Women's Congress*

Waarom was hulle hier? *Why were they here?*
Wie is die coconuts? *Who are the coconuts?*

Zanu(PF) *Zimbabwe African National Union (Patriotic Front)*

Index

Abrahams, Ivan 172
Adams, Fasiegh 146, 147
affirmative action 36, 37, 38, 43–44, 67, 211
African National Congress (ANC)
see also Mandela, Nelson; Mbeki, Thabo; Zuma, Jacob
challenges 104–106
dissatisfaction of electorate 118–119
failures 106–108
partnership with NNP 125–127
African Renaissance 47, 61, 63
African Union (AU) 233, 234, 235
Agliotti, Glen 171, 173
Ahrends, Chris 19
Alexkor 70
apartheid 27, 56, 63, 169–170, 237
see also race and racism
Aristide, Jean-Pierre 160, 203, 227, 235–237
arms deal 16, 71, 74, 120, 121, 123, 124, 170, 174, 188, 212–213, 243
Asmal, Kader 68, 235
Atlantis 152–153

Baddely, Felix 29
Balfour, Ngconde 65–66
Battersby, John 9, 208
BEE (black economic empowerment) 30–32, 34, 58, 81, 189, 242
Bernstein, Hilda 113, 203

Big Bay scandal 126, 135, 139, 140–141
Bikitsha, Nikiwe 36
Biko, Steve 26, 230
Bizos, George 22, 23
black economic empowerment see BEE
Black Sash 10, 120, 183
Blair, Tony 132, 226
Blendulf, Susanne 29
Bloom, Kevin 216–217
Bloom, Richard 164, 167
Boesak, Allan 13–14, 19, 23–25, 172, 176, 249
Boraine, Alex 102, 103
Botha, Pik 113, 133
Botha, PW 18, 56, 169, 206–207, 210, 212
Brink, André 197
Bristow-Bovey, Darrel 201
Bruce, Peter 206, 214
Bullard, David 201
Bush, George 132, 208, 232–233
Buthelezi, Mangosuthu 116, 163
Butler, Anthony 127–128, 130–131

Cachalia, Amina 21
Calland, Richard 51, 52, 108, 237, 238, 239
Campbell, Alistair 209
Carolus, Cheryl 144
Charlton, Harry 91, 163
Chikane, Frank 19

255

civic organisations *see* NGOs
Coetzee, Ryan 123, 244
Collinge, Jo-Anne 68
coloured people 10, 16, 26–27, 134, 146–148, 152, 249–250
constitution 20–21, 56, 71, 145, 169, 189
Cosatu 30, 112–113
Cox, Pieter 31
crime 164–169, 171, 172, 190–191, 193–194
  see also women, abuse
Cronjé, Geo 51–52

Dandala, Mvume 18
Daniels, Glenda 118–119, 120
Davids, Quinton 53
Davis, Dennis 61
death penalty 87, 88, 166, 193–194
Declaration of Commitment 74–76
De Klerk, FW 75, 133
De la Rey song 133, 134–135
De Lille, Patricia 15–17, 86, 97, 108, 116, 117–118, 120, 135, 202, 250, 251
Democratic Alliance (DA) 10, 16, 75, 104, 138–139, 146, 173, 187, 202, 204, 206, 211, 251
Desai, Siraj 73, 172, 187
Desmond, Cosmos 24
Didiza, Thoko 186
Diederichs, N 27
Dipico, Manne 155, 160, 186
Dlamini-Zuma, Nkosazana 10, 99, 177, 230, 244
Dolny, Helena 156, 159, 160, 186, 200–201
Duarte, Jessie 176
Du Plessis, Tim 52
Du Preez, Max 133, 210

Dyantyi, Richard 136
Dyssel, John 29

education 34, 36, 41, 65
  see also universities
emigration 35, 36–38, 39, 40
Erwin, Alec 32, 155
Esack, Farid 23, 24, 25
e.tv 212, 213, 215

Fakie, Shauket 91
February, Judith 108
Feinstein, Andrew 123, 125, 177
Forrest, Drew 66
Forum of Black Journalists (FBJ) 60
Foxcroft, John 23, 25
Fraser-Moleketi, Geraldine 79, 237
Freed, Jocelyn 95
Friedman, Steven 60, 89, 108

gangsterism 148–150, 165–166, 166–167, 168
Gauntlett, Jeremy 46
Geldenhuys, Estelle 95
gender equity
  see also women
  Gender Commission 82, 87, 96–98, 192, 247
  Gender Equity Unit 7, 91, 247
  need for equality 86, 89–90, 93, 198
Gibson, Douglas 205
Ginwala, Frene 123
Gleason, David 210
Gobbato, Angelo 64, 65
Godi, Themba 43
Goldin, Brett 164, 166
Goniwe, Mbulelo 156, 157, 173, 175
Gqola, Pumla 81
Grindrod, Simon 135

Grootboom community housing case 70–71, 120
Guest, Robert 31, 174, 185
Gumbi, Mojanku 230, 231
Gunda, John 117

Hamnca, Prince 201
Harber, Anton 196
Harksen scandal 126, 145, 187, 211, 219
Harris, Cyril 19
Hassim, Shireen 81
health care 35, 68, 77, 95, 177–178, 180, 184, 198
see also HIV/AIDS; Tshabala-Msimang, Manto
Heath, Willem 55, 219
Hefer, Joos 172, 187
Henry, Richard 29
HIV/AIDS
see also Tshabalala-Msimang, Manto
effects 80, 82, 88, 97–98, 170, 193
failure of prevention message 83
Mbeki's denialism 10, 11, 84–86, 107, 160, 243–244
programmes 95, 96
treatment 70, 94, 98, 160, 180–181, 244
Hlophe, John 45–46, 72, 73
Holiday, Anthony 1, 62, 63, 74
Holman, Michael 227–228
Holtshauzen, Evelyn 8
Hout Bay scandal 125, 211, 219
Human Rights Commission (HRC) 8, 49–50, 54–55, 60, 60–61

Impumelelo Innovations Award Trust 36, 96, 183, 247
Independent Broadcasting Association (IBA) 119, 122

Independent Democrats (ID) 16, 108, 116–118, 202
Industrial Development Corporation (IDC) 32–33, 187
Inkatha Freedom Party (IFP) 104, 116
Isaacs, Abie 146

Jack, Bonile 200, 201
Jacobs, Achmat 134
Jali commission 190, 191
Jansen, Johnny 134
Jewellery City project 135, 139
Jiyane, Ziba 116
Johnson, Shaun 122
Johnson, Victoria 218, 219
Jones, Colin 19
Jordan, Archibald Campbell 39, 40
Jordan, Pallo 39
Jozana, Mbuyiselo 117
judiciary 25, 45, 70–73

Kane-Berman, John 222, 223
Kasrils, Ronnie 221
Kathrada, Ahmed 21
Kebble, Brett 171, 173
Keene, John 29–30
Kilroe, Stephanie 95
Kirby, Robert 201
Klebsiella deaths 178, 184, 198
Kluever, Henri 177
Komphela, Butana 18
Kriegler, Johann 72, 73
Kruger, Jimmy 229–230
Kupe, Tawane 209

Land Bank 155–156, 159–160, 186, 187, 200
Langa, Mandla 215
Lehutso, Rusj 138
Lekota, Mosiuoa 30, 188

Leon, Tony 55, 75, 107–108, 186, 202, 204, 206, 207, 217, 220, 251
Louw, Lionel 18

Mabona, Steve 176
Macozoma, Saki 30, 210
Madam (Movement Against Discrimination of Indigenous African Minorities) 133–135
Madikizela-Mandela, Winnie 18, 79, 121, 145, 188
Maduna, Penuell 121, 123, 177
Mafolo, Titus 57, 58
Mahlangu, Ndaweni 176
Makgoba, Malegapuru 46, 142
Makgoba, William 61–62, 63, 64, 65
Makhanya, Mondli 130, 132, 206–207
Makwetla, Tsepiso 195
Malatsi, David 144, 145
Mama, Amina 81
Mamoepa, Ronnie 240
Mandela, Nelson 8, 21, 22, 55, 76, 115–116, 131
Mandela, Winnie *see* Madikizela-Mandela, Winnie
Mangcu, Xolela 246
Mani, Makhaya 199
Manuel, Trevor 43, 187, 210
Mapisa-Nqakula, Nosiviwe 47, 155
Marais, Peter 144, 145, 218, 219
Marinus, Quintin 117
Marshall, Joan 95
Masala, Benjamin 134
Mashabane, Norman 82, 99–101, 176
Masilela, Godfrey 156
Masondo, David 108
Matlare, Peter 215, 248
Max, Lennit 117
Mazwai, Thami 113–115, 214

Mbatha, Hawu 40
Mbeki, Thabo
 allegation of corruption 158–159
 approach towards Mugabe 47, 102, 170, 187, 208, 209, 221, 223–225, 225–226
 double standards 91–92, 173
 failures of leadership 11–12, 35, 102
 HIV/AIDS denialism 10, 11, 84–86, 97, 107, 160, 180–181, 243–244
 obsession with race and racism 47, 53–54, 84–86
 reaction to criticism 8, 111–112, 113–115
 reaction to Selebi's case 171–173
 state of nation speech (2005) 160–162
 versus Zuma 116, 130, 131
 and women's issues 11, 81, 84–86
Mbele, Rose 23
Mbete, Baleka 103, 123, 156–157, 176
Mdladlana, Membathisi 154–155
media 121–122, 199, 200–201, 204–209
 see also SABC
Meshoe, Kenneth 163
Meter, Shantaal 219
Meyer, Roelf 20
Mfeketo, Nomaindia 15, 44, 135, 138, 142–144, 216
Mgoqi, Wallace 44, 135, 138–139
military police 29–30
Mkhatshwa, Smangaliso 19
Mlambo-Ngcuka, Phumzile 31, 82, 136–137, 163, 187, 204, 205
Modise, Tim 120, 142, 233, 241
Mogale, Nathabiseng 98–99
Mohlahlane, Phil 159, 160
Mokaba, Peter 107
Mokwena, Thabo 43, 139

Moldenhauer Commission 176
Molefe, Phil 209
Moosa, Valli 101
Morkel, Gerald 150, 187
Morobe, Murphy 205
Morrell, Rob 142
Morris, Mike 142
Motlanthe, Kgalema 12, 155, 160, 186, 202, 210
Motsepe, Patrice 30
Movement for Democratic Change (MDC) 103, 195, 223
Mpafi, George 29
Mpofu, Dali 195–196, 204
Msomi, S'thembiso 208
Mthombothi, Barney 161, 217
Mufamadi, Sydney 136, 150
Mugabe, Robert
  attitude towards whites 76
  as dictator 19, 46, 54, 114, 221, 223–228, 229, 231, 233
  on homosexuality 14
  judiciary 72
  lack of criticism 82
  Mbeki's attitude 47, 102, 170, 187, 209, 221, 224, 225–226, 230
Mukoki, Alan 156
Mulder, Corné 204
Muller, John 176, 177
municipalities 16, 28, 35, 44, 104–105, 162, 173–174
Munusamy, Ranjeni 201, 209
Mushwana, Lawrence 137, 187
Mvoko, Vuto 202

N2 Gateway Housing project 143
Nassif, Clinton 173
National Development Agency 43, 73, 161
National Prosecuting Authority (NPA) 111, 124, 130, 243
Native Club 26–27, 28, 56–58
Nattrass, Nicoli 9–10
Naudé, Beyers 24
Ncamazana, Dumisane 190
Ncame, Xolile 156
Ndungane, Njongonkulu 92
Nepad 61, 63, 233–235
Netshitenzhe, Joel 43
Ngcuka, Bulelani 201, 205
Ngonyama, Smuts 30, 31, 99–100, 101, 229
NGOs (nongovernmental organisations) 119–120, 181–183
Ngqula, Khaya 32
Nkosi, Agnes 94–95
Nqakula, Charles 29, 49, 70, 155, 198
Ntsebeza, Dumisa 72, 73
Nujoma, Sam 152, 227, 233
Nxedlana, Ike 138
Nzimande, Blade 128

Oilgate scandal 91, 111, 186, 187, 188
Omar, Dullah 9, 149, 165
opposition parties 102–104, 120
Owen, Ken 39, 108

Pagad 148–150
Pahad, Essop 101
Palmer, Robin 108
Pamodzi Investment Holdings 155–156, 160, 186
Pan Africanist Party (PAC) 16
Parliament 121, 123–125, 131, 162–164, 189, 217, 252
Perlman, John 36, 182, 206, 241
Phomolong revolt 162
Pierce, Nigel 52

Pityana, Barney 55, 61, 75
police service 28–30, 49–50
prisons 190–191
Progressive Women's Movement (PWM) 81–82, 83–84

Qoboza, Percy 210
Qunta, Christine 66

race and racism 45–46, 47–48, 50–55, 57, 59–61, 68–69, 143, 200, 206–207, 211, 249–250
see also affirmative action; xenophobia
Radebe, Jeff 155
Ramaphosa, Cyril 19–21
Ramatlakane, Leonard 49, 146, 198, 199
Ramogale, Marcus 142
Rasool, Ebrahim 10, 16, 28, 126, 136, 220, 250, 252
Reddy, Govin 40
Reed, Veronica 219
road safety 184–185
Roodefontein scandal 126, 144

SABC (South African Broadcasting Corporation) 54, 113, 114, 122, 195–197, 201–202, 204, 208, 209, 212, 213, 214–216, 241, 247–248
Sachs, Albie 14
Sampson, Courtney 19
Saunders, Cliff 215
Saunderson-Meyer, William 146, 198, 213
Scopa 28, 43, 131
Scorpions 103, 124, 130, 131, 176
Sebanyoni, Mpho 96
Seepe, Sipho 46, 60

Seipei, Stompie 176
Selebi, Jackie 59, 157, 168, 171–173
Semenya, Ishmael 72, 73
service delivery 11–12, 104–105, 162, 173–174
Sese Seko, Mobutu 33–34
Setsetse, Paul 215, 247–248
sexism hearings 96–97
Sexwale, Tokyo 101, 126
Shaik, Schabir 90, 109, 111, 174, 249
Sibuyi, Cordelia 117
Sigcau, Stella 125, 220
Sisulu, Albertinia 22–23
Sisulu commission 195, 196
Sisulu, Elinor 21
Sisulu, Walter 21–23, 225
skills shortage 34–35, 37–38, 39, 41–42, 66
Skosana, Ben 191
Skwatsha, Mcebisi 28
Smith, Charlene 8, 84–85, 98–99, 107
Smith, Ian 229
Smit, Johan 218
Soko, Stanley 176
Solomons, Gasant 19
Sonn, Percy 66
Sono, Themba 117
South African Broadcasting Corporation *see* SABC
South African Communist Party (SACP) 112–113, 120, 127–129
South African Local Government Authority (Salga) 43, 139
Southern African Development Community (SADC) 223
Sparks, Allister 50–51, 113–115, 200
sport 65–66
Squires, Hilary 92, 112, 243
Staggie, Rashied 148, 149

Stavenhagen, Rodolfo 134
Steenkamp, Freddie 25
Strydom, GHF 27
Strydom, Miranda 209, 214
Suzman, Helen 3, 71, 173, 243–244
Swart, Lara 100–101

TAC (Treatment Action Campaign) 70, 77, 147, 148, 180, 182, 231
Taljaard, Raenette 16, 125
tendering processes 138, 139, 140–141, 187
Terblanche, Juanita 123
Todd, Judith 229
Townsend, Mark 240–241
Trahar, Tony 206
Travelgate scandal 72, 91, 111, 124, 156, 174, 187, 222
TRC (Truth and Reconciliation Commission) 24, 75, 165, 190
Treatment Action Campaign *see* TAC
Trikamjee, Ashwin 172
tripartite alliance 103
Tsedu, Mathatha 201
Tshabalala-Msimang, Manto 9, 14, 70, 80, 92–94, 154, 163, 181, 184, 198, 203, 214, 244
Tshwete, Steve 126
Tsvangirai, Morgan 195, 223
Tutu, Desmond 17–19, 24–25, 114, 230
Tyamzashe, Mthobi 176

Umsobomvu Fund 43
unemployment 193
United Democratic Front (UDF) 13–14, 104, 112, 131
universities 59–60, 61–65, 68–69
University of the Free State 47–48, 59
University of the Western Cape 7, 27, 91

Van Blerk, Bok 133
Van der Merwe, Willem 92, 108
Van Rooyen, Brian 126
Van Schalkwyk, Marthinus 111, 112, 126, 133, 144, 196–197, 206, 235
Verryn, Paul 24, 48
Verwoerd, Betsie 55
Verwoerd, Hendrik 27, 40
Vosloo, Ton 210

Wadee, Ahmed 68
Welz, Martin 210
Wills, Mike 216
women
  see also gender equity
  abuse 80, 83, 84–85, 86–88, 98–99, 192–193, 198
  initiatives 94–96, 246–247
  in leadership 79–84, 97–98
Woods, Donald 210
Woods, Gavin 16, 123

xenophobia 47, 48, 49, 49–50, 60, 143, 221–222
Xingwana, Lulama (Lulu) 82, 155, 159, 160

Ya-Nakamhela, Udi 146
Yengeni, Tony 107, 123, 136, 145, 157
Young, Richard 212, 213

Zapiro 219–220
Zikalala, Snuki 195, 209, 214–215
Zille, Helen 74, 104, 105, 135, 138, 146, 216–218, 251, 251–252
Zimbabwe 103, 120, 187, 195, 208, 209,

223–227, 227–229, 233–234, 238
see also Mugabe, Robert
Zuma, Jacob
  ANC president 35, 60, 231
  corruption allegations 59, 242, 243
  firing by Mbeki 163, 172, 178
  patron of moral regeneration campaign 173, 219–220
  rape trial 90–92, 108–110
  use of state resources 205
  versus Mbeki 111, 116, 130, 131